Vegetable

GARDENING

THE Colonial Williamsburg Way

18th-CENTURY METHODS

FOR TODAY'S ORGANIC GARDENERS

WESLEY GREENE

PHOTOGRAPHY BY BARBARA TEMPLE LOMBARDI

RODALE

To Denise and Don,

soul mate and garden mate

Rodale books may be purchased for business or promotional use or for special sales. For information, please write to:
Special Markets Department, Rodale Inc., 733 Third Avenue, New York, NY 10017.

Printed in the United States of America
Rodale Inc. makes every effort to use acid-free ♾, recycled paper ♻.

Photographs by Barbara Temple Lombardi

Book design by Christina Gaugler

Library of Congress Cataloging-in-Publication Data

Greene, Wesley.
    Vegetable gardening the Colonial Williamsburg way : 18th-century methods for today's organic gardeners / Wesley
Greene ; photography by Barbara Temple Lombardi.
        p.   cm.
    Includes index.
    ISBN 978–1–60961–162–0 hardcover
    1. Vegetable gardening–Virginia–Williamsburg–History–18th century.   2. Organic gardening–Virginia–
Williamsburg–History–18th century.   I. Lombardi, Barbara Temple.   II. Title.
SB320.7.V8G74   2011
635.09755'42–dc23   2011031475

Distributed to the trade by Macmillan

2 4 6 8 10 9 7 5 3 1   hardcover

We inspire and enable people to improve their lives and the world around them.

www.rodalebooks.com

Contents

Introduction

When the first colonists arrived in Virginia in the spring of 1607, they were greeted by a vast wilderness populated by the many tribes of the Powhatan Nation. It was a wilderness for which the colonists were woefully unprepared. When Captain Christopher Newport set sail for the return trip to England on June 22, 1607, he left behind 104 colonists at the new settlement of Jamestown. Within a month, 21 were dead. By the time the first supply ship returned in January 1608, only 38 were still alive.

The Jamestown colonists relied on the native population to supplement their food supply. In 1609, Chief Powhatan, in an attempt to starve the colonists out, blockaded the settlement and withheld all provisions. His strategy almost worked. Of the nearly 500 colonists living at Jamestown in the fall of 1609, only 60 remained by the spring of 1610. This period is remembered as "the starving time." Everyone felt the "sharpe pricke of hunger," as the colony's governor wrote.

Nevertheless, the English held on and learned to provide for themselves. In July 1610, the newly resupplied colony submitted this surprisingly optimistic report to the London Company of Virginia: "We have made triall of our owne English seedes, kitchen hearbes, and rootes, and find them no sooner putt into the ground then to prosper as speedily and after the same quallitie as in England." For the rest of the century, most accounts attested to the fertility of the soil and the luxuriance of the produce, though Virginians were apparently slow to take advantage of this good fortune. Robert Beverley recorded in *The History and Present State of Virginia* (1705): "A Garden is no where sooner made than there. . . . And yet they han't many Gardens in the Country, fit to bear that name."

Beverley may have been too harsh. Virginia in the 17th century was still a wilderness with most households practicing subsistence farming. Corn was, by far, the most important crop, followed by field peas and beans. Livestock thrived, and hogs ran wild through the woods. A vegetable garden provided luxuries rather than staples, and though its produce was a much appreciated diversion from a monotonous diet of meat and grain, it was not always dependable.

In the 18th century, towns such as Williamsburg (founded in 1699) were populated by a professional class of merchants, tradesmen, lawyers, doctors, and clerks with the wealth and leisure to pursue vegetable gardening. For instruction, they turned to the English garden works of Philip Miller, Richard Bradley, John Abercrombie, and others. The Virginian climate was very different from the English climate, so the garden information found in these works had to be adapted to suit local conditions.

The first American garden book, *A Treatise on Gardening,* was written in Williamsburg by John Randolph, the last royal attorney general for the colony of Virginia. There are no copies of his original work, and later editions are attributed only to "a native of this State." We have deduced that Randolph was the author based on citations from several contemporary sources, one being Thomas Jefferson's reference to the *Treatise* as the work of John Randolph.

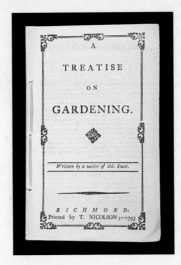

It is not known exactly when the *Treatise* was written. Randolph was a loyalist and returned to England in 1775, so he must have written his treatise before then. Most evidence points to the middle years of the 1760s. The only known 18th-century copy of this little book is a 1793 edition published in Richmond and kept at the Wyndham Robertson Library at Hollins University in Roanoke, Virginia.

Randolph closely followed the advice found in Philip Miller's *The Gardeners Dictionary,* published in England. A comparison of the two works reveals Randolph was working from either the 1752 folio or the 1754 abridgement of *The Gardeners Dictionary.* Randolph's *Treatise* was not, however, merely a copy of Miller's more famous work. Randolph was clearly writing from his own experience in the New World. Most notably, he changed the planting dates to suit the Virginia climate. He also observed, for example, that the multiple spring sowings of spinach recommended for England resulted, in Virginia, in plants bolting and going to seed.

Like Randolph, we use 18th-century English garden works as guides to keeping our Colonial Garden and Nursery on the Duke of Gloucester Street in Colonial Williamsburg's historic area. Like Randolph, we have adapted this information to suit the Virginia climate; we also have altered his advice to suit the 21st-century climate. It was much colder in 1765 Virginia than it is here today.

Most of the tools used in our garden are made in the shops and yards of our historic tradespeople. The blacksmith makes our metal tools, the coopers make the buckets, and our watering cans are made by one of our multitalented gunsmiths. The wheelwrights make our wheelbarrows, the joiners make our frames, and the basketmakers weave our baskets. Bricks come from our wood-fired kiln, and the paper for our frames is provided by our printers. Glass and glass bells come from abroad, as they would have in the 18th century.

The modern gardener would recognize most of our hand tools, and many gardening tasks have spanned the centuries relatively unchanged. Often the difference is in the materials rather than the method. For example, we provide bottom heat to our seedbed by using fermenting manure, while the modern gardener uses electric mats. We cover our hoops with oiled paper, while the modern gardener uses plastic. The materials may be different, but the method and results are the same.

For some tasks, technology has made a dramatic difference in the way we garden. The ability or inability to water the garden has been the single most important limiting factor to gardening throughout history, particularly in southern climates. Many of man's earliest inventions (the Assyrian shaduf, the Roman aqueduct, the Greek Archimedes screw) were devices for moving water. In 18th-century Williamsburg, water had to be hauled from a well.

We have found, in our small ¼-acre garden, that with hauling water from the well, filling up the cistern, and using watering cans, the two of us can move 4,000 pounds (about 200 gallons) a day and still not keep up with our needs when summer stays dry. In 18th-century Williamsburg, the garden was the responsibility of the lady of the house, and she was at the mercy of the weather. Only families wealthy enough to afford slave labor to move the water could reliably keep a summer garden.

Even then, it was an overwhelmingly difficult task. John Custis, who kept a 4-acre garden on the edge of town, lamented in a 1738 letter to Peter Collinson: "I kept 3 strong Nigros continually filling large tubs of water and put them in the sun and waterd plentifully every night, made shades and arbors all over the garden allmost; but abundance of things perishd; notwithstanding all the care and trouble, so that my garden is very much impaired."

Landon Carter, who owned a plantation on the Rappahannock River in Virginia, complained on April 29, 1771: "Gardiner Johnny is growing a Villain again; he pretends to have been watering, but the earth is crackt where he waters."

The unreliability of water in the garden was the primary reason that 18th-century Virginia households did not depend on the garden to feed the family. Williamsburg residents then, as now, relied on the market to provide their staples.

The 18th-century gardener was an organic gardener without any interest in being one. The common philosophy was to kill anything that hopped, wiggled, or flew, but the colonists just weren't very good at it. However, some of their methods work quite well now. Limewater has proved to be a very

effective control for aphids, although it can be used only on mature plants as it will harm most seedlings. A simple trap made of boards to capture slugs and snails within the lettuce frames has achieved a tolerable control. Handpicking is an ancient tried-and-true method for controlling caterpillars, but the gardener must be diligent.

In some cases, we are forced to battle insects that the 18th-century Virginia gardener would not have known, such as the Mexican bean beetle and Colorado potato beetle. There is also the case of the imported cabbage caterpillar, which was well known in England but did not find its way to Virginia until the 19th century. We particularly resent these modern interlopers in the colonial garden, but like our 18th-century predecessors, we have learned to live with blemishes on our vegetables and accept what damage we cannot prevent.

For fertilizer, we use manure or dung: primarily horse dung, but also poultry, sheep, and cattle dung. Authors of the 18th century were very particular about the advantages of various manures. *The Farmer's Magazine* made these distinctions in 1776: "Horse-dung best suits cold soils, and cow-dung the loose burning ones: sheep-dung suits most soils. . . . Hog's-

Tools of the trade; preparing lime slurry and applying to melons

dung was formerly rejected from the notion of its producing weeds, but it is now found to be perhaps the
richest and fattest of any we have . . . a little of it suf-
fices. Fowls and pigeons, living principally upon
grain, their dung makes a very warm manure, but
cannot well be obtained in large quantities."

However, animal manure may pose health risks if
not used correctly. Pet manure should never be used
in the vegetable garden, nor should hog manure.
Fresh manure of any type must never be used in the
garden. Unseasoned horse manure is full of weed
seeds, and fresh poultry manure will burn plants. Six
months is generally a sufficient time to age the dung,
and the temperature in the manure pile should reach
140°F. Composted manure applications should be
timed so that at least 60 days pass between applying
the manure and harvesting the crop. When harvesting, care should be taken in washing vegetables, particularly those that are used raw.

The 18th-century gardener primarily used animal
dung, but a few also experimented with vegetable
"dung" in the same way that modern gardeners use
composted vegetable waste. While not as nutrient
rich as animal dung, vegetable dung provides an
excellent way to build a healthy soil and is the safest
compost for the modern gardener. For all 18th-
century references to dung provided in this book's
instructions for growing vegetables, vegetable dung
or compost may be substituted.

Perhaps the most challenging aspect of recreating
the 18th-century garden is finding the appropriate
historic varieties of plants. Most vegetables are
annual or biennial plants in our climate, making
them very susceptible to varietal extinction. Once the
last seed is planted and not collected, the variety is
gone. Many heirloom varieties, such as the 'Rouncival' pea, are probably extinct. Others, like the 'Hotspur' pea, survive in the form of their 19th-century
progeny, in this case the 'Prince Albert' pea. The
18th-century gardener viewed the task of seed saving
in a very different way than we do today. We are try-
ing to freeze time and save heirloom varieties in as
pure a form as possible. The 18th-century gardener
was happy to discover any trait that improved a vegetable variety and would start saving seed from the
newest improvement. Over time, the older form
would disappear or be absorbed into the newer form.

Colonial Virginians had most of the vegetables with
which the modern gardener is familiar. A few plants
that were not found in the 18th-century garden—and for
that reason are not found in this book—are sweet corn,
Brussels sprouts, and rutabaga. Asian vegetables, such
as mustard greens, bok choy, and soybeans, are also
missing. On the other hand, the 18th-century gardener
grew some vegetables that are seldom found in the modern garden, such as salsify, scorzonera, and cardoon.

What connects all generations of vegetable gardeners is the optimism of committing seed to earth. It
is an unpredictable endeavor, and yet generations of
garden writers have dared to predict that a seed
planted in April will provide a harvest in July. In this
book, we give you the best advice for the management of your kitchen garden from the most notable
gardeners and botanists of the 18th century.

This is how we garden in the town of Williamsburg today, and after long experimentation with
these ancient methods, we humbly submit them for
the inspection and benefit of gardeners everywhere.

"TO GENTLEMEN and LADIES, who delight in Gardening.
WE the underwriten, having been regularly bred to the several branches of Gardening,
and practiced that art for many years; and finding, upon mature consideration . . .
recommend this Book of Gardening to your particular regard and attention."

—James Garton, *The Practical Gardener, and Gentleman's Directory* (1770)

CHAPTER 1
of
Beans and Peas

The vegetables we know as beans and peas, called legumes, are members of the large Fabaceae family and represent some of the most important vegetable staples known to humankind. They were also among the first vegetables to be domesticated and helped to lay the foundation for three of the world's great centers of civilization. Mesopotamia was blessed with a luxury of legumes that included the field pea, chickpea, lentil, and broad bean. Of this group, the pea and the broad bean migrated west and north to become staples in medieval Europe. English colonists brought them to Virginia in the first decade of settlement. The New World kidney bean was domesticated in Peru about 8000 BCE, and its culture spread north, reaching today's southeastern United States by 5000 BCE. It became the most common New World vegetable on European tables. The soybean was a relative latecomer, first domesticated in China a little more than 3,000 years ago. It made its first tentative appearance in North America in the 18th century but was not adopted as a field crop until early in the 20th century, so it was of no consequence in colonial American gardens.

Legumes are rich protein sources, which made them the perfect companion crop for the world's three major grains: wheat from Mesopotamia, corn from Mesoamerica, and rice from ancient China. It was this dietary combination of legumes and grains that allowed these cultures to flourish.

Garden legumes are notable for "fixing" nitrogen through a symbiotic relationship with soil-borne bacteria, called rhizobia, which live in nodules formed on the plants' roots. This relationship enables peas and beans to thrive without extra nitrogen fertilizers and helps to enrich the soil for crops that follow, making legumes near-perfect nutritional and organic garden elements.

BROAD BEAN
Vicia faba

Pliny the Elder, Roman chronicler of the ancient world, recorded that the Greek mathematician Pythagoras forbade his students to eat broad beans. Pythagoras's reason for this ban on beans has been debated for more than a thousand years. One reason Pliny offered was the belief that departed souls resided within the beans. Thomas Hale, writing in 1756, had a different interpretation: "What he [Pythagoras] meant by this was, that they should abstain from meddling with the Affairs of the Republick; because the Antients used Beans in the electing of their Magistrates." In ancient times, apparently, a black bean was cast for a "no" vote and a white bean for a "yes." Whatever his reason for forbidding his students from eating beans, Pythagoras himself ate them quite frequently.

Old World History

The broad bean, better known today as the fava bean, originated in the area east of the Mediterranean basin and was initially gathered in the wild as a small-seeded bean. Also known today as the horse or field bean (*Vicia faba* var. *equina*), this bean produces a small hard seed used primarily for feeding livestock, although its strong and rich flavor is prized by Mediterranean chefs for making falafel, a bean paste often served fried in balls in a pita. The larger-seeded broad bean (*V. faba* var. *major*) was being grown in Egypt by 2400 BCE. From there, the broad bean spread throughout the European continent and became one of the most important staple crops of the medieval period. Monastery records document harvests in the hundreds of pounds. By the 17th century, broad beans came to be associated with the diet of the lower class and fell into disfavor with the gentry. John Parkinson, apothecary and botanist to King James I,

referred in 1629 to "our ordinary Beanes, serving for foode for the poorer sort for the most part."

These beans enjoyed a resurgence in popularity in England in the 18th century, largely because of the great variety of broad beans that had been developed by curious and inventive gardeners, as well as the varieties brought from abroad. There were beans for the spring season and beans for winter, white-flowered beans, red-flowered beans, large beans, and small beans, and they were once again among the commonest components of the kitchen gardens for all classes of English.

To the New World

The broad bean never achieved the same degree of popularity in the American garden, but as late as 1865, Fearing Burr was able to list 19 varieties of broad, or "English," beans in *The Field and Garden Vegetables of America*. The broad bean remains a common vegetable in Europe, but few Americans grow or eat broad beans today. There are several reasons; chief among them is our climate. This useful vegetable prefers a mild, wet climate, such as is found along the central to northern coastal regions of the western United States, which is where you are most likely to encounter the broad bean. The climate over the rest of this country is often too cold in winter, too hot in summer, and too dry at all times to easily grow the broad bean.

The second reason for our uniquely American oversight is that the preparation of the broad bean for the table is somewhat more demanding than that of the common green bean. Broad beans must first be shelled from the pod, as you would a lima bean. Broad bean skins contain a bitter property that some people find unpleasant. This can be greatly lessened by lightly steaming and then gently pinching each bean, causing the skin to slip off. While it sounds tedious, it actually goes quite quickly, once you master the pinching technique.

Broad Bean Varieties

Of the early varieties of broad bean, the most prized in 18th-century England and Virginia was the 'Mazagan'. *The Complete Farmer* (1766) described this bean as "the first and best sort of early beans at present known." The 'Mazagan' was imported from a Portuguese settlement of the same name on the coast of Africa. Unfortunately, the 'Mazagan' bean seems to have disappeared as a distinct variety, but a number of other early varieties are available from English seed suppliers. 'The Sutton' is perhaps the smallest and finest of modern varieties and may be similar to the 'Mazagan'.

Of the larger, later beans, the most popular 18th-century variety and the variety most commonly available today is the 'Windsor' bean. *The Complete Farmer* describes it as "the best of all the sorts for the table," explaining that, "when these are planted on a good soil, and are allowed sufficient room, their seeds will be very large, and in great plenty; and when they are gathered young, are the sweetest and best tasted of all the sorts."

Broad bean in flower; 'Windsor' beans

The Williamsburg Gardener's Assistant

Sowing the bean seed. In mild climates (coastal Virginia and southward), the broad bean is sown in late fall. In colder climates, it should be sown as early in spring as you can possibly work the soil. In Williamsburg, we sow the seed in late November, and it is usually Christmas week before the plants appear aboveground. Germination can be hastened by soaking the seeds, as described by John Abercrombie in 1790: "It is proper, before planting, to soak them several hours in river or pond water, that, when planted, they may come up more freely and regular together." At the same time, you can check the viability of the seeds: Beans that float will not germinate and may be discarded.

Broad bean seeds are quite large and are best planted with a sharpened stick, known as a dibble, at about 2 inches deep and 6 inches apart, in rows that are 2 feet apart (asunder). After planting, lightly mulch the bed with well-rotted manure. The manure will serve several purposes, as Samuel Trowell advised in 1747: "Put some of the Manure along each Row, but not too thick, for a little will do, which will not only preserve the Bean at the first appearing from Slugs, Snails, or any other Vermin from eating it; and every Shower will feed the Roots." While we have not been troubled by slugs or snails in Williamsburg, a light dressing of composted manure will disguise the newly planted beans from the squirrels, who will take every seed if they discover them. After the seeds are planted, water the rows to set the seed and hasten germination.

What diligence is required in the care of beans. When beans are planted in fall, the aim of the gardener should be to have plants that are not larger than 2 or 3 inches tall before cold weather arrives. We have found that it is at this size they best stand the trials of winter. In the colder months, it is necessary to provide some cover from the frost. Philip Miller, the best known of the 18th-century English

Sowing broad beans with a dibble

*(Top) Mature beans and Tusser's trellis;
(bottom) topping the bean plants and
harvesting beans*

garden writers, advised a mulch of "Peas-haulm, Fern, or some other light Covering, which will secure them from the Injury of Frost." In the Colonial Garden in Williamsburg, we use a somewhat more elaborate device that was recommended in 1573 by the English poet and farmer Thomas Tusser for the raising of strawberries:

> *If frost do contin[u]e we, take this for a lawe,*
> *the strawberies looke, to be covered with straw.*
> *layde overly trim, uppon crotchis and bowes*
> *and after uncoverd, as weather alowes.*

In Williamsburg, we find that this loosely woven table, fashioned from tree branches and covered with straw, is equally serviceable for the protection of broad beans. In spring, we reuse it by cutting the lattice in half and standing the sections on end to support the cucumbers.

Once the danger of frost is over and the plants have begun their spring growth, the woven frame may be removed so that the gardener can work among the plants. By the middle of April in Williamsburg, the plants are "topped" and the suckers removed as explained by Batty Langley in 1728:

"When your Beans are in full Blossom pinch off their Tops, and carefully cut away all Suckers that may break out, and grow from the bottom of their Roots." Topping and suckering your plants will produce an earlier crop of fewer but better-formed beans.

An ingenious method for prolonging the bean harvest. You can split the harvest between an early and a late crop of beans by following an ingenious method related by Richard Bradley in 1718: "I have been told by Mr. *Furber* of *Kensington* . . . that if we set the Rows about a Foot assunder, suffering them to grow 'till they are almost ready to blossom, and then cut down every other Line within two or three Inches of the Ground, we shall then have a double Crop of *Beans* from the same Sowing."

By the middle of May in Williamsburg, the beans will be ready for harvest. They should be picked as young as possible, for they will be less bitter. Modern gardeners have also discovered that the broad bean makes an excellent "green manure" or compost.

> "The Bean having very great Varieties, it would be endless, and well as useless, to describe all its several Kinds."
>
> —Batty Langley (1728)

Seed Varieties

Varieties listed in 18th-century Virginia

- **'Windsor'**: Large, late season bean, most common of the 18th-century varieties

- **'Long Podded'** and **'White Blossom'**: Both are likely varieties of the 'Windsor' bean.

- **'Mazagan'**: Small, early season bean that is often described as the finest of all varieties; the 'Mazagan' or its ancestor apparently survives in southern Europe.

- **'Lisbon'**: Another of the Portuguese beans, such as the 'Mazagan'

- **'Sandwich'** and **'Toker'**: These two varieties are described as mid-season beans, larger than the 'Mazagan', but smaller and earlier than the 'Windsor'. 'Toker' was advertised in England several years ago.

- **'Nonpareil', 'Battersea',** and **'Hotspur'**: These three names are used for a number of vegetables. "Nonpareil" is a declaration of quality (without equal). "Battersea" refers to the Battersea area of London where large market gardens were operated in the 18th century. "Hotspur" was more commonly associated with the pea and denoted a smaller-statured early season variety.

Heirloom varieties for the modern gardener

- **'Windsor'**: Cold-hardy, with long pods

- **'The Sutton'**: Small early bean, perhaps similar to the 'Mazagan'

- **'Aquadulce'**: Very similar to 'Windsor', very hardy

BROAD BEAN ESSENTIALS

PLANTING In areas where the ground does not freeze, sow in late November, as the last leaves fall. In colder climes, sow as soon as the ground can be worked in spring, when the snowdrops bloom and crocus leaves begin to lengthen.

SPACING Broad beans can be grown in rows or in a rectangular bed. For row planting, plant the seeds with a dibble 1 to 2 inches deep, 6 inches apart, in rows 2 feet asunder. For beds, plant the seeds on 6-inch centers. Water well.

FOR BEST GROWTH Broad beans require a long cool season with ample moisture. Removing the top flowers hastens the harvest and provides better-formed beans.

HARVESTING Pick the beans while the pods are small and before the bean seeds develop a thick skin. Very young beans can be used without skinning the individual beans and are less bitter than older, tougher beans.

TO SAVE PURE SEED Separate varieties by 1 mile.

COLLECTING AND STORING SEED Allow beans to dry within the pod while on the plant. Seed saving is more difficult in the South, as the seeds do not develop reliably in hot weather. Shell seeds from pods and store in airtight containers. Refrigerate seeds to prolong viability.

SEED VIABILITY 6 years

PEA

Pisum sativum

The green pea was one of the most fashionable of all garden vegetables for 18th-century Virginia gentlemen to grow. Thomas Jefferson famously engaged in a yearly competition with his neighbor, George Divers, to see who could bring the peas in first; the winner had the honor of hosting the other to dinner. Divers generally triumphed, but one year Jefferson's peas were ready first. According to his grandson, Thomas Jefferson Randolph, "When his family reminded him that it was his right to invite the company, he [Jefferson] replied, 'No, say nothing about it, it will be more agreeable to our friend to think that he never fails.'"

The Ancient Pea

Peas are among the most ancient of all agricultural crops. The progenitor of the modern pea has never been found and is likely extinct, but it is thought to have originated somewhere in central Asia between Afghanistan and northern India. By 5000 BCE, pea cultivation had spread to Egypt. From there, peas moved to Greece, the Balkans, and into central Europe by 4000 BCE.

There is no record of the pea in England until after the Norman Conquest in 1066, but once the pea arrived, it quickly became a staple crop among all classes. The ancient pea was used only as a pulse, or dry seed, and today is known as the field pea (*Pisum sativum* var. *arvense*). It was far too bitter to be eaten as a green shelling pea and was more commonly found in the field among grains than in the garden among cabbages. The 'Carlin' pea dates to the 12th century and is one of the oldest varieties of pea still available. Like all field peas, the flowers are colored, and the pea is used when dry.

The Green Pea

The 'Hastings' pea appeared in the historic record in the 15th century as the first recognizable green pea

Garden pea; colored flowers on field pea; white flowers on green pea

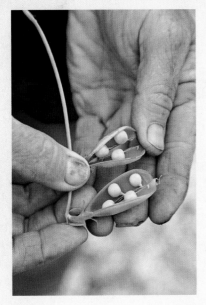  

'Prince Albert' pea; 'Sickle' pea; harvesting 'Blue Prussian' pea

(*P. sativum* var. *sativum*). Like all peas eaten in the green stage, it bore white flowers. By the end of the century, the 'Rouncival' pea was developed in the gardens of the Hospital of St. Mary of Roncesvalles at Charing Cross, London. In 1573, Thomas Tusser recorded instructions for laying a garden that included, "And set (as a Deintie) thy runcivall pease." This pea remained a popular garden variety for the next 300 years. In the 18th century, Stephen Switzer recorded in *The Practical Kitchen Gardiner* (1727) that peas were "justly accounted one of the greatest delicacies of the garden." Seed merchants, eager to profit from this obsession with peas, created dozens of names for varieties with very similar attributes, causing Richard Bradley to lament in 1718, "I have often wonder'd at the Indiscretion of some People, who take a Delight in giving cramp Names to Plants, and make it their Business to multiply Species without Reason, as if a Fruit would be the better for a Name."

Green Pea Varieties

Of all varieties, the early season peas were, and are, the sweetest. The premier early season pea of the 18th century was the 'Hotspur', described in England for the first time by Leonard Meager in *The English Gardener* in 1683. Many varieties of 'Hotspur' were developed over the next century, but the most popular and most widely grown was the 'Charlton Hotspur'. This pea was probably the parent of the 'Prince Albert' pea. Developed in England before 1837 and named for the husband of Queen Victoria in 1842, the 'Prince Albert' may be the last 'Hotspur' pea still available.

Most 18th-century peas were consumed as shell peas, but the sugar, or edible podded, pea (*P. sativum* var. *saccharatum*) was also known. This pea was often called the sickle pea, for the crooked, sickle-shaped pods, and was the sweetest of all varieties, a distinction that came with its own problems. As explained by John Mortimer in 1707: "The great inconveniency that doth attend them is, that their extraordinary sweetness makes them liable to be devoured by Birds."

The larger, late season peas, such as the 'Marrowfat' and 'Blue Prussian' (*P. sativum* var. *medullare*), can be used in either the green or dried state. These peas were enormously important to the English cook and provided the "pease porridge" made famous in the children's nursery rhyme. Today they are used to make wasabi peas.

The Williamsburg Gardener's Assistant

Sowing the pea seed. Peas are the first crop planted in spring. In Williamsburg, we endeavor to have them in the ground by Valentine's Day. The greatest impediment to these early plantings is the condition of the soil. In early spring, the ground is slow to dry, and a rainy season often exacerbates the situation. As a remedy, it was a common practice for 18th-century gardeners to dig the soil in rough furrows in fall. The resulting ridges dry much more quickly in spring and can be leveled out to provide a seedbed.

Peas are adaptable to many soils, but they are most prolific in a "strong" soil, since well-composted ground retains the moisture that they crave. Walter Nicol observed in 1798, "The ground is seldom manured for them, as they generally follow some crop that required manuring or fallowing." This is because peas, like all legumes, are able to capture atmospheric nitrogen that not only nourishes the plant, but also replenishes the soil, as long as the peas' roots are tilled into the garden rather than removed with the vines once the harvest is over.

Various methods of trellising your peas. Most varieties of peas require trellising to keep them off the ground and to facilitate harvesting. The easiest method that we have found was explained by John Rutter in *Modern Eden* in 1767: Plant the seeds in two rows, approximately 1 foot apart, setting the peas with a dibble at 2 inches one from the other. "When they are half a foot high," Rutter advised, "some boughs, with all the twigs upon them, should be stuck into the ground, for them to climb upon." In this manner, two rows of peas are trellised by a single row of twigs. This system is particularly suited for the smaller early season peas. Once the pea season is over, the entire row of sticks and pea vines can be rolled up and easily discarded.

For the late season peas, which are more robust climbers, we fashion a tentlike trellis of sticks over a single row of peas. Not only does this provide a much more substantial support for these larger peas, which will often grow 7 feet tall or more, but it can also be used to keep rabbits from the peas, a common prob-

Twig trellis; constructing the stick trellis; stick trellis with rabbit excluder

lem in Williamsburg. Poke two rows of 6- to 8-foot sticks into the ground, one stick paired to another, on either side of the row of peas. Tie the paired sticks together over the center of the row and attach long horizontal sticks across the top and at various heights along the sides of the trellis to bind it all together. This provides a form for the peas to climb on as well as a structure around which to wrap cheesecloth to effectively exclude rabbits. If well constructed, this trellis can also be used to grow pole beans after the peas are harvested.

Preserving the peas from injurious pests and other harms. It is in their earliest stage, just after they emerge aboveground, that the peas are most susceptible to injury. Batty Langley warned in 1728, "When your Pease begin to appear above Ground, be diligent in surveying them every Morning, and to destroy all the Slugs you can find near them." If slugs or snails should trouble the young seedlings, Langley provided this recipe: "Slack'd Lime, and Sea Coal Ashes strewed upon the Drills, before the Pease are come up, will

Peas in hotbed

prevent their being destroy'd; be careful to do the same after Rains." Slaked lime is also called hydrated or pickling lime (readily available at garden centers and most grocery stores), and wood ashes may be substituted for coal ashes. As Langley observed, this mixture must be reapplied after every rain until the peas begin to climb and are safe from further damage.

Once the peas begin to flower, they are greatly annoyed by any disturbance to their roots, so any weeding should be done with great care and with as little disruption to the peas' roots as possible. It will serve the gardener well to conduct a thorough weeding while the peas are young and the weeds are small.

Care and harvesting of peas. "When the crops of peas arrive to bearing," wrote Samuel Fullmer in 1795, "let the pods be gathered as often as they succeed to perfection, while young and green; permitting them to grow plump, but not leaving them till they get old, for the closer they are gathered when fit, the longer they will continue blossoming and bearing; besides, when peas are moderately young they are greatly superior for eating."

The harvest of this excellent vegetable may be extended by planting several varieties of early and late season peas. In Williamsburg, the 'Prince Albert' is harvested first, followed by the sickle pea, the 'Blue Prussian', and finally the 'Marrowfat'. For those gardeners who wish to have a particularly early crop of peas, the ingenious Langley provided a method in 1728: "Observe to stop them . . . that is, pinch off their leading Shoots, and 'twill cause them to ripen a full Fortnight before the others which are not so stopt."

For an even earlier crop, John Rutter gave this advice in *Modern Eden* (1767): "Peas may be forwarded by a hot-bed in spring, so as to come in yet considerably earlier than any in the open ground; and as there is little trouble in this, a good garden should not be without the advantage." In Williamsburg, we never fail to sow a row of peas along the back wall of our early hotbed. From a January sowing in the warm soil, we expect to harvest peas by the middle of April.

PEA ESSENTIALS

PLANTING Sow the seeds as early as the soil can be worked, after the snowdrops spread their petals and the first crocus blooms.

SPACING For peas trellised in double rows, plant seeds 1 to 2 inches deep and 2 to 3 inches apart, in rows 1 foot asunder; plant 3 feet asunder for peas grown on trellises.

FOR BEST GROWTH Peas are cool season plants that wither in the heat and become tough and bitter if plagued by drought. Lay a thin layer of compost to preserve moisture and discourage weeds once peas appear above ground.

HARVESTING For the best quality, harvest peas assiduously while the pods are smooth and green and before they yellow and roughen.

TO SAVE PURE SEED Separate varieties by 200 feet.

COLLECTING AND STORING SEED Allow peas to dry within the pod on the vine. It is sometimes necessary to protect the peas from birds. Shell the peas from the pod and store in airtight containers. Refrigerate to prolong viability.

SEED VIABILITY 3 years

Seed Varieties

Varieties listed in 18th-century Virginia

♦ **'Hotspur', 'Charlton Hotspur', 'Early Golden Hotspur', 'Ormand Hotspur', 'Master Hotspur', and 'Reading Hotspur'**: 'Hotspurs' were the most popular pea of the 18th century. As a whole, they were early season, smaller-statured shell peas. The variety 'Prince Albert', developed in the 1830s, is said to descend from the 'Charlton Hotspur'.

♦ **'Leadman's Dwarf', 'Early Frame', 'Six Weeks Pease', and 'Nichol's Early'**: These were extra early, very dwarf pea varieties that were grown in frames for an early harvest.

♦ **'Green Rouncival', 'Marrowfat' or 'Dutch Admiral', 'Dwarf Marrowfat', and 'Egg Pea'**: Large, late season peas. 'Rouncival' was one of the first green shelling peas. The 'Marrowfat' took the place of the 'Rouncival', also known as the 'Egg Pea', in the 18th century.

♦ **'Spanish Morrotto'**: Another large, late season pea, probably similar to the 'Marrowfat'

♦ **'Sugar Dwarf'**: Edible-podded pea

Heirloom varieties for the modern gardener

♦ **'Prince Albert'**: Small-statured, early season pea

♦ **'Marrowfat'**: Large, mid- to late season pea, usually allowed to dry for soup

♦ **'Champion of England'**: A large 'Marrowfat' type pea

♦ **'Blue Prussian'**: Large pea, with blue-green seeds, very late, that can be used green or dry

♦ **'Sickle'**: Small- to medium-statured, edible-podded pea

NEW WORLD BEANS
Phaseolus spp.

Barbary pirates sailing out of Mediterranean bases to attack the Spanish treasure fleets captured not only gold and silver, but also vegetable seeds from the Western Hemisphere. These exotic seeds were often sent to the Balkans, where the Ottoman Empire managed agricultural lands, and from there were introduced into Europe, causing much confusion as to their origin. The history of the New World bean, erroneously called the French bean, was further confused by Henry Phillips, who recorded in *History of Cultivated Vegetables* (1822) that it was now known that these beans were not native to France after all, but rather, "We may conclude this excellent and wholesome vegetable is a native of the eastern extremity of Europe, or that part of Asia now belonging to the Turks."

The New World bean acquired the name *bean* because it reminded early explorers of the European broad bean. Thomas Hariot, botanist for the 1585 expedition to Roanoke Island in present-day North Carolina, explained: "Called by us *Beanes,* because in greatnesse & partly in shape they are like to the Beanes in England; saving that they are flatter, of more divers colours, and some pide [speckled]."

The Kidney Bean

The kidney bean (*P. vulgaris*) was the most common of three species of *Phaseolus* found in early American gardens. It is not native to North America, but by the time the first colonists reached Jamestown in 1607, the "Three Sisters"–corn, beans, and squash–were agricultural staples for some native tribes and were quickly adopted by the English settlers. The kidney bean was first described in England by William Turner in *Names of Herbes* (1548): "Called in english Kydney beane, because the seede is lyke a Kydney." It has carried this name ever since, but not until late in the next century did it become a common vegetable on the English table. John Parkinson, apothecary to

Dwarf kidney beans; 'Caseknife' bean

James I, wrote in 1629 that these beans were found "more oftentimes at rich mens Tables." By 1683, John Worlidge recorded that they "within the memory of Man were a great rarity here in *England,* although now a known and common delicate food."

Once adopted, the kidney bean–especially when used as a snap, or edible-podded, bean–became the most important New World vegetable on European tables. Subsequently, it appears that it was from Europe that the first snap bean varieties emerged. One of the first of these varieties was recorded by Giacomo Castelvetro in 1614: "The least well known and the largest, we call 'Turkish' . . . beans." These "Turkish" beans were a climbing variety that could be used, when young, as a snap bean. Adriaen van der Donck explained in *A Description of the New Netherlands* (1655), written in what later became New York: "The Turkish beans which our people have introduced there [in America] grow wonderfully . . . and are much cultivated. Before the arrival of the Netherlanders, the Indians raised beans of various kinds and colours, but generally too coarse to be eaten green, or to be pickled." In a curious example of a reintroduction of a native crop in a different form, Peter Kalm recorded in his *Travels in North America* in

1748: "The Indians likewise sow several kinds of beans, which for the greatest part they have secured from the Europeans."

Kidney beans come in both climbing (pole) varieties and dwarf (bush) varieties. The dwarf bean of the 18th century had a very stringy pod and could not be used as a snap unless gathered at a very young stage. The first true dwarf snap bean varieties, such as 'Refugee' and 'Early Mohawk', appeared early in the 19th century. Today, almost all of our snap beans, whether from the store or from the garden, come from dwarfs.

The 18th-century snap beans came almost exclusively from pole varieties. The most common pole bean in England and Virginia was the 'White Dutch', known as the 'Caseknife' bean today. By modern standards, this is a tough-podded bean, but it was still superior to the dwarfs available to John Randolph in 18th-century Williamsburg. Randolph wrote: "The Dutch sort are not so apt to be stringy, which the dwarf sort are." The modern gardener has a truly amazing selection of beans to choose from, and among snaps in particular, it is a tenderer, tastier, and less stringy lot than that raised by our colonial predecessors in their gardens.

The Runner Bean

Runner beans (*P. coccineus*) are climbing varieties native to the mountains of Mexico and Guatemala that prefer a cooler, more humid environment than the common kidney bean does. Runner beans suffer in the hot, often dry summers on the coastal plain of Virginia, but were very well suited to the English climate.

The first runner bean to arrive in England was the scarlet runner, introduced by the renowned English gardener John Tradescant early in the 17th century. By the 18th century, it was widely grown as both an ornamental and a culinary crop. Philip Miller recorded in the 1754 edition of *The Gardeners Dictionary* that it was often used "to cover Arbours and Seats." This same bean was likely among the "arbor beans" listed by Thomas Jefferson at Monticello. As for its edible quality, James Justice related in 1771 that it ". . . is clear from the strings that are so troublesome in the fruit of the other kinds." To this day, the scarlet runner bean is one of the most attractive inhabitants of the kitchen garden.

The Lima Bean

The lima or butter bean (*P. lunatus)* was often called the bushel or sugar bean in 18th-century Virginia. It has long been thought to be a native of both South and Central America and was apparently domesticated from the wild *P. lunatus* var. *sylvester* in two separate locations. The larger form was domesticated in

Scarlet runner bean

Sieva bean

South America sometime before 6000 BCE, and the smaller was domesticated somewhat later in Mesoamerica. The smaller, more heat-tolerant variety is often referred to as the sieva or butter bean and is sweeter than the larger, often starchy lima bean. Some writers separate the varieties, classifying the smaller butter bean as *P. lunatus* and the large lima as *P. limensis.*

John Lawson was likely referring to the sieva bean in North Carolina when he referred in 1709 to the "Bushel-Bean" that the native people trained on poles. All 18th-century lima and sieva beans were pole varieties.

In the 19th century, a small-seeded dwarf variety of butter bean was discovered in the mountains of Virginia and is now the most popular form of this bean for the home garden.

The Williamsburg Gardener's Assistant

Sowing the bean seed. All of the *Phaseolus* beans are warm season plants and are best sown once warm weather has firmly settled in. The gardener gains little by rushing the season, as the seeds do not germinate reliably in a cool soil. The condition of the soil is equally important, for there is not a plant in the garden, according to *The Practical Kitchen Gardiner* (1727), that "requires a finer richer soil than kidney beans do; which ought to deter any body from planting them on a stubborn clay."

This partiality for a lighter soil by all types of beans is due to the very large seed leaves that must curl out of the ground as the seed germinates. They are greatly obstructed by a heavy soil. This condition may be aggravated by a wet season or from overgenerous watering, which not only promotes rot, but also, as gardeners have long observed, causes the surface of the soil to form a crust, impeding the seeds from extending their leaves above the ground.

The gardener is best served by a well-composted ground, but those who are encumbered by a wet, heavy soil may improve their situation by following the advice of Richard Bradley, who recorded in *New Improvements of Planting and Gardening* (1718): "We sow *Kidney-Beans* . . . making *Drills* from *North* to *South,* laying the *Beans* in them about four Inches a-part, and covering them with Earth, rais'd in a Ridge to keep the Wet from them." This slight ridge over the seeds will shed the rain and remain loose and amenable to seed germination.

If you garden in a lighter soil, a dibble will serve even better to set the seeds. Stretch a string line to space the rows at 2 feet asunder. Using your dibble, make 1- or 2-inch deep holes, 4 inches apart, and drop one bean into each hole. Cover the beans by

Bean seed leaves

(Top) Seeding in ridges; (bottom) seeding with dibble

"The Bushel-Bean, which is a spontaneous Product. . . . They are
set . . . at the Feet of Poles, up which they will climb. . . . white and
mottled, with a purple Figure on each side it, like an ear . . . very flat."

—John Lawson, *A New Voyage to Carolina* (1709)

raking over the top of the row, which will provide a loose soil over each individual bean and promote even germination. The gardener may hasten germination, particularly for midsummer plantings, by following the advice of Philip Miller (1733): "Soak the *Beans* six or seven Hours in Water before you plant them, which will greatly forward their Growth."

To harvest beans in their perfection. Once the plants have flowered and set their fruit, the gardener must be diligent in harvesting the beans. As Charles Marshall recommended in 1798: "A crop produces more, and lasts longer, the *oftener* the beans are gathered: It is proper, therefore, to gather them constantly whilst *young* and good." The younger the bean is picked to eat as a snap, the more succulent will be the product of your labor.

The bean varieties and how they are trellised. While the dwarf varieties are the most common form grown in the modern garden, the advantage of growing pole beans for snaps is that the plants will bear throughout the season. The dwarf varieties provide only a few pickings and must be replanted for season-long production.

Pole beans, both kidney and butter or lima beans, may be trained on arbors, sticks, or poles. Most can be maintained with horizontal supports made from twigs, which renders the picking much easier. In Williamsburg, we reuse the tentlike trellises that were constructed for spring peas and grow our summer beans on them. For the stronger climbers, such as the butter beans, or for the gardener who is constrained by space, poles may be the better choice. Most gardeners fashion three-pole tepees, but we have found that a row of poles, tied together and braced accordingly, will provide more beans in a smaller space and with fewer poles. In erecting this arbor, it is necessary that the poles be supported from several directions, so that they will withstand the stronger winds that often come late in the season when the beans are in their perfection. You will need a ladder to pick them, but for those gardeners who have more vertical space than horizontal, this method will provide bushels of beans in a small area.

Beans on pea trellis; harvesting beans; pole trellis

NEW WORLD BEAN ESSENTIALS

PLANTING After danger of frost, when the peach blossoms fall and the dogwood tree blooms.

SPACING Plant your seeds 1 to 2 inches deep, 3 to 4 inches apart for bush beans, 4 to 6 inches apart for pole and runner beans. Make your rows 2 feet asunder for bush beans, and space your poles or trellises 3 feet asunder for pole or runner beans.

FOR BEST GROWTH All beans need a warm, light soil to germinate and grow successfully. A continually moist soil is critical from blossom to pod set for a well-formed crop of beans.

HARVESTING When harvested for green beans, pick the pods before the seeds are visible in the pod. The smaller pods will be crisper and less stringy. For shell beans, pull the pods as they start to change color. For dry beans, let the pods dry on the plant.

TO SAVE PURE SEED Separate varieties by 200 feet for all types of kidney beans (*P. vulgaris*); by ½ mile for runner beans (*P. coccineus*); and by 1 mile for lima beans (*P. lunatus*).

COLLECTING AND STORING SEED Allow the beans to dry in the pods on the plants. Shell seeds from pods and store in airtight containers. Refrigerate seeds to prolong viability.

SEED VIABILITY 4 years for all types of kidney; 5 years for runner beans; 3 years for lima

Seed Varieties

Varieties listed in 18th-century Virginia

- **Yellow, scarlet, white,** and **black:** There were many colored beans used in a dry state.

- **'French', 'Speckled French',** and **'White Dwarf Kidney':** "French beans" were generally understood to mean dwarf, or bush, beans in the 18th century.

- **'Canterbury Dwarf Kidney':** A very common, white-seeded bean with a dwarf to half-runner habit. Identified as a flageolet bean in the 19th century

- **'White Dutch':** A pole bean, 'White Dutch' was the most common green or snap bean variety in the 18th century. Known as 'Caseknife' bean today.

- **'Scarlet Blossom':** A scarlet runner bean

- **'Hominy':** A commonly listed white-seeded pole bean. Often grown in cornfields and probably similar to a taller great northern bean

- **'Goosecraw':** There were many regional beans said to originate in the craws of turkeys or geese.

- **'Lima', 'Carolina White',** and **'Large Sugar':** All types of lima or butter bean. The smaller-seeded sieva type, such as 'Carolina White', seemed most prevalent.

Heirloom varieties for the modern gardener

- **'Caseknife':** Pole bean, flat podded, somewhat coarse, used as snap bean

- **'Amish Nuttle':** Pole bean, speckled seed, cutshort seed (seeds closely packed diagonally in pods), used as dry bean

- **Cannellini:** Dwarf bean, small white seed, used green when very young, later as dry bean

- **'Refugee':** Dwarf bean, round pods, speckled seed, used as snap bean

CHAPTER 2
Of the
Cabbage Family

Huddled along the Atlantic coast of Western Europe, one of the world's most versatile plants makes its home in windswept, barren enclaves. Wild sea kale, *Brassica oleracea* var. *sylvestris,* tolerates salt spray and limestone soils but does not tolerate competition, so it is restricted to habitats too harsh for its more robust competitors. From this seemingly unremarkable plant, one of our most beloved groups of vegetables has evolved. Its leaves have been refined to give us cabbages, collards, and kales. Its flowers have been modified to provide broccoli and cauliflower. Its stem has swollen to produce kohlrabi, and its buds have enlarged to produce Brussels sprouts.

The Celts were apparently the first to cultivate the ancient cole or cabbage plant, and it is from the Celtic word *bresic* that the Latin genus for all cole crops, *Brassica*, derives. Along routes lost to history, the first cole crops migrated to the northern shore of the Mediterranean Sea. There they were refined and returned to northern Europe in their many different forms.

The heading cabbage was first listed in England in the 14th century. The English word *cabbage* derives from the French *caboche*, suggesting that it was introduced from France. Cauliflower appears to have been developed in Cypress or the Levant (eastern Mediterranean) and was introduced into Italy around 1490. Sprout broccoli was developed in the eastern Mediterranean and was introduced into England from Italy early in the 18th century.

In 1812, Thomas Jefferson was the first American to grow Brussels sprouts. Long held forth as the "poster child" for vegetables that Americans love to hate, Brussels sprouts contain a bitterness that we now know some people are genetically predisposed to taste. Other people are not and prize them as a delicacy.

COLEWORT, COLLARD, and KALE
Brassica oleracea var. *acephala*

The 16th-century French work, *L'Agriculture et Maison Rustique,* translated into English as *Maison Rustique; Or, The Countrey Farme,* recorded: "First of all we are to speake of Coleworts, both because they are most common, and also most aboundant of all other sorts of hearbs." By the middle of the 18th century, however, these open-headed cabbages had fallen into disfavor and were considered food fit only for the poor. Early in the 19th century, the original colewort disappeared, and a similar plant was adopted in the southern United States with the name of *collards,* a phonetic corruption of colewort. Collards also had a reputation for feeding the poor, but as Princess Pamela, the 20th-century Southern cook, put it: "Somebody said something 'bout God musta liked the common people 'cause he made so many of them."

The Ancient Colewort and Its Demise

The colewort and the closely related kales are the closest, in form, to the ancestors of all cabbage family plants and were the first to be domesticated. Stephen Switzer recorded in *The Practical Kitchen Gardiner* (1727): "The antient *Greeks* divided the Brassica into three distinct species; *viz.* the first, *crispa,* with curl'd or short leaves, and but few stalks; the second, *lea,* the leaves growing on long stalks, for which it was call'd *cauleda,* perhaps our coleworts; and the other, *crambe,* with smaller leaves, but more indented than any of the former; which undoubtedly belongs to the borecole, broccoli, or seakele."

When the great 16th-century herbals were written, there were curled coles and apple coles, swollen coles and red coles, coleworts for winter months and

'Georgia' collards; 'Black Tuscan' kale; marrow-stem kale

coleworts for summer months. By the middle of the 18th century, the English colewort had been reduced to a single variety generally known as 'Dorsetshire' kale. By the end of the century, it had largely disappeared from the English garden and was finally declared extinct in the first quarter of the 19th century. The reason for its demise was explained in *The Complete Farmer* (1766): "COLEWORT, or *Dorsetshire Kale,* is a species of cabbage, formerly much cultivated in gardens, but at present little known, cabbage-plants being substituted in its room." What this refers to is the substitution of cabbages, harvested before they mature and form heads, in place of the true colewort that provided a milder, more tender green.

The American Collard

The collard is a uniquely American vegetable that appeared late in the 18th or early in the 19th century and has always been associated with Southern cuisine. Lt. William Feltman recorded in his journal on August 17, 1781, as the Continental Army marched through Hanover County, Virginia, on its way to battle at Yorktown: "The negroes here raise great quantities of snaps and collerds. They have no cabbage here." It is not clear if this is an early reference to the modern collard or to the ancient colewort.

One of the oldest varieties of collards still available is 'Green Glaze', developed from the 'Green Glaze' cabbage early in the 19th century. The 'Green Glaze' collard is a smaller plant than the modern 'Georgia' or 'Vates' collard. The leaves are bright green and somewhat coarse. 'Green Glaze' is seldom bothered by the imported cabbage caterpillar, a common pest for the other varieties.

Kale and Its Kinds

"Kale" is simply an alternative pronunciation of "cole," primarily in the northern part of the British Isles. The name derives from the Latin *caulis*, meaning "stem," in reference to the leafy stalk of the ancient brassica. However, by the 18th century, kale was generally understood to refer to varieties of coles

imported from the Netherlands. They were also known as *borecoles,* from the Dutch *boerenkool* or "peasant's cabbage." Borecoles differed from the common colewort in having curled and frilled leaves. Initially they were treated as a garnish, as was explained by Richard Bradley in *The Compleat Seedsman's Monthly Calendar* (1738): "*Curl'd Coleworts*, or *Curl'd Worts*, is a Sort of Cole with jagged cut Leaves, strip'd with many Colours; it serves to garnish Dishes, but is never boil'd or eaten, that ever I have heard of."

By the middle of the 18th century, there were several varieties and colors of borecole, but the most popular form was called Scotch kale, a name it retains to this day. The 18th-century Scotch kale was quite a bit larger than the modern variety, as related in *The Gardener's Kalendar* (1777): "Bore-cole, or, as it is often called Scotch-Kale, is a very useful plant. . . . There are two sorts of it, the brown and the green. The plants run up with very long stems, sometimes three, four, or five feet high." The modern Scotch kale, except when in flower, seldom grows taller than 18 inches.

Thomas Jefferson's favorite kale was sprout kale, and while this variety has not been identified with certainty, it may have been similar to one of the Siberian kales (*B. napus*). These are milder flavored than most European kales (*B. oleracea*), such as Scotch kale. The Russo-Siberian kales are also prized for the flower sprouts they produce in spring. In addition to the common Scotch and Siberian varieties, there are heirloom kale cultivars, such as 'Red Russian' and 'Black Tuscan', which give a range of taste and texture to these excellent greens.

"The common Colewort is now almost lost near *London,* where their Markets are usually supplied with Cabbage or *Savoy* Plants, instead of them."

—Philip Miller, *The Gardeners Dictionary* (1754)

The Williamsburg Gardener's Assistant

Collards and kales and their seasons. Collards and kales are staples in the fall and winter garden, and in the South, produce both a fall and a spring harvest. They are easy plants to grow, but like all members of the cabbage family, are heavy feeders, so the ground you place them in should be well composted. The more luxuriant their growth is, the more delectable their flavor will be.

In Williamsburg, the seeds for collards are sown in late summer and transplanted to the garden with the first cool weather in September. At the same time, kales are seeded in drills, or rows, spaced 18 inches apart. When the kale seedlings appear, thin them to stand 2 inches apart. This is done more quickly and with less damage to the remaining plants by cutting down the unwanted plants with scissors, rather than pulling them out. When the kales have five to seven leaves, thin them to stand 6 inches apart. This should be all the care that they require.

Collards are not as tolerant of the cold as are kales, so in colder climates, the gardener should plan to have fully formed plants before the temperature drops below 20°F. Kales will generally survive winter in all but the coldest climates. In the North, lay down a thick layer of straw about the plants. This will usually be enough to preserve them through winter, especially if they are protected by snow.

What protection is necessary to defend against the caterpillar. Modern collards are greatly bothered by the imported cabbage caterpillar, whose white butterfly every gardener knows. In areas with long, mild autumns, the plants must be protected by diligently rubbing the eggs off the leaves, by collecting the cat-

Thinning kale seedlings

Siberian kale; sprouts on kale stem; kale flowers

erpillars as they hatch, or by applying an elixir to the leaves to repel the caterpillars. We have found that a solution of tansy leaves, steeped in water overnight and sprinkled on the collard leaves in the morning, will discourage the caterpillar if applied every other day. A small amount of dish soap added to the solution will help it stick to the leaves. The most effective measure is a covering of gauzy fabric to keep the butterflies off until frost destroys them for the season. Kales are not nearly as susceptible to this bothersome pest, but gardeners must watch for damage while the weather is warm.

To harvest collards and kale in their perfection. The harvest of collards and kales begins after the first frosts of autumn. As explained by John Mills in 1763, "They should not be eaten before the frost has rendered them tender; for till then they are tough and bitter." This is the result of a natural response to cooler weather: Plants protect themselves from freezing by converting starch to sugar, which is the reason all greens are sweeter after a frost. In Williamsburg, we are able to harvest collards and kale in November and December and again in spring, before the plants begin shooting to flower.

The largest kales will produce sprouts along their stems. As explained in *Every Man His Own Gardener* (1776), "In the months of February and March their long stems will be loaded, from the very bottom to the top, with fine young sprouts; all of which, as well as the principal head at top, will boil remarkably green and tender." The smaller, modern kales produce flowering stems in spring that are equally tasty. Collards should be harvested before the flowers appear.

"Kilmaurs or *Scotch* Kail are the best of any for boiling in winter, but they will not eat tender, until they are well pinched with the frost."

—James Justice, *The British Gardener's New Director* (1771)

COLLARD AND KALE ESSENTIALS

PLANTING Sow collards for transplants in late summer, when the phlox and asters bloom. Transplant when seedlings have five or six leaves.

SPACING Kale seed is sown in rows or plots, ¼ inch deep, when the goldenrod blooms. Collards are planted 2 feet apart in rows 2 feet asunder. Kale seedlings should be thinned to stand 6 inches apart in rows 12 to 18 inches asunder.

FOR BEST GROWTH Kale and collards are cool season plants that are best grown in a rich soil. Caterpillars are serious pests on collards.

HARVESTING Both collards and kales are harvested after the first frost for best flavor. In areas where the ground freezes, collard plants should be pulled before severe frost. Kales will stand winter in all but the coldest climes. Kale flowers harvested before they open in spring are a tasty bonus.

TO SAVE PURE SEED All collards and most kales will cross with other kales and collards as well as with all other members of the *Brassica* genus, so must be isolated by 1 mile.

COLLECTING AND STORING SEED Collards and kales are biennial plants that must pass through a winter season to flower. Flower stems often require support. Seeds are held in slender pods that are left to dry on the plant and may require protection from birds.

SEED VIABILITY 4 to 5 years

Seed Varieties

Varieties listed in 18th-century Virginia

♦ **'Common Colewort'**, **'Curled Colewort'**, **'Winter Colewort'**, and **'Summer Colewort'**: The most ancient of brassicas. Coleworts appear to have gone extinct around 1815.

♦ **'Curled Green Kail [sic]'** and **'Siberian Borecole'**: Green kale was similar to the modern Scotch kale, though larger; it is now classed as *B. oleracea* var. *acephala*. 'Siberian Borecole' was likely a *B. oleracea* var. *napus* cultivar.

♦ **'Large Field Colewort'**: Also known as cow cabbages for their use in feeding livestock; probably similar to 'Jersey' kale

Heirloom varieties for the modern gardener

♦ **'Green Glaze' collard**: Coarse dark green leaves, smaller than the modern 'Georgia' or 'Vates' collards

♦ **'Dwarf Green Curled' kale**: Small, hardy kale with dark green crinkled leaves

♦ **'Black Tuscan' kale**: Tonguelike, dark green wrinkled leaves, least cold-hardy of group

♦ **Siberian kale**: Blue-green tender leaves in loose whorls, very hardy

♦ **'Red Russian' kale**: Sharply indented, purple leaves, very mild flavored

CABBAGE

Brassica oleracea var. *capitata*

The Weekly Entertainer of 1819 recorded: "The Cabbage is a sovereign remedy for curing intoxication from wine, and that it has the power of preventing it; for we are informed, that by eating a certain quantity of Cabbage before dinner, we may drink as much wine as we please. . . . the phenomenon is indisputable, and the recipe, which was declared to be effectual by the ancient Egyptians, is now universally adopted in Germany." The reason for this effect was explained by the Greek botanist Theophrastus, who wrote in the 4th century BCE work *Enquiry into Plants*: "For they say that the [wine grape] vine scents the cabbage and is infected by it." As a result, he wrote, cabbage is able to "expel the fumes of drunkenness." Today, cabbage and bratwurst are more commonly served with beer than with wine at Oktoberfests around the world.

Origins of the Modern Cabbage

"Heading" cabbages (those that form heads) were known in Germany by the 12th century and may have been introduced into England as early as the 14th century, but these were likely plants that formed very loose heads and had limited distribution. John Evelyn wrote in 1699, "Tis scarce an hundred Years since we first had *Cabbages* out of *Holland*. Sir *Anth. Ashley* of *Wiburg St. Giles* in *Dorsetshire*, being (as I am told) the first who planted them in *England*."

The first cabbages were of the round form that John Gerard pictured in *The Herball* (1597) as the "White cabbage Cole." The 'Copenhagen' cabbage, developed in the 19th century and still common today, is of this type. By the 18th century, flat varieties had also been developed. Stephen Switzer, in *The Practical Kitchen Gardiner* (1727), writes of the 'Dutch' cabbage as "being the flattest and the largest of all" the forms of cabbage. The 'Flat Dutch' cabbage known to gardeners today is of this type. These large cabbages are very cold-tolerant and are the best choice for a winter crop.

'Oxheart' cabbage; 'Copenhagen' cabbage; 'Flat Dutch' cabbage

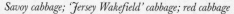

Savoy cabbage; 'Jersey Wakefield' cabbage; red cabbage

Origin of the Savoy Cabbage

Even more cold-hardy are the savoy cabbages that are characterized by crinkled, blistered leaves. They are the sweetest of all cabbages. These distinctive cabbages originated in the former Duchy of Savoy, a small province in northern Italy. They arrived in France in the 16th century with Marie de Medici, who was married to the French king, Henry IV.

Early Season Cabbage

The early season cabbages are usually conically shaped and are grown for both a spring and fall crop. One of the oldest cabbages of this type was called the 'Sugar Loaf', first noted in England early in the 17th century. It remained the premier variety of early cabbage for the next 200 years. John Randolph wrote of it in 18th-century Williamsburg: "The SUGAR LOAF, which is the finest. . . . should be sown every month and transplanted every season." Unfortunately the 'Sugar Loaf' is now extinct, but there are a number of early, conical-shaped cabbages available to the modern gardener. 'Jersey Wakefield', a 19th-century cabbage, is probably the best known of this group today.

Red Cabbage

Red cabbages are as old as the round white cabbages. They are described in Germany as early as 1150, and a red cabbage is pictured in Leonhart Fuchs's *Vienna Codex*, completed around 1563. In 1885, the 'Red Dutch' cabbage was described in Vilmorin-Andrieux's *Vegetable Garden* as "of a violet-red colour, sometimes slightly mixed with green." These cabbages were used almost exclusively for pickling.

Cabbage Comes to the New World

Cabbages were introduced into Virginia with the first settlers at Jamestown and became one of the most important greens in the diet of colonial Virginians. As the population grew and English agricultural practices were established in the New World, cabbage was planted on a large scale for feeding livestock. Some varieties were grown almost exclusively for livestock, such as the "Scott's" cabbage that George Washington planted between corn rows in 1788. *The Complete Farmer* calculated in 1766 that 12 cabbages a day was the proper quantity for one cow and that a field of cabbages had three times the value as the same acreage of turnips.

The Williamsburg Gardener's Assistant

Sowing and transplanting cabbages. Cabbages are planted both spring and fall on well-composted ground. In Williamsburg, spring cabbages are sown on a hotbed in January and transplanted to the garden in early April. For a fall crop, the seeds are sown in a nursery bed the first of August and set out in the garden with the first cool days of fall.

The cabbages are ready to transplant when the plants have five or six leaves. Plants grown in the hotbed or nursery, without the benefit of pots, must be handled with considerable care. It is very important that they are not allowed to wilt when first set

(Top) Cabbage transplants; (bottom) cheesecloth frame and cheesecloth row cover

Cabbage coleworts; cabbage sprouts; brush cover

out. For this reason, they are best moved on a cool, overcast day. As explained in *The English Pocket Gardener* (1794): "Chuse a moist day, and an hour before sun-set. . . . and give them a few careful waterings."

To transplant, use your trowel as a spade, plunging it into the ground to the full depth of the trowel and slightly slanted under the plant. Once you have cut a circle around the seedling and separated it from the surrounding soil, it may be lifted from the bed. Seedlings generally benefit from being sheltered under a bell glass for the first week. If the weather becomes warm, prop up one side of the bell glass with a shard of pottery for ventilation. If bell glasses are not available, evergreen boughs stuck in the ground on the west and south sides to shade the plants will serve nearly as well. If your seedling plants become leggy, which is often the case in fall, bury the stem up to the first set of leaves.

To produce cabbage coleworts. To produce a crop of coleworts, space the transplants 1 foot apart in rows 1 foot asunder. Once the plants are well grown, but before they cabbage (form heads), pull every other plant for use as coleworts. This allows the remaining plants 2-foot intervals to cabbage. The early season cabbages generally make the finest coleworts. In this manner, you will produce two crops from the same ground.

The dressing and harvesting of the cabbage crop. For the larger, later season cabbages, draw the earth around their stems as they grow. This, explained Thomas Hitt in 1771, "will equally strengthen them and forward their growth." It will also hold the heads upright as the season progresses. As the cabbages begin to head, John Evelyn suggested in *Kalendarium Hortense* (1706): "Remember to cut away all rotten and putrify'd Leaves from your *Cabbages*, which else will infect both *Earth* and *Air*." There are few smells as objectionable as those that come from rotting cabbage leaves, and the gardener will find that a tidy garden is a more pleasingly fragrant garden.

The early cabbages are the first to come to harvest, and careful attention must be paid to their progress, as most will head in a short time and burst if not cut soon. The 'Jersey Wakefield' is particularly prone to bursting, especially if the weather stays wet. The early varieties are not as cold-tolerant as are the late cabbages, so they must all be cleared from the fall garden before hard frosts arrive.

The late season cabbages, once they reach a mature size, can be left far into winter with only a little protection. In Williamsburg, we lay boughs of privet, pollarded for this purpose (see how in the "Growing Sticks" chapter), over the cabbage rows, and the dead air space created will preserve the plants well into January. Even when the cabbage freezes, you need only to pull off the outer leaves to find the interior fresh and green and extraordinarily sweet.

To produce cabbage sprouts. When the cabbage is ready for harvest, it should be cut from the stalk with a sharp knife, rather than pulled up roots and all. As Batty Langley advised in 1728: "When the Heads of Cabbages are cut from the Stalks, observe to cut them off sloping, with the Slope or Cut towards the South; as also to cut away from the Stalk all the bottom Leaves, to give Liberty for the free Growth of their Sprouts, which are preferable to the Cabbages themselves." The small sprouts that form on the stems of the cut cabbages provide a small but very sweet and mild harvest.

What measures may be employed to defend against the caterpillar. Cabbages, like collards, are very susceptible to damage from the imported cabbage caterpillar. Gardeners in 18th-century Williamsburg would not have been bothered by this pest, as it did not arrive in this country until the middle of the 19th century. It was well known in England, however, and its potential ravages were calculated by Richard Bradley in 1720: "Those *Caterpillars* which feed upon the *Cabbage,* and change into the common White Butter-flies, breed twice every Year, each of them laying near 400 Eggs at one time; so that from the second Brood of one single *Caterpillar* we may reasonably expect 160000."

When the plants are young, the caterpillars and the eggs that produce them can be easily found and removed, but once the plants begin to form heads, the caterpillars migrate to the heart of the plants and cannot be easily reached. We have had some success with an elixir made from tansy leaves, as explained earlier for collards. For complete control, a covering that excludes the butterfly is the easiest solution. We cover the plants with cheesecloth laid over a simple frame of sticks. The modern gardener has several fabrics available from garden supply stores that may be employed in a like manner.

Savoy and red cabbages are not as susceptible as the common early and late season cabbages are, but they, too, are occasionally attacked and should be closely monitored.

CABBAGE ESSENTIALS

PLANTING Sow seeds for spring cabbages ¼-inch deep, 4 to 6 weeks before last frost or when the first crocus blooms. Sow seed for fall cabbages in late summer, when the phlox and asters bloom. Transplant when seedlings have five or six leaves.

SPACING If planted for coleworts, separate plants by 1 foot in rows 1 foot asunder. For early season cabbages, plant 2 feet apart in rows 2 feet asunder. For larger late season cabbages, plant 2½ feet apart in rows 3 feet asunder.

FOR BEST GROWTH Cabbages require a rich soil and are best when heads mature in cool weather. Savoys are hardiest and best suited for winter. Red cabbage is better suited for spring. Caterpillars are serious pests on cabbages, but less so on savoys and red cabbages.

HARVESTING Double-crop early season cabbages by thinning for coleworts. Harvest remaining plants as soon as heads are formed and before they split. Late season cabbages are best after a frost in fall.

Both early and late season cabbages should be harvested while the heads are still tight.

TO SAVE PURE SEED Separate brassicas by 1 mile.

COLLECTING AND STORING SEED Cabbages are biennial plants that must pass through a winter season to flower. Flower stems often require support. Seeds are held in slender pods that should be left to dry on the plant and may require protection from birds.

SEED VIABILITY 4 to 5 years

Seed Varieties

Varieties listed in 18th-century Virginia

♦ **White, 'Early Dutch'**, and **'White Dutch'**: Large round and flat-headed cabbages; many were long season varieties grown as winter cabbages.

♦ **'Large Winter'**, Scotch, and **'Large Hollow'**: These large cabbages were developed for feeding livestock.

♦ **'Sugar Loaf'**, **'Battersea'**, **'Early York'**, **'Yorkshire'**, and **'Russia'**: These were the early season cabbages and were typically conical in shape.

♦ **'Yellow Savoy'** and **'Green Savoy'**: Crinkled-leaf cabbages, the sweetest and most cold-hardy of the group

♦ **Red**: The red cabbage of the 18th century had much more green on its leaves than modern varieties have.

♦ **'Madeira'**: An obscure variety that is possibly a Portuguese kale, such as 'Couve Tronchuda'.

Heirloom varieties for the modern gardener

♦ **'Copenhagen'**, **'Brunswick'**, **'Glory of Enkhuizen'**, and **'Danish Ballhead'**: Round cabbages similar to the common white of the 18th century

♦ **'Flat Dutch'**: Very large, flat-headed cabbage typical of the 18th-century 'Dutch' cabbage

♦ **'Jersey Wakefield'**, **'Winnigstadt'**, and **'Oxheart'**:

Early season conical heads similar to 'Early York' and 'Battersea'

♦ **'Winter King'**: Very hardy, open-pollinated savoy cabbage

♦ **'January King'**: 19th-century semi-savoyed cabbage similar to the 18th-century red cabbage in coloration, though very different in flavor

CAULIFLOWER

Brassica oleracea var. *botrytis*

John Randolph, the last royal attorney general for the colony of Virginia, recorded in *A Treatise on Gardening* (1793): "CAULIFLOWERS, Must be sown *critically to a day,* or else there is no dependence on the success of them. I cannot, nor do I find any one else capable of assigning a good reason for this, but the experience of this country, as well as England, verifies the proposition. We must therefore receive this fact as we do many others, rest ourselves satisfied, that the thing certainly exists, tho' the mode of existence is an impenetrable secret to us." In Virginia, he tells us, the proper days are April 12 and September 12.

The Origin of Cauliflower

Cauliflower was first described in England by John Gerard in his *Herball* of 1597 as one of the finest members of the cabbage family. It is listed by every author after this time as one of the delicacies found almost exclusively in the gardens of gentlemen. Its origin is obscure, but John Worlidge recorded in 1716 that: "Seeds are brought out of *Italy,* and the *Italians* receive it from *Candia,* and other of the *Levantine* parts." Candia is present-day Crete. Other authors place cauliflower's origins farther to the east.

The English Embrace the Cauliflower and Its Culture

By the 18th century, the English had acquired a taste for cauliflower and a proficiency in growing it that was equal to that of any nation on the European continent. Philip Miller recorded in the 1754 edition of *The Gardeners Dictionary*: "Cauliflowers have of late Years been so far improved in *England,* as to exceed in Goodness and Magnitude what are produced in most Parts of *Europe.*" In fact, the fascination with cauliflower and the desire by the English to have them available at all seasons was one of the forces behind the development of specialized gardening techniques that allowed innovative market gardeners to raise crops out of season. Richard Weston recorded in 1769: "Of all the crops raised by the kitchen-gardeners, none yield so much profit as those of collyflowers raised under glasses; and indeed the large expenses attending them require some extraordinary profit; nor are there many gardeners who . . . can afford to sink so much money as the glasses cost."

The Cauliflower in America

Cauliflower was an early introduction into the American colonies but remained a crop grown primarily by the gentry. William Hugh Grove kept a diary of his travels through Tidewater, Virginia, in 1732, and recorded: "Curl'd Savoys are Plenty but few Colyflowers or Hartichoak tho' the Gentry sometimes rayse a few."

This elite status was due to the difficulty of raising cauliflowers. John Rutter attested to this in 1767: "WE enter here upon the culture, not only of the nicest of the cabbage-kind, but perhaps the most delicate plant in the kitchen-garden." He then cautions: "If every article be not observed, it will never succeed in due perfection."

Cauliflower under bell glass

The Williamsburg Gardener's Assistant

The seasons for the best growth of cauliflower. Cauliflowers grow best when the weather remains cool and are nearest perfection when the curds that form the cauliflower head are developed at temperatures between 58° and 68°F. As most varieties of cauliflower mature between 60 and 85 days from the date of transplanting, you must plan your sowing dates accordingly.

For this reason, cauliflowers are most easily grown as a spring crop in the northern states and as a fall crop in the South. Any impediment to their growth will result in buttoning, when tiny ill-formed cauliflowers develop to the ruination of the plant. In spring, the plants must not be set so early that they are exposed to hard frosts, for this will often cause them to button. Rootbound transplants will often button, and poor soils, dry weather, or unseasonably hot weather will also cause them to go off before their time.

For the fall crop, the plants must form their curds before freezing weather arrives. Then they will tolerate mild frosts with only slight protection. For the spring crop, the plants must form their curds before the temperature reaches 85°F, or the resulting cauliflower will be of very poor quality.

When cauliflowers are sown. Seed your plants for a spring crop in a hotbed frame or conservatory 6 to 8 weeks before the average date of the last spring frost. In Williamsburg, we start them in hotbeds in the middle of January. We sow fall cauliflowers near the first of August in a nursery bed sheltered from the afternoon sun. Every precaution against drought and insect damage must be taken at this time, for weak seedlings produce weak plants that are far more likely to button.

Cauliflower pests and their various controls. The greatest danger to the spring planting within the frames is from slugs and snails. If they should appear, lay some slaked lime and ashes among the plants. Also set boards or tiles against the sides of the frames and check them every morning for these pests. If these measures should fail, the gardener may experiment with a method suggested by James Justice in

Cauliflower seedlings; cauliflower transplants; watering cauliflower

1754: "If they still persist, lay a good Mulch of Tobacco Stalks, steeped in Vinegar, around the lower Parts of your Collyflowers, and this will quite finish them at once."

The greatest danger to the fall plantation is from the cabbage caterpillar. A finely woven net will best serve to defend your plants from the butterfly that spreads the caterpillar. It is also important to keep the nursery bed free from weeds and well watered.

To manage your cauliflower transplants. When the plants have five or six leaves, they will be ready for transplanting. In Williamsburg, we follow the advice of Leonard Meager, who directed in 1683: "The ground . . . ought to be made rich with dung [now compost], and then [the cauliflowers planted] in some handsome order about two foot asunder."

If your transplants have become leggy, which often happens with fall plants, bury the stems so that their first leaves are immediately aboveground. This is best done in rainy or cloudy weather or late in the day. It will be advantageous to cover them with bell glasses to preserve fall plantings from the white butterfly and spring plantings from chilly nights and bothersome rabbits. If the weather remains hot in fall, raise the glasses on one side to admit the air.

Once the plants have rooted well, remove the bells and till the ground between the plants. Cauliflowers must not be allowed to suffer drought, so to prevent this, we dig a trough between the rows to hold water. As Bradley explained in 1718: "The *Alleys* between the *Plants* are floated with Water, which will nourish them much more than common Watering."

If the weather remains mild, this is all that is required to bring them to perfection in fall. If hot

Blanching cauliflower

weather persists, brush or boughs stuck into the ground on their south side will shade the plants.

To know when cauliflower is in its perfection. When the cauliflower begins to appear, bend some of the largest leaves over the curd and fasten them with a small twig or with twine to blanch the curd and keep it white. Modern cauliflowers will often fold their leaves over the heart of the plant by natural inclination, but the gardener may ensure the process with but a little effort.

As the curd begins to expand, take notice of the outermost florets. As explained in *Modern Eden* (1767): "The cauliflower should be left to grow till the outside pieces [of the curd] begin to spread. This is a proof that it is at the full growth, and it should be cut. The proper time of cutting them is about nine o'clock in the morning."

The gardener will find that enjoying a well-grown cauliflower comes both from its delicate flavor and the satisfaction of successfully cultivating one of the more demanding residents of the kitchen garden.

Seed Varieties

Varieties listed in 18th-century Virginia

♦ 'Early Colliflower' and 'Late Colliflower'

Heirloom varieties for the modern gardener

♦ 'Early Snowball' and 'All the Year Round': Cauliflower forms have not changed dramatically.

CAULIFLOWER ESSENTIALS

PLANTING Sow seeds for spring transplants ¼ inch deep, when the first crocus blooms. Sow seeds for fall transplants ¼ inch deep, when phlox and asters bloom.

SPACING Transplant when seedlings have five or six leaves. Set 2 feet apart in rows 2 to 2½ feet asunder.

FOR BEST GROWTH It is critical that cauliflower seedlings are well tended, as any stress may result in buttoning. Seedlings should not be exposed to temperatures below 45°F and curds must form in temperatures below 80°F.

HARVESTING Tie outer leaves over curds to keep curds from yellowing. A head is fully formed when outer florets begin to separate.

TO SAVE PURE SEED Separate brassicas by 1 mile.

COLLECTING AND STORING SEED Cauliflower is a biennial that must pass through a winter season to flower and produce seed. It is also less cold-hardy than other members of the cabbage family and will not survive temperatures below 25°F without protection. The 18th-century gardener would dig the cauliflower before severe weather set in and transplant it to a pile of sandy soil in the cellar. Whichever plants survived winter were planted back out in spring to produce seed. Store seeds in airtight containers and refrigerate.

SEED VIABILITY 4 to 5 years

BROCCOLI

Brassica oleracea var. *italica*

The original broccoli plants produced florets of several colors, but were not "stable" varieties and required continuous selection to maintain the preferred purple. As Rev. William Hanbury wrote in *A Complete Body of Planting and Gardening* (1773): "The Purple Broccoli is the most delicate of all the sorts, and admits of several varieties; such as the Green, the Brown, the Blue, and others of different tints, which will all rise from the same seed, if it is not properly saved. The Purple is called the best sort, and in that colour the Gardener is ambitious of preserving his Broccoli: The others, especially the Green and the Yellowish-coloured, are looked upon as spurious, and are frequently thrown away."

The Origin and Naming of Broccoli

The Latin root, *brachium*, for the word *broccoli* means an arm or branch and refers to the young flower shoots that all kales produce. These flower stems have been consumed by humankind since the beginning of written record. Exactly when a superior form of kale became sprouting broccoli has not been discovered. It is thought that broccoli or its predecessor originated in the eastern Mediterranean and from there found its way to Italy, for it was Italian gardeners who developed the first distinct forms of broccoli sometime before the middle of the 16th century.

By the time it was introduced into England early in the 18th century, there were several forms. As Stephen Switzer recorded in 1728 in *A Compendious, but More Particular Method*: "There are three several Kinds that I have had growing in my Garden . . . That with small whitish-yellow Flowers, like the cauliflower; others like the common Sprouts and Flowers of a Colewort; and a third, which is, in my humble Opinion, the best of all, that with purple Flowers: All

which come mix'd together, none of them being as yet (at least that I know of) ever saved separate."

The cultivation of broccoli differed from that of other members of the cabbage family. John Laurence explained in *A New System of Agriculture* (1727): "The *Brocauli* is an *Italian* Plant, brought lately from *Rome* by the present Earl of *Burlington*, who has given it a Reputation among those who love Novelties. . . . Although it is of the *Cauli* Kind; yet it requires a *particular* Management, and therefore *particular* Directions. Many,

'Roman' broccoli

ignorant of the Plant, will be sowing it in the *Spring*; but it should not be sown till about *Midsummer*, and not much *after* . . . that it may attain Strength to get over the Winter." The ancient broccoli, sometimes called sprout broccoli, must be planted in fall to grow over winter and form its florets in spring. Spring-planted broccoli produces only leaves.

Broccoli and Its Kinds

Purple broccoli was also known as 'Roman' broccoli and produced a succession of small florets throughout the spring season. White broccoli was called 'Naples', 'Neapolitan', or 'Colliflower Broccoli' and was very similar to the cauliflower. James Justice, author of *The British Gardener's New Director* (1771), declared: "I prefer the White Brocoli, or what is called the *Neopolitan* Brocoli. . . . it is a crop [that] will hold [remain good] for a considerable time, and many persons esteem them more than they do the best Collyflowers." This plant was likely similar to what is known today as long leaf, winter-hardy cauliflower. The broccoli cultivar known as 'Nine Star Perennial' is probably very much like the original cauliflower broccoli. The botanic relationship between cauliflower and broccoli is very close, distinguished by the morphology of the flower buds. Most broccoli flower buds will open to form flowers, while most cauliflower buds will not.

Introduction into America

Broccoli arrived in Virginia at a surprisingly early date: It was first noted by William Hugh Grove in 1732. Its introduction was very likely through the active trade with the Portuguese wine islands of Madeira and the Azores, rather than directly from England.

"The Roman Brocoli is the proper sort to cultivate, *otherwise called the Italian Brocoli.*"

—John Randolph, *A Treatise on Gardening* (1793)

The large-headed green broccoli available in stores today has long been known in Europe as *calabrese,* named for the Italian province of Calabria, where it presumably originated. Calabrese broccoli arrived in this country with Italian immigrants late in the 19th century, but remained a distinctly ethnic vegetable until 1927. That was the year the D'Arrigo family began growing it in the Santa Clara Valley of northern California and shipping it to the East Coast, where it became an immediate success.

The purple sprouting broccoli of the 18th century is rarely grown today, but in many ways is superior to the calabrese for the home gardener. The plants produce a longer season of harvest in spring and are much easier to manage, because pest caterpillars are more easily found in the smaller, purple-colored heads.

'Nine Star Perennial' broccoli

The Williamsburg Gardener's Assistant

The season of sprout broccoli. The management of purple sprouting broccoli is different from either calabrese broccoli or cauliflower. Sprouting broccoli is only sown in fall. Calabrese broccoli is grown as an annual and can be sown both in spring and fall at the same time that cabbages are planted.

In Williamsburg, we sow broccoli seeds in the first week of August in a seedbed under an arbor and set the transplants in the garden in September. Sprout broccoli plants are heavy feeders and grow to a large size, so the advice offered by William Hanbury in 1773 holds true to this day: "The situation should be naturally warm, and well-sheltered; the ground should be light, double-dug, and some rotten dung [compost] worked to the bottom of each trench . . . the plants should be set in rows two feet and an half asunder, and a foot and an half from each other in the rows." If the transplants have become leggy, which is often the case, they should be buried up to their lower set of leaves.

What protection is required for winter months. As the season progresses and the weather cools, the broccoli will shoot up to nearly 3 feet tall and due care must now be taken. As explained by John Hill in 1757: "The same good Growth that forwards it at this Time, exposes it more to the coming Frosts; to protect it from these, and at the same Time encrease its Vigour, proceed thus: Break the Earth between the Plants, very thoroughly, to the Depth of five Inches, and draw a good deal of it about their Stalks." Mounding soil around the stems not only protects the plants from the weather, but it also supports them from being blown down over the course of winter.

Broccoli is extraordinarily cold-hardy, but as a precaution against severely cold weather, we build a simple structure described by John Gerard in 1597: "Cover [the plants] with Hoopes and poles, that you may the more conveniently cover the whole bed or bancke with Mats, olde painted cloth, strawe or such like, to keepe it from the injurie of the colde frostie

Plant broccoli seedlings to first set of leaves; protecting broccoli from severe weather; broccoli under bell glass

Harvest broccoli with 4 inches of stem.

nightes." We use sticks to construct the hoop framework and cover the plants with a paint tarp on the coldest nights.

In northern climates, the gardener will have better success over winter by well mulching small plants with straw and covering them with bell glass.

To harvest broccoli in its perfection. As soon as the weather warms in spring, the plants will begin to grow and put forth their sprouts. The first florets of the purple sprouting broccoli are the largest, though still small compared to the modern calabrese broccoli. When harvesting the florets, cut about 4 inches of stem with the flower head. The stems will taste like asparagus and the heads like familiar green broccoli.

The greatest advantage of purple broccoli is explained by William Hanbury in *A Complete Body of Planting and Gardening* (1773): "After the heads are cut off, the stalks will send forth many side-shoots, or smaller heads, which may be gathered when the others are over; for they are equally sweet, or sweeter than the general heads, and are by many preferred before them." This second harvest is, indeed, extraordinarily sweet and will continue for many weeks if the florets are harvested regularly.

Seed Varieties

Varieties listed in 18th-century Virginia

♦ **'Roman', 'Italien', 'Early Purple',** and **'Late Purple'**: Purple sprouting broccoli was the most common variety in 18th-century Virginia.

♦ **'Colliflower Broccoli'**: Very similar to cauliflower in appearance

♦ **Green** and **Yellow**: Broccoli varieties of the 18th century were not stable; these color permutations were generally considered inferior.

Heirloom varieties for the modern gardener

♦ **'Purple Sprouting'**: Both early and late varieties are available from English seed houses.

♦ **'Nine Star Perennial'**: Similar to the 18th-century cauliflower broccoli

BROCCOLI ESSENTIALS

PLANTING Purple sprouting and cauliflower broccoli are sown in fall, when phlox and asters are in bloom, and transplanted in September or October. Calabrese is sown at the same time as sprout broccoli in fall and when crocuses bloom in spring. Transplant fall and spring calabrese when the plants have five or six leaves.

SPACING Sprout broccoli should be planted 2 feet apart in rows 2 to 2½ feet asunder. Plant calabrese 1½ feet apart in rows 2 feet asunder.

FOR BEST GROWTH Sprout broccoli must be planted in fall and often requires support for winter months. Caterpillars are a serious problem on calabrese broccoli, but seldom bother sprout broccoli.

HARVESTING Sprout broccoli should be harvested before florets open and with about 4 inches of stem. Calabrese broccoli is harvested before the florets begin to separate on the outer edges of the head and yellow flower buds appear.

TO SAVE PURE SEED Separate brassicas by 1 mile.

COLLECTING AND STORING SEED Sprout broccoli has to pass through a winter season to flower. Calabrese broccoli will often flower over summer from spring plantings. Refrigerate seed in airtight containers.

SEED VIABILITY 4 to 5 years

KOHLRABI or TURNIP CABBAGE

Brassica oleracea var. *gongylodes*

Kohlrabi was first described in England by John Gerard in 1597 as the "Round rape Cole," but the name didn't stick. By the 18th century, it was generally known as the turnep cabbage, but it was also called the cabbage turnep and the turnep colewort, and at least one author called it a turnep brocoli. The Germans proved to be more decisive: They named the plant kohlrabi and stuck with it. *Kohl* is derived from the German word for cabbage, while *rabi* derives from turnip, so in German it is the cabbage-turnip; and to this day, the Germans are the world's most enthusiastic eaters of kohlrabi.

The Ancient Turnep Cabbage

Kohlrabi is certainly one of the odder members of the cabbage family; it may also be one of the oldest. Pliny the Elder described a variety of cabbage in his *Natural History* (circa 77 CE) that "has a thin stalk near the root but grows thicker between the leaves." This may be an ancient kohlrabi, or it may be a description of the marrow-stem kale, the likely parent of kohlrabi.

Kohlrabi never became a common vegetable on English tables, but did have some admirers. As recorded by Richard Bradley in *The Compleat Seedsman's Monthly Calendar* (1738): "*Cole Rape*, or *Cole Turnep*, is rais'd in some Gardens . . . this Plant has a large Bunch or Knob as big as a large Turnep, just above Ground, and upon that there grow Leaves like Coleworts."

The turnep cabbage of the 18th century was a coarser, stronger-flavored plant than the modern kohlrabi. In Williamsburg, John Randolph wrote in his *Treatise*: "There's a Turnep CABBAGE, which being very strong is fit only for soup." In fact, when the turnep cabbage was grown at all in the colonies, it was generally grown for livestock. C. Varlo in 1785 Philadelphia reported: "Cabbage-turnep and turnep-rooted cabbage, American . . . are chiefly intended for cattle."

Both the white and purple 'Vienna' kohlrabi grown by gardeners today are sweeter, milder plants.

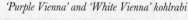

'Purple Vienna' and 'White Vienna' kohlrabi

The Williamsburg Gardener's Assistant

The culture of kohlrabi. Of all the members of the cabbage tribe, kohlrabi is the easiest to grow. At Williamsburg, they are sown in spring and fall at the same time that the cabbages are planted and are transplanted to a rich soil while they are still young (with no more than six leaves).

As they are small plants, they may be spaced at only 1 foot apart. They will be ready for harvest about 2 weeks before the earliest cabbages. For the sweetest flavor, harvest kohlrabi when it is no more than 2 inches in diameter. As kohlrabi is ready for harvest within 6 weeks from setting out, multiple crops may be sown in the middle and southern states. Plan your sowings so that your plants are ready before the ground freezes in fall and before hot weather commences in summer.

Kohlrabi seedlings

KOHLRABI ESSENTIALS

PLANTING Kohlrabi is sown in spring when the crocuses bloom and in fall when phlox and asters are in flower. Succession plantings may be made every 3 weeks until warm weather begins in spring and cold weather begins in fall.

SPACING Kohlrabi may be grown in 1-foot squares, either in rows or in plots.

FOR BEST GROWTH It is an easy plant that only requires a well-composted soil and adequate water.

HARVESTING Harvest while bulbs are small for best flavor and texture. Small bulbs are often eaten raw or sliced for hors d'oeuvres. Oversize bulbs tend to split and harden in the middle.

TO SAVE PURE SEED Separate brassicas by 1 mile.

COLLECTING AND STORING SEED Kohlrabi must pass through a winter season to flower and seed. Plants can be stored in sand in the cellar or protected under bells or frames in the garden.

Seed Varieties

Varieties listed in 18th-century Virginia

♦ **'Turnip Cabbage'** and **'Turnip Colewort'**: The 18th-century turnip cabbage, or kohlrabi, was a coarse, strong-flavored vegetable.

Heirloom varieties for the modern gardener

♦ **'Purple Vienna'** and **'White Vienna'**: Well-flavored 19th-century introductions

CHAPTER 3

of
Salad Greens

Leafy greens were likely among the first vegetables used by humankind, particularly in early spring when young, tender leaves first emerged from soil and branch. All areas of the world have indigenous greens, but most of the salad greens familiar to modern gardeners, including lettuce, spinach, endive, chard, and parsley, originated between India and the Mediterranean basin.

The English word *salad* derives from the Latin *herba salata,* or salted herb, which referred to the first salad dressing. Many of the common salad greens were introduced into England from Italy, often by way of France. John Evelyn wrote in *Acetaria: a Discourse of Sallets* [Salads] in 1699: "The more frugal *Italians* and *French,* to this Day, gather *Ogni Verdura,* any thing almost that's *Green* and Tender . . . so as every Hedge affords a *Sallet."*

In addition to the familiar salad greens, many, many other plants–purslane, burdock, orache, salad burnet, sea kale, dandelion, sorrel, and alexander–have been used as greens. Flowers also have been added to the salad bowl. Leonard Meager in *The English Gardener* (1683) listed the flowers of cowslip, borage, bugloss, and gillyflowers (stock) as salad ingredients. Perhaps the most common flower used in salads since its introduction into Europe from the West Indies in the 16th century has been the peppery-flavored nasturtium.

The English were not great salad eaters until the 18th century. Giacomo Castelvetro, an Italian refugee in London, commented in 1614 on the English aversion to vegetables: "The vast influx of so many refugees from the evils and cruelties of the Roman Inquisition has led to the introduction of delights previously considered inedible, worthless or even poisonous. Yet I am amazed that so few of these delicious and health-giving plants are being grown to be eaten."

LETTUCE
Lactuca sativa

Min, the Egyptian god of fertility, was often depicted with offerings of lettuce, considered an aphrodisiac by the ancient Egyptians. In Greek mythology, lettuce gained a very different reputation. The beautiful Adonis, lover of Aphrodite and Persephone, was killed by a boar while hiding in a garden of lettuce. The association of lettuce with the death of Adonis pretty much ruined its reputation as a sexy salad green, and for thousands of years it was associated with impotence and lack of libido. The Pythagoreans, that most dour of ancient sects, extolled a variety of lettuce known as eunuch because it "relaxes desire." Today, the lettuce salad has regained a measure of romance as an appetizer on candlelit tables.

Lettuce in the Ancient World

The earliest depiction of lettuce is found at the temple of Pharaoh Senusret I at Karnak, Egypt, indicating that lettuce has been known and cultivated for at least 4,000 years. These ancient varieties of lettuce were of an upright, open-headed form, much like the modern romaine lettuce, and were possibly used as a sedative rather than as a salad ingredient. The lettuce genus, *Lactuca*, derives from the Latin *lac*, or milk, in reference to the milky sap called lactucarium contained in the stems of wild lettuce. This compound is often known as lettuce opium and has long been used for its hypnotic and sleep-inducing properties.

The Roman naturalist Pliny the Elder described a variety of lettuce that was already ancient in the 1st century CE "called 'meconis,' a name which it derives from the abundance of milk, of a narcotic quality." Pliny added: "In former times, this last was the only kind of lettuce that was held in any esteem in Italy." As late as 1831, John Loudon recorded in *An Encyclopædia of Agriculture*: "The lettuce might be grown for its milky juice, as a substitute for, or rather a variety of opium."

By the 1st century CE, varieties of lettuce that contained much less lactucarium and were much less bitter were available. These were being used before the main course as an appetizer very much the way lettuce salads are used today. Pliny described these lettuces as "possessed of cooling and refreshing properties, for which reason it is, that they are so highly esteemed in summer; they have the effect, also, of removing from the stomach distaste for food, and of promoting the appetite."

The First of the Modern Lettuces

Cos is one of the oldest varieties of lettuce available today. It was named for the Isle of Cos in the Aegean Sea, where it likely originated. From there it was introduced into Italy and from Italy to northern Europe and England with the Roman legions. By 1629, Parkinson recorded in *Paradisi in Sole:* "There are so many sorts, and so great diversitie of Lettice, that I doubt I shall scarce be beleeved."

The Cabbage Lettuce and How It Heads

The first "cabbaging" lettuce appeared in the middle of the 16th century. Most gardeners considered these heading lettuces superior to the older cos or Roman lettuces, but how to get the lettuce to consistently form heads remained a mystery. Charles Estienne and John Liebault wrote in the French work *L'Agriculture et Maison Rustique* (1564) that lettuce could be made to form heads by trampling on the plants. John Gerard, the imaginative author of the *Herball* (1597), suggested that: "by manuring, transplanting, and having regarde to the moone and other circumstances"

Cos lettuce

lettuce may be made to form heads like a cabbage.

As late as the 1760s, when John Randolph wrote *A Treatise on Gardening* in Williamsburg, he recorded that the common leaf lettuce was nothing more than "the Cabbage Lettuce degenerated as all seed will do that is saved from a Lettuce that has not Cabbage closely." This seemed to suggest that lettuce somehow acquired its cabbaging properties from the cabbage plant.

'Tennis Ball' and 'Brown Dutch' Lettuces

The 18th-century gardener could choose from many varieties of lettuce. Two of the most popular and best-tasting lettuces known to colonial Virginians and still available to the modern gardener are the 'Capuchin' and 'Brown Dutch' lettuces. In Williamsburg, John Randolph wrote: "The DUTCH BROWN, and green Capuchin are very hardy, will stand the winters best, and remain in the heat of summer 3 weeks longer than any before they go to seed." The 'Capuchin', better known today as 'Tennis Ball' lettuce, is very similar to the modern Boston lettuce. 'Brown Dutch' forms a small, loose head with attractive brown leaf colorings that can range from a blush on the margins of the leaf to the entire leaf. Both are excellent salad lettuces.

The Prince of Salads

Lettuce was among the most popular of garden plants in 18th-century Virginia. In a disparaging assessment of Virginia gardeners, Francis Michel, a Swiss traveler who was in the Williamsburg area from October 1701 until December 1702, recorded in his journal, "The inhabitants pay little attention to garden plants, except lettuce, although most everything grows here." This mirrored the sentiment in England, where Stephen Switzer observed in 1727: "It ever was, and still continues to be the principal foundation of the universal tribe of sallets." This is a distinction that lettuce holds to this day.

'Tennis Ball' lettuce; 'Brown Dutch' lettuce

The Williamsburg Gardener's Assistant

What care is necessary to grow lettuce in fall. Lettuce should be grown for every season of the year. For the fall crop, sow your seeds in late summer in a bed well sheltered from the afternoon sun. As it is a small seed, a suitable method for sowing in the nursery bed was suggested by John Rutter in 1767: "Sow the lettuce-seed not too thick: sift over it a quarter of an inch of mould [fine, organically enriched soil], and water the bed lightly every morning. When the plants come up, weed the ground by hand, and draw away a few of the lettuces, where they rise very close; then water them, and let them stand till they have a little strength [for transplantation]."

When the lettuces have four or five leaves, they will be ready to move from the seedbed into the garden, where they will stand for harvest. In Williamsburg, we space them according to the recommendations given by William Hanbury in 1773: "Draw out the strongest, and plant them in well-prepared beds, at about a foot distance from each other. At this time give them a moderate watering,

and repeat it every morning until they have taken root." Lettuce plants set in the garden by the middle of September will be ready for harvest in late October and early November.

Raising lettuce transplants for winter months. The winter crop of lettuce is sown as the days begin to cool in fall. In Williamsburg, this is near the first of October. The seedlings are sown into a nursery bed and managed in the same manner as the fall planting. When they have achieved the proper size and have four or five leaves, they are transplanted into cold frames as instructed by Walter Nicol in 1798: "These are to be planted . . . under a frame and lights [window sashes], [taking care that] they are to be duly refreshed with water, have air freely admitted to them in fresh weather, and defended from severe frosts."

A method for blanching cos or romaine lettuce. Winter is the proper season for planting cos or romaine lettuces that are intended for tying up and

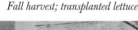
Fall harvest; transplanted lettuce

Tying cos for blanching; unwrapping the cos; blanched cos hearts

blanching. These are the coarsest and bitterest of the lettuce tribe, and to remedy this, gardeners have long "whited," or blanched, them. One method was explained by Giacomo Castelvetro in 1614: "Our ingenious gardeners tie [the lettuce] tightly together round a cane, so that the insides blanch as white as snow and become wonderfully crisp."

To blanch cos lettuce, let the plants grow within cold frames until the outer leaves begin to fall and then take a stout thread and bind them. Begin by tying a loop, not too tight, at the base of the plant and around a stick or cane. Gather the leaves together and spiral the string around them to the top of the leaves, making a proper head. In a fortnight [2 weeks], the lettuce will head handsomely, and the inner leaves will turn a creamy whitish color, which vastly improves their flavor.

What care is necessary to preserve lettuce in winter. As colder weather arrives, the cold frames are left closed on cloudy days, but whenever the sun shines, the window sashes must be vented or removed. Take every opportunity to inspect the plants. As advised by Robert Edmeades in 1776:

"During the Winter, look those over which are in the frame, pick off all decayed leaves, moss and weeds, and gently stir the surface of the earth." If you are bothered by slugs or snails within the frames, try the simple method for removing them given by William Thompson in 1779: "If you place bricks, tiles, or boards, hollow against your pales and walls, the snails will creep under them for shelter, and may then be taken." We use boards set on the inside of the south walls of the frames and inspect them every morning for slugs and snails.

When the temperature is forecast to be lower than 25°F, cover the glasses at night with straw and lay a tarp over all as added insulation. Winter lettuce is the finest crop of the year. Not only is it sweeter, as all greens are when touched by frost, but the lettuce is slower to bolt, or run to flower, providing a much prolonged harvest. In Williamsburg, we can begin to harvest the outer leaves in December. The plants head up and mature in February and March.

Starting spring lettuce in hotbeds. For the spring crop of lettuce, the seed should be sown within a hotbed or in a conservatory by the middle or end of

January. In the hotbed, cover the seeds with ¼ inch of fine, organically enriched soil. Water them lightly with water that has been heated so that it's warm (not hot) to the touch. This will set the seeds and not retard the heat in the bed.

We find that it is easiest to sow the seeds thickly and reset them as soon as their first set of leaves develops. To accomplish this, lift the entire row while the plants are in the two-leaf stage, carefully tease them apart, and lay them in a basket. You can then level the soil and remove any weeds that have sprouted. After firming the soil with your hand or the flat of your trowel, make evenly spaced holes with a dibble about 3 inches apart to receive the plants.

Take the individual seedlings from your basket, being careful to handle them by the leaves and not the stems. Drop them into the holes and lightly firm them in. Once this is accomplished, water them with water that has been warmed to the heat of the bed. This will set them and nourish them.

Some of the excess seedlings that are not replaced within the frames can then be moved to the garden under bell glasses, setting three plants per glass. These will remain until they are wanted to supply the garden in spring.

(Clockwise from top) Slug and snail traps; winter lettuce crop; covering frames in severe weather

(Top) Lettuce seedlings in hotbed; (bottom) handle seedlings by the leaves; separating seedlings; seedlings reset in hotbed

When the seedlings within the hotbed frame have five or six leaves, transplant them to the cold frame. These will provide the first spring salads, to be followed by the plants under bell glass transplanted to mature in open ground. From these plantings, lettuce can be supplied until the end of May.

What is required for a summer harvest of lettuce?
For the summer crop, the gardener is best served by the small lettuces that include varieties such as 'Oakleaf', 'Black-Seeded Simpson', and 'Red Sails'. These lettuces, often called cutting lettuce, are meant to be cut young and mixed with other small salad greens,

often called a mesclun mix today. William Hanbury in *A Complete Body of Planting and Gardening* (1773) explained how to manage them: "Keep them clean from weeds; and when they are very small, they may be thinned for table use . . . and thus may the practice be repeated all summer, only with this difference . . . if they are stationed in too warm a place, they will run up, for the most part, to seed."

We find that it is easiest to sow the seed thickly and lift the seedlings for replanting at about 2-inch intervals when they are still in the seed-leaf stage, in the same manner that we manage the seedlings in the winter hotbed. Once they have taken root, thin them to 4 inches apart. Summer lettuce is grown within our cold frames, otherwise idle during this time of year, which allows us to easily shade the seedlings by fastening cheesecloth over them. If well managed, this planting will provide tender and colorful salad greens throughout most of the summer months.

(Top) Cutting lettuce seedlings; lifting seedlings; dibble holes; (bottom) separating seedlings; placing seedlings; summer lettuce under cheesecloth

LETTUCE ESSENTIALS

PLANTING Lettuce is sown throughout the year. Spring and fall plants are sown to form mature heads, summer lettuce is cut small, and winter lettuce is sown for heading and blanching.

SPACING Heading lettuce should be spaced at 1 to 1½ feet asunder, depending on variety. "Cutting lettuce" for summer months should be grown on 4- to 6-inch centers.

FOR BEST GROWTH The finest lettuce is grown during cool weather in a moist, rich soil. For the coarser lettuce, such as cos, a light freeze greatly improves flavor and texture.

HARVESTING Spring and fall lettuces must be harvested soon after heading, for they will soon bolt. Winter lettuce can be left in the bed much longer without bolting. Summer lettuces must be cut while still young and sweet.

TO SAVE PURE SEED Lettuce varieties seldom cross, but should be separated by 25 feet to discourage any occasional occurrences.

COLLECTING AND STORING SEED Some varieties of heading lettuce have difficulty pushing seed stalks through their heads. This can be facilitated by cutting a slice in the top of each head. The seedheads of many varieties require staking for ease of seed harvest. Refrigerate seed in airtight containers.

SEED VIABILITY 3 years

Seed Varieties

Varieties listed in 18th-century Virginia

- ‘White Cass,’ ‘Black Cass’, ‘Egyptian Coss’, ‘Versailles Coss’, ‘Roman’, and ‘Italian Loaf’: Upright open-headed lettuces similar to modern romaine

- ‘Aleppo’: Upright romaine-type lettuce with purple speckles

- ‘Curled’: Open lettuce with curled leaves, described as an endive-leaved variety

- ‘Cabbage’ lettuce: Perhaps the first heading lettuce, a variable variety considered inferior by the 18th century

- ‘Ice’: Somewhat open, oblong-headed lettuce with blistered, shiny leaves

- ‘Imperial’: Large oblong- and loosely headed winter hardy lettuce

- ‘Brown Dutch’: Tender, loosely headed lettuce with brown coloration, particularly on leaf margins, but sometimes entire leaf

- ‘Capuchin’, ‘Tennis Ball’: Loosely headed lettuce similar to Boston lettuce

- ‘Silesia’: A large, loosely headed lettuce with wavy, often red-tinged leaf margins

- ‘Nonpareil’: Common variety name of uncertain attributes

Heirloom varieties for the modern gardener

- ‘Tennis Ball’, ‘Brown Dutch’, ‘Aleppo’, ‘Egyptian Cos’, and many others

SPINACH

Spinacia oleracea

Spinach came to Europe by way of Spain and was one of the last of the salad greens to be adopted by the English. William Turner recorded in 1568 that spinach was "an herb lately found and not long in use." Once adopted, it became one of the most popular greens on the English table. An extraordinary example of the English affection for spinach was recorded in the *Memoirs of the noted Buckhorse* in 1756: "Yesterday Mr. *Suet*, a Tallow-chandler of great Business, cut his Throat from Ear to Ear, owing, it is said, to his Wife's having over-boiled a Leg of Lamb and Spinage; a Dish it seems he was extremely fond of. The Coroner's Inquest . . . brought in their Verdict, *accidental Death.*"

The Origin and Classification of Spinach

Spinach was probably developed from the wild *Spinacia tetranda* that is still gathered in the Turkish countryside. It was known in Persia by the 3rd century CE, but was not known by the ancient Greeks or Romans. From Persia it was introduced into Moorish Spain, where Ibn Hajjaj in 1047 wrote a monograph on spinach.

The etymology of spinach follows a clear path from Persia to Spain and from there to the rest of Europe. From the Persian *ispanai* (meaning "green hand") we get the Spanish *espinaca*. From the Spanish word we get the Old French *espinache,* and from this

Thick-leafed spinach; young prickly-seeded spinach leaves

Prickly-seeded spinach; smooth-seeded 'Viroflay' spinach

we get the English *spinach*. The first European to illustrate spinach was the German botanist Leonhart Fuchs, who called it "*Spinachia*" in *De Historia Stirpium* (1542) and recorded that it was a Spanish vegetable resembling "*Mangolt*" (Swiss chard).

It is not clear when spinach was first introduced into England. The Archbishop of Canterbury wrote of "spynhach" at Lambeth in 1322, and "spynoches" are included in an English cookbook from 1390 called *The Forme of Cury*. However, it is possible that these references actually referred to orach (*Atriplex hortensis*). When Gerard's *Herball* was published in 1597, he said of spinach, "I rather take it for a kind of Orach." Spinach became more common in 17th-century English gardens, but the confusion over where to fit it into the botanic system lasted for well over 100 years. In 1710, William Salmon wrote in *Botanologia*: "Some Authors will have it to be a Species of the *Araches*; others of the *Beets*; others again of the *Blites*: but I think it has no Relation to any of these Plants, but is a particular kind of its own."

Prickly- and Smooth-Seeded Spinach

The first spinach grown in Europe was the prickly-seeded form, which was a particular favorite of Catherine de Medici, a native of Florence, Italy, and wife of the 16th-century French king, Henry II. She was very likely responsible for the culinary treatment referred to as "à la Florentine," in which dishes are prepared on a bed of spinach.

Smooth-seeded spinach, which is the variety that is universally grown today, was known by the early 17th century. John Parkinson wrote in *Paradisi in Sole* (1629) that there were three sorts of spinach: two prickly and "the third that beareth a smooth seede, which is more daintie, and noursed up but in few Gardens."

By the 18th century, both the smooth- and the prickly-seeded spinaches were well known in Williamsburg, but smooth-seeded spinach was the preferred variety. The prickly-seeded spinach, often called winter spinach by 18th-century authors, had a light green, distinctly triangular leaf and the inconvenient habit of bolting and running to seed much sooner than the modern smooth-seeded varieties.

The Williamsburg Gardener's Assistant

The proper season for the sowing of spinach. In the middle and southern states, spinach is sown in autumn after the weather cools. Gardeners are often disappointed by poor germination in the fall garden, which is usually a result of sowing the seeds before the weather cools. Most varieties of spinach germinate very poorly in temperatures above 80°F, so rushing the season is generally a waste of seed. The greatest advantage of fall-sown spinach, other than the extraordinary sweetness of the leaves after the first frost, is that these plants will be ready for harvest much sooner in spring than will plants that are sown in spring.

In the northern states, spinach is sown as soon as the weather cools in late summer for a fall harvest. If protected with a straw mulch, spinach will usually stand the winter for a spring harvest in all but the most severe climates. In areas where spinach will not stand the winter, it can be sown as soon as the ground thaws in spring.

Stephen Switzer observed in 1727 that spinach, "is one of those kitchen plants that requires the best ground, or at least that which is most amended by dung [compost]." Spinach delights in a rich, continually moist soil. This is especially true for seedlings, so every effort to improve your ground will be rewarded with more robust growth, fewer problems from insects, and a more succulent harvest.

The method of sowing spinach. The area where you intend to sow spinach should be finely raked and leveled. The seeds are either sown in rows or in bands. In either case, cover the seeds with no more than $\frac{1}{4}$ inch of soil and gently water them in. When the weather remains dry, it is important that the ground remains continually moist with gentle watering.

If the spinach is meant for broadcasting, the seed is raked in, as explained by Samuel Fullmer in 1795: "Dig an open compartment of ground, and

Frosted spinach; spinach seedlings; harvest entire plant in spring.

directly sow the seed thinly on the surface, thread it evenly down, and rake it in regularly; and when the plants have got leaves an inch broad . . . thin them to three or four inches distance." For fall harvest, gather the outer leaves, leaving the crown of the plant to continue growing. In spring, as the plants expand and become crowded, you may thin them by pulling entire plants by the roots.

The smooth-seeded spinach will last from fall to spring, but the prickly-seeded kind comes to perfection much quicker and bolts much sooner. In Williamsburg, we make a second sowing in November or early December to furnish the spring garden. As soon as the ground thaws in the spring, both sorts of spinach may be sown for an early harvest of baby spinach leaves.

Seed Varieties

Varieties listed in 18th-century Virginia

♦ **'Summer'**, **'Broad leaf'**, and **'Round'**: Rounded, often blistered leaves, generally thicker than winter spinach

♦ **'Winter'** or **'Prickly'**: Light green, smooth, triangular leaves

Heirloom varieties for the modern gardener

♦ **'Prickly'**: Seeds are prickly.

♦ **'Viroflay'**: Italian variety with large, relatively smooth, dark leaves

♦ **'Giant'**: Thick, rounder leaf, moderately savoyed

SPINACH ESSENTIALS

PLANTING In the middle and southern states, sow spinach in the fall after the weather cools, when goldenrod is in full bloom. Germination is enhanced by refrigerating seeds for 2 weeks before sowing. In northern states, fall-sown plants will often overwinter with a loose mulch and the natural insulation provided by snow. Spring plantings, particularly in the north, will provide an extended season of baby spinach leaves.

SPACING Plant seed no more than $1/2$ inch deep, in rows 12 to 18 inches apart. Thin plants to 3 inches apart.

FOR BEST GROWTH Spinach is a cool season plant, performing best in weather below 70°F. Ensure a continually moist soil with plenty of compost.

HARVESTING Harvest outer leaves in fall and entire plants in spring. Remove entire planting as soon as plants show signs of bolting to seed.

TO SAVE PURE SEED Spinach is wind pollinated, and pollen can be carried for miles under favorable conditions.

COLLECTING AND STORING SEED Allow seed to dry on the plant, if possible. If the weather remains wet, seed can be harvested and dried indoors. Use gloves to harvest prickly-seeded spinach. Refrigerate seed in airtight containers.

SEED VIABILITY 4 to 5 years

ENDIVE

Cichorium endivia

Endive and Chicory

Endive has been used either medicinally or as a pot herb since at least Roman times and likely much longer. It is often confused with the very closely related succory, or chicory (*Cichorium intybus*), in the ancient garden books. A 1616 English translation of the French *L'Agriculture et Maison Rustique* (1564), *The Countrey Farme,* records: "Endive . . . is more serviceable in Physicke than any other wayes, and is not planted in Gardens, because it is alwaies bitter." This is almost certainly a reference to chicory.

This same confusion between the two *Cichorium* species is seen in *The Gardener's Labyrinth* (1577): "The Endyve, otherwise named the Sycorie, or soure Lettuce, serveth rather for the use of Medicine, than for other purposes."

Both endive and chicory are bitter herbs, but chicory is far more bitter than endive. As recorded by Stephen Switzer in *The Practical Kitchen Gardiner* (1727), "Succory, when it is yet green, is so bitter that there are but few can eat it raw." Endive can be made less bitter and more palatable through blanching. This process was first explained by John Parkinson in *Paradisi in Sole* (1629): "Of many eaten greene, but more usually being buried a while in sand, that it may grow white, which causeth it to lose both some part of the bitternesse, as also to bee the more tender in the eating."

The Forms of Endive and Their Properties

Parkinson listed two forms of endive: the smooth or broadleaf endive known today as escarole or 'Batavian' endive (*C. endivia* var. *latifolium*) and the curled endive (*C. endivia* var. *crispa*). He also observed that "the curld Endive is both farre the fairer, and the tenderer." This sentiment was shared by almost all authors after this time, and it is often the only endive available at market today. Broadleaf endive blanches to a creamy yellow, rather than to the purer white of the curled, and has a more robust flavor that is not without its admirers.

Even when blanched, endive is not liked by everyone. Batty Langley wrote in *New Principles of Gardening* (1728): "Endive is an excellent Winter and Spring Sallet, and highly deserves our Care." Ten years earlier, Richard Bradley wrote: "*Endive,* when it is blanch'd, is much used about *London* in *Winter Sallets;* tho', in my Opinion, it is a Plant hardly worth our trouble, as it has neither Taste nor Flavour."

'Batavian' endive; curled endive

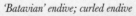

The Williamsburg Gardener's Assistant

What diligence is required in the sowing of endive. Endive is best sown for a fall and winter crop, as it is much improved by cooler weather. It is generally started in a nursery bed in late summer and then transplanted to the garden. Stephen Switzer observed in *The Practical Kitchen Gardiner* (1727) that endive is one of the class of vegetables "which succeed not without being transplanted."

Once the seeds have germinated in the nursery bed, we follow the instructions given by John Reid in *The Scots Gardener* (1766): "When they have five

leaves, transplant them into a rich border," spacing them a foot or 18 inches apart, and "watering them well until they root; so soon as they turn bushy or thick of stalk . . . tie them up regularly with . . . strings in dry weather."

Various methods for the blanching of endive. Endive can be blanched either by covering it with a pot or by burying the entire plant. John Randolph employed the latter method in 18th-century Williamsburg, explaining that endive was transplanted to trenches and earthed up in the manner of celery. We prefer the former method. Begin by gathering the leaves together and then tying them up with twine, taking care that they are perfectly dry. Any amount of moisture on the foliage will cause the leaves to rot. Cover the plants with a clay pot that is large enough so that the leaves do not touch the inside of it. For perfect blanching, care should be

(Top) Tying endive; (bottom) endive under pots; blanched endive; endive under paper frame for spring harvest

taken that no amount of light is allowed to enter the pot. To ensure complete darkness, plug the drainage hole with a peg and earth up around the pot's rim. With proper care, the endive will be sufficiently blanched in 10 days.

Once blanched, the endive must be used immediately, for it does not store well. For this reason, the plants should be blanched a few at a time. As explained by Stephen Switzer in 1727, "Tie it up with bass mats to whiten it, tho' not all together, but some one time and some another, as occasion requires, it being apt to rot when it has been long tied up." In Williamsburg, the last of autumn endive

is blanched and ready for the table during the Christmas season.

What care is required to have endive for the spring season? If a spring harvest is desired, plants may be sown in October and transplanted under paper frames to stand winter. (See the "Gardening under Cover" chapter for information on frames.) As explained in *The Practical Gardener* (1778), "Those who desire to have endive all the spring, should cover the plants in hard winters." This crop of endive is most often used green, for as soon as warm weather arrives, it is not possible to blanch the endive without rotting it.

ENDIVE ESSENTIALS

PLANTING Seed in late summer, when the phlox and asters bloom. Transplant to the garden when plants have five or six leaves. In the South and middle states, a second crop may be sown in fall, as tree leaves begin to color.

SPACING Sow seeds not more than ½ inch deep and transplant seedlings 8 to 12 inches apart, in rows 18 to 24 inches asunder. If meant for blanching under pots, space according to diameter of pot rims.

FOR BEST GROWTH Endive is tolerant of many soil conditions, but the leaves are more tender in a richer soil. Plants that are overwintered are best preserved under row covers.

HARVESTING Endive is much sweeter when blanched for 10 to 14 days before harvest. Freezing weather improves flavor by lessening bitter properties.

TO SAVE PURE SEED Separate varieties by half a mile.

COLLECTING AND STORING SEED Endive is a biennial plant that must grow over a winter season to flower and set seed. Seed stalks often require staking, and finches will occasionally take the seeds. Refrigerate in airtight containers.

SEED VIABILITY 8 years

Seed Varieties

Varieties listed in 18th-century Virginia
♦ 'Curled' and 'Broadleaf'

Heirloom varieties for the modern gardener
Endive varieties have changed very little through the centuries.

PARSLEY

Petroselinum crispum

Both the flat- and curled-leaf varieties of parsley have been known for thousands of years. The method of obtaining the different leaf forms, however, was long a mystery. Thomas Hill advised in 1577: "If the owner or Gardener would have the leaves growe verye broade then let him attende to the words of the worthy Greeke Florentinus, who willeth to take up of Parselie Seedes at one tyme, as muche as can handsomly be holden betweene three of the fingers, and these after the tying up in a thinne or well worne linnen cloth, to be set into a shallowe hole with dung [compost], handsomly mixed in. . . . The Parsely may the Gardener cause to growe crisped in leafe, if he thrust and bestowe the Seedes a little before the sowing in a ball stuffed with them, whiche [are then] broken somewhat with a staffe."

The Genesis of Parsley and Its Kinds

Parsley is another ancient resident of southern Europe and has been used both as a medicine and a culinary plant for thousands of years. Pliny the Elder wrote in 1st-century Rome that not a salad or a sauce was served without it. It was likely that the Romans first introduced parsley into England. Aelfric of Eynsham, an English abbot, listed parsley in a Latin vocabulary composed in 995 CE.

The most common variety of parsley throughout most of its history has been the flat-leaf, or Italian, parsley. Curled parsley was known in England by the time Thomas Hill wrote the *Gardener's Labyrinth* in 1577, but was the less common of the two sorts and remained a curiosity for another two centuries. In 1741, Philip Miller recorded that curled parsley was found only in "curious Gardens, for garnishing Dishes" and noted that the flat-leaf was the variety of parsley preferred by cooks.

The Preference of Hares

Rabbits, on the other hand, seem to prefer the curled parsley, judging by our current experience in the Colonial Garden in Williamsburg, as well as the experience of John Randolph in 18th-century Williamsburg. Randolph wrote: "Where you breed Rabits it may be sown in the fields, Hares and Rabits being remarkable fond of it, will resort to it from great distances." This may have been advantageous at a time when a rabbit browsing in the garden in the morning would very likely have been found in a pot in the kitchen by the afternoon. In the modern garden, rabbits are more often a pest than a dinner entrée.

'Flat-Leaf' parsley; 'Curled' parsley; turnip-rooted parsley

The Utility of Parsley in the Kitchen and on the Plate

Parsley's greatest fame and utility for cooks throughout history has been as a member of the group of sweet herbs that also contains rosemary, sage, and thyme. As Stephen Switzer observed in *The Practical Kitchen Gardiner* (1727): "The cook can never be without it, there being nothing more proper for stuffing . . . and other sauces." Once the meal is over, we may follow the advice of Thomas Hill: "There is nothing that doth like sweeten the mouth, as the freshe and greene Parselie eaten." This is the best use of the curled parsley, which is generally the sweeter variety.

The Turnip-Rooted Parsley

The turnip-rooted or 'Hamburg' parsley has been a curiosity in the garden throughout its history. It appears to have been introduced into England in the 18th century. Philip Miller wrote in *The Gardeners Dictionary* (1754): "The great-rooted Garden Parsley is now more known in *England* than it was some Years ago: in *Holland* it is very common in all their Markets." Then, as now, the roots were generally peeled and used in soups.

"He that will have it curled, must bruise the seed with a pestle of Willow, to the end that the huske may breake and fall off, and afterward wrap it in a Linnen Cloth, and so put it in the ground. Otherwise, without thus much to doe, it may be made to curle howsoever it be sowne, if you draw a Rowler upon it so soone as it beginneth to grow."

—*The Countrey Farme* (1616) (Translation of *L'Agriculture et Maison Rustique,* 1564)

The Williamsburg Gardener's Assistant

What patience is required in the sowing of parsley. When sowing parsley, patience is the gardener's best companion. In 18th-century Williamsburg, John Randolph recorded the common wisdom that "the seed goes nine times to the devil" before coming up. He is alluding to parsley's notoriously slow rate of germination: It sometimes takes 6 weeks to appear aboveground.

Parsley is a biennial plant, and as with all members of its tribe, is in its perfection in fall. It then grows through winter to flower and seed in spring. For the main crop, start the seed in late July on a moist, partially shaded bed that has been long cultivated and free of weeds. This ensures that the plants are not covered over by weeds during the time they take to germinate. In September, the seedlings will be of a size to move to the garden, where they will stand the winter.

The cultivation of swallowtail butterflies. In many parts of the country, parsley plants will be visited in fall by the caterpillar of the black swallowtail butterfly. If not plucked from the plant, the caterpillars will strip the leaves entirely to the ground. The gardener who likes to have these pleasant caterpillar "ornaments" about the garden should always have some parsnips growing nearby, so that the caterpillars may be placed upon them. They will thrive on the parsnip foliage and do no damage to the parsnip root.

Securing parsley for winter months. Walter Nicol cautioned in *The Scotch Forcing and Kitchen Gardener* (1798): "A winter store is better secured by covering with a frame and lights, or hand-glasses." We have found that bell glasses and a generous straw mulch answer this purpose best and will preserve the foliage in perfection throughout January and February.

Parsley transplants; black swallowtail caterpillars

(Clockwise from left) 'Curled' parsley under bell glass; turnip-rooted parsley; summer parsley

What care is necessary to have parsley in summer months? In spring, the plants will quickly run to flower, set their seeds, and die. As parsley is in constant demand in the kitchen and at the table, it should also be sown in spring to have a summer crop. The disadvantage of summer parsley is that hot weather will turn it bitter if the plant is allowed to grow too large. To remedy this, Benjamin Townsend suggested in 1726: "You must keep it cut down, and it will shoot a-fresh, for the Nicety of it is to have it young." These young cuttings are sweet. The gardener may find it more convenient to raise summer parsley in pots. These are easier to water and can be moved to the shade in the hottest weather.

Cultivation of the turnip-rooted parsley. Those who wish to grow 'Hamburg' parsley need only follow the advice of Samuel Fullmer: "The large-rooted parsley is by many admired for its large wholesome root, being long, taper, white, and carrot-shaped, attaining a handsome size, good to boil and use as carrots, and in soups. . . . It is propagated by seed, sowed every Spring, in February, March, or April, in an open quarter of light ground, which being properly digged, sow the seed, either on the surface, tread it down, and then raked in lightly; or in shallow drills six inches asunder, and covered in [soil] about half an inch deep."

Fullmer continues: "The plants will increase fast in growth, some will be fit to draw young in July or August, &c. [etc.] but the roots will not acquire full growth till October. . . . [They may then be] housed in layers of sand for the Winter, as advised for carrots." In more temperate climates where the soil can be kept from freezing, the plant may be left in the ground and pulled as required over winter months.

PARSLEY ESSENTIALS

PLANTING Sow seed in late summer, when the phlox and asters bloom, and transplant to the garden when plants have five or six leaves. Spring and summer sowings are best made in shady borders or in pots and harvested while young.

SPACING Sow seeds ¼ inch deep and set plants 6 to 12 inches apart, in rows 12 to 18 inches asunder.

FOR BEST GROWTH In the middle and southern states, the main crop is grown in fall and protected over winter under bell glass. In the north, start plants in a conservatory 6 to 8 weeks before the last frost. Summer plants should be harvested while the leaves are small and less bitter.

HARVESTING Harvest individual leaves from fall to spring from mature plants. Harvest immature leaves in summer.

TO SAVE PURE SEED Separate varieties by 1 mile.

COLLECTING AND STORING SEED Parsley is a biennial that must pass through a winter season to flower and produce seed. Seeds will fall from the plant soon after they ripen, so must be harvested when individual seed clusters become ripe. Refrigerate seed in airtight containers.

SEED VIABILITY 3 years

Seed Varieties

Varieties listed in 18th-century Virginia

♦ 'Curled' or 'Double'

♦ 'Common' or 'Roman'

Heirloom varieties for the modern gardener

Parsley varieties have changed very little over the centuries. They are still divided between the curled and the flat-leaf Italian.

♦ 'Curled': Several varieties are available with double- or triple-divided leaves.

♦ 'Flat-Leaf' or 'Italian'

"The cook can never be without it, there being nothing more proper for stuffing . . . and other sauces."

—Stephen Switzer, *The Practical Kitchen Gardiner* (1727)

CHARD

Beta vulgaris var. *cicla*

Chard has long been prized for its colored leaves. John Gerard recorded in *The Herball* that a remarkable specimen "grew with me [in] 1596. to the height of viii. cubites [approximately 12 feet], and did bring foorth his rough and uneeven seede very plentifully: with which plant nature doth seeme to plaie and sport hirselfe: for the seedes taken from that plant,

which was altogither of one colour and sowen, doth bring foorth plants of many and variable colours, as the worshipfull gentleman master *John Norden* can very well testifie, unto whom I gave some of the seedes aforesaid, which in his garden brought foorth many other of beautifull colours."

Theophrastus's Beet

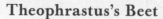

Chard is one of the most ancient of salad greens adopted by humankind. It was known in the 4th century BCE as Sicula, identifying it as an import from Sicily. From Sicula is derived the species name for the chard, *cicla*. The Romans called the chard *Beta*, its current genus and source of its common name, beet. The chard beet was the first culinary plant to arise from the highly variable wild sea beet (*Beta maritima*), which would also give rise to the red beet root, the *mangel wurzel*, and finally the sugar beet more than a thousand years later. Chard was known as the white beet in English garden works of the 17th and 18th centuries, and like those of the modern chard, the leaves came in many colors. John Parkinson wrote in *Paradisi in Sole* (1629): "There are many diversities of Beetes, some growing naturally in our own Country, others brought from beyond Sea; whereof some are white, some greene, some yellow, some red."

The Mysterious Origin of the Swiss Beet

When and why it became known as *Swiss* chard is a bit of a mystery. It is often postulated that it was named in honor of a mysterious Swiss botanist by the name of Koch in the 19th century. However, its association with the Swiss dates to at least the 18th century. John Rutter described it in 1767 as the "Swiss chard beet." James Justice also related it to the Swiss

in *The British Gardener's New Director* (1771): "The White Beet with a large stalk, commonly called Beetchard, or Swiss Beet."

The Etymology of Chard

The French name *chard* refers to its large stem, as recorded by John Evelyn in *Acetari: A Discourse of Sallets* (1699): "The *Costa*, or Rib of the *White Beet* (by the *French* call'd the *Chard*) being boil'd, melts, and eats like Marrow." The French word arises from the Latin *cardus*, which described an edible thistle known as cardoon.

A Poor Man's Green

The white beet or chard was known in colonial Virginia, but there are few references to it compared with other greens. In fact, the English have never been particularly fond of chard. Thomas Hill wrote in *The Gardener's Labyrinth* (1577) that chard is "more often eaten at poor mens tables." In 1754, Philip Miller noted in *The Gardeners Dictionary*: "At present they are not so much esteem'd as they have been, and are but in few Gardens." Perhaps the English carried this prejudice with them to the New World.

"This Kind differs nothing from the former *White Beet,* but only that it is not so great, and that both the Roots and Leaves are somewhat red."

—William Salmon, *Botanologia* (1710)

The Williamsburg Gardener's Assistant

The season for sowing chard. Chard is generally sown where you intend it to remain for harvest. If grown in pots for transplants, it must be set in the garden while the plant is still young. Plants that become pot-bound in the container often prove to be inferior plants when placed in the garden.

In Williamsburg, the chard is sown before the end of April, as it germinates better in a cool soil. All greens perform better in a fertile soil, but a rich soil is particularly important for chard, whose leaves can be coarse and strong flavored when grown in a poor soil.

A curious manner of thinning chard was explained by John Rutter in 1767: "When the plants are come up . . . clear them to four inches distance; three weeks after this hoe the bed again, and then clear them to six inches distance; and after three week more clear the bed again, and leave only the best of the plants at thirteen inches asunder." This, of course, is impossible. Once plants are thinned to 4 inches apart, they cannot be thinned to 6 inches. This should be a parable to all gardeners: The best lessons are learned in the ground, not on the page. Regardless of the method, 1 foot apart is a serviceable spacing. The plants thinned from the row can be used in the manner of spinach.

A proper method for harvesting chard. After the final thinning, the leaves are harvested individually from the plants. As Rutter further explained, "The outer leaves only are to be cropped off when wanted; and thus the young ones left in the center will grow larger, and there will be a constant supply for the season." The outer leaves must be harvested regularly, or they become hard and bitter, and the entire plant suffers as a result. Under proper management, chard will continue to produce new leaves from the heart of the plant throughout summer, supplying the table long after other greens, such as spinach, are gone for the season.

When autumn arrives, stir the soil and dress your plants with dung [compost]. They will revive remarkably and produce abundant greens long into the season and of equal or better quality than the spring and summer crops. In the middle states and southward, chard will often overwinter with a good mulch laid around the plants; harvest early sprouts in spring before they run to flower.

Thinning chard; harvesting chard; earthing up chard

CHARD ESSENTIALS

PLANTING Sow seeds in spring, when the daffodils bloom. If started from transplants, set plants out with four or five leaves.

SPACING Sow seed 1 inch deep and thin plants to stand 1 foot apart, in rows 18 to 24 inches asunder.

FOR BEST GROWTH Chard must be maintained in vigorous growth to produce the best quality of leaves and stems. Fertilize with a side dressing of compost in spring and fall to encourage new tender growth.

HARVESTING Harvest leaves routinely to stimulate young leaves from the heart of the plant.

TO SAVE PURE SEED Both chard and beetroot are wind pollinated and will cross with each other. Pollen can travel up to 5 miles. Isolation cages provide the surest results.

COLLECTING AND STORING SEED Chard is a biennial that must pass through a winter season to flower and set seed. In cold climates, chard plants can be dug in fall and overwintered in frames. Chard seeds are formed in clusters and are sometimes broken apart before storage. This, however, may reduce germination percentage. Refrigerate seed in airtight containers.

SEED VIABILITY 6 years

Seed Varieties

Varieties listed in 18th-century Virginia

♦ **'White Beet':** Chard was seldom listed by 18th-century gardeners in Virginia, but it was probably white stemmed with green leaves.

Heirloom varieties for the modern gardener

♦ **'Fordhook Giant':** An early 20th-century variety probably similar to 18th-century plants

"[The spinach beet] grows in gardens and tilled land everywhere."

—Leonhart Fuchs, *De Historia Stirpium* (1542)

The "SMALL SALADS"

Stephen Switzer wrote of salads in 1727: "There are about thirty or forty species that are by some learned naturalists appropriated to this purpose." Other than the common greens—such as lettuce, spinach, endive, and chard—there were those collectively known as the small salads, which were a common feature in the colonial diet.

The small salads are plants, such as cresses, that have been consumed since before recorded history, but that have never developed much beyond their primeval appearance. Many of them, to this day, can be gathered in the wild. The small salad disappeared for a time from the American diet and was reinvented by 20th-century gardeners as mesclun mix.

THE TYPES OF CRESSES

There are a number of plants that carry the name of cress, but the four primary culinary cresses are watercress (*Nasturtium officinale*), winter or upland cress (*Barbarea vulgaris*), garden cress (*Lepidium sativum*), and Indian cress (*Tropaeolum*), which is called nasturtium today.

Cresses are among the most ancient of salad greens and have been used by humankind since records have been kept. The first European reference

to cress comes from a German monk named Walafrid Strabo (Walafrid the Squint-Eyed). He mentioned cress in *Hortulus* in 840 CE, though there is no way to know which cress he meant.

Watercress grows in shallow water, preferring the edges of streams. Throughout history, it has been gathered wild and seldom grown in gardens. It is not advisable to gather watercress from the wild today, as it may carry a particularly nasty liver fluke that is most prevalent in pastures where sheep have grazed.

Winter cress, also known as scurvy grass, is a widely dispersed European herb named for Saint Barbara. It long ago took up residence in this country as the common, roadside yellow rocket. Winter cress is the hardiest and strongest flavored of the cresses. Its wayfaring habit has long been noted. John Gerard described this plant in the 1597 *Herball*: "It groweth in gardens among pot herbes, and very common in the fields, neere to pathes and high waies, almost every where." To this day, winter cress, known as "creasy greens" to Southern cooks, is gathered in the wild along paths and highways. A close relative known as upland cress (*B. verna*) is the preferred variety and the one that is sometimes brought into the garden.

By the 18th century, winter cress had largely fallen out of favor. Philip Miller wrote of winter cress in *The Gardeners Dictionary* (1768): "These were formerly eaten in winter sallads, before the English gardens were furnished with better plants; since when they have been rejected, for they have a rank smell, and are disagreeable to the palate."

The "better plants" Miller was referring to were the several forms of garden cress, *L. sativum*, also known as peppergrass. This is the most common cress sold at market and grown in the garden today. It is better flavored than the winter cress but not nearly as cold-hardy.

Garden cress was probably introduced into England in the 16th century. John Gerard listed and illustrated several types of cress in the *Herball* (1597). His description read: "Garden Cresses or Towne Cresses, hath small narrow jagged leaves, sharp and burning in taste." Garden cress has both smooth and curled leaf forms. The curled form has been the most esteemed variety throughout history by most authors, but William Cobbett wrote in *The American Gardener* (1821): "The curled is *prettiest,* and is, therefore, generally preferred; but, the plain is the *best.*"

The Celebrated Indian Cress

There are two forms of the celebrated Indian cress or nasturtium: *Tropaeolum minus,* the dwarf form with small leaves and generally of a bushy habit, and *T.*

majus, the larger-leaved climbing form. Both forms are native to Peru, but the first plants exported to Europe originated in the West Indies; hence the name of Indian cress.

John Parkinson wrote in *Paradisi in Sole* (1629): "Indian Cresses, or yellow Larkes heeles . . . is of so great beauty and sweetnesse withall, that my Garden of delight cannot bee unfurnished of it." Stephen Switzer wrote in *The Practical Kitchen Gardiner* (1727): "Of the cresses there are three or four sorts that are admitted into the garden. . . . the *Indian* kind is recommended above all." Switzer added that it is of use for "quickning the drooping spirits, purging the brain, and of singular effect in the scurvy, so that all *Englishmen* can't eat too much of this herb, or chew it too much."

The smaller *T. minus* was introduced into Europe first, but was quickly replaced by the larger *T. majus,* introduced in the 1680s. In Virginia, John Randolph recorded: "If stuck they will climb a great height and will last till the frost come, and then totally perish. It is thought the flower is superior to a radish in flavour, and is eat in sallads or without." In Philadelphia in 1806, Bernard McMahon recorded: "[The seedpods] make one of the nicest pickles that can possibly be conceived."

(Top) Watercress; (bottom) winter cress; garden cress; Indian cress

The Williamsburg Gardener's Assistant

The various cresses and their seasons. Winter cress and garden cress are sown in the garden in early fall, at the same time that spinach is planted. Winter cress, or the upland cress, will survive winter in most parts of the country for a late winter or early spring harvest. Garden cress will not stand the frost, but is a very fast grower and can be sown every 10 days until about a month before hard frost sets in. After this, it can be sown in frames.

Both cresses are easily cultivated. As explained by Samuel Fullmer in *The Young Gardener's Best Companion* (1795): "For each sowing, draw very shallow, flat drills [shallow furrows], with the edge of the hoe held horizontally, sow the seed very thick, and cover it lightly with earth; or instead . . . smooth the surface, by fine raking it, and sow the seed thereon quite thick, smooth it down with the back of the spade, and sift earth over it half a quarter or an inch deep."

Cresses are best when harvested very young. As Fullmer explained: "The plants are commonly in best perfection for sallads, when in the seed-leaves, or not above a week or fortnight old; either cutting them clean up within the surface, or cut off above ground, to shoot again."

While the fall sowing of cresses requires the least management, provisions must be made for spring and summer. As stated in *Adam's Luxury, and Eve's Cookery* (1744): "THIS Plant is very much esteemed for mixing in Sallets, and is to be cultivated all the Year." To accomplish this, you can start sowing the garden cress out of doors after the danger of frost in spring and continue throughout summer. You will find that the summer crop is best grown in containers. As suggested by Walter Nicol in 1798: "With the addition of a few boxes, tubs, or large pots, [garden cress] may be had every day in the year, in abundance, by the trouble of sowing once a week, or ten days, as occasion shall require."

The Indian cress, or nasturtium, is sensitive to both frost and hot weather. The seeds are quite large, and germination is hastened by soaking them overnight. Nasturtium seeds should be planted $\frac{1}{2}$ inch deep, as they must have darkness to germinate. In Williamsburg, we sow the seed in late August. While it will germinate and grow in the heat of August, nasturtium does not come into its own until the weather cools in late September. In cooler climates, nasturtium will grow throughout summer.

Garden cress seedlings; harvesting cresses and other small salads

The SEVERAL KINDS of MUSTARD

There are quite a number of plants that have carried the name "mustard" over the centuries, but the principal ones are white mustard (*Sinapis alba)*, brown mustard (*Brassica juncea*), black mustard (*B. nigra),* and Ethiopian mustard (*B. carinata*). In the modern condiment, the white mustard gives the spicy quality, while the brown or black gives the mustard its pungency. The term *mustard* comes from the use of the seeds to form a sweet "must," a component of old wines. The crushed seeds were formed into a paste called "hot must" or *mustum ardens.*

The mustard green used in Southern cooking today is an Asian plant *(B. juncea)* and was not known in colonial America.

White Mustard

White mustard is a native of the Mediterranean basin and southern Europe and provided one of the earliest spices known to humankind. It is mentioned in Sanskrit records dating to around 3000 BCE and was first noted in England by Aelfric of Eynsham in 995 CE.

As a salad green, white mustard has always been the preferred species. In *Adam's Luxury, and Eve's Cookery* (1744), it is observed: "THERE are two Sorts of Mustard, White and Red; but the White only being cultivated in the Kitchen-Garden. . . . This is propagated by Seed for Sallets to mix with Cresses, &c. [etc.], all the Year."

White mustard was an indispensable component of the English diet. Stephen Switzer observed in 1727: "The young mustard plants . . . when they are just peeping out of the bed, are of incomparable effect to quicken and revive the spirits, they strengthen the memory, expel heaviness. . . . In short, it's the noble *embamma* [sauce], and so necessary an ingredient in all cold raw salleting, that it is very rarely, if at all, left out."

White mustard arrived in North America some-

time in the 17th century and quickly made itself at home. It is now found growing wild in almost every state of the continental United States and in most parts of Canada.

"Mustard . . . is exceeding hot and biting, not only in the seed, but the leaf also, and more especially in the seed."

—Stephen Switzer,
The Practical Kitchen Gardiner (1727)

White mustard

The Williamsburg Gardener's Assistant

The sowing and harvesting of mustard. Mustard is as easy or easier to grow than cress. It germinates quickly and is often ready as a sprout within a fortnight (2 weeks) of sowing. This prompted Stephen Switzer to observe in 1727 that mustard can be raised for seasoning "during the roasting a joint of meat."

It prefers a sweet soil, so the addition of marl, or lime, is often beneficial. Sow the seeds on a well-prepared bed, not prone to crusting, in shallow drills, or broadcast and gently rake the seeds in. Once the seeds are covered, tamp the ground lightly with the end of a rake and water regularly. The seeds will germinate in 3 or 4 days, and harvest can begin within 10 days or 2 weeks and continue until hard frosts arrive.

Mustard can then be sown in frames for a winter crop. For the summer season, mustard is best sown in pots, often mixed with other small salad greens such as cress and rocket. Some shade in the afternoon is beneficial during the hottest months.

If the seed is desired, the pods will be ready for harvest in 8 to 10 weeks. The leaves are unfit to eat once the seedpods have formed and may even be toxic.

Mustard seedlings; mustard seed pods

"The goodnesse of the seede is knowen in the breaking
or cracking of it betweene the teeth."

—Thomas Hill, *The Gardener's Labyrinth* (1577)

CORN SALAD and Its VARIOUS NAMES

Corn salad (*Valerianella locusta*) is also known by the English as lamb's lettuce, by the French as *mâche*, and by the Germans as *feldsalat*. The English call it lamb's lettuce because it is one of the few greens available to spring lambs.

The names "corn salad" and *feldsalat* (field salad) recognize its origin as a plant gathered from the wild, which man has been doing for a very long time. Evidence of corn salad has been found among the remains of Swiss lake dwellings dating from the Late Stone Age, and it has likely been gathered from the wild since prehistoric times.

Corn salad

The Historic Use of Corn Salad

John Parkinson described corn salad in *Paradisi in Sole* (1629) as a salad green sown in autumn for winter salads. Its primary importance has long been to supply the table in the colder months when other salad greens are scarce. A hundred years later, Batty Langley wrote in *New Principles of Gardening* (1728) that "Corn Sallet . . . is now received into our Gardens, and was introduced by the *French* and *Dutch*, who were the first that eat it in Sallets in *England*."

Corn salad was never a prominent green in English gardens. By the time Philip Miller published the 1768 edition of *The Gardeners Dictionary*, corn salad had fallen out of favor: "It is propagated as a sallad herb for the spring, but having a strong taste which is not agreeable to many palates, it is not so much in use as it was formerly." In 1821, William Cobbett wrote in *The American Gardener*: "This is a little insignificant annual plant that some persons use in salads, though it can hardly be of any real use, where lettuce seed is to be had. It is a mere *weed*."

Weed or not, the modern cook has once again discovered the culinary value of this hardy little green.

"The *Lamb Lettuce*, which is call'd *Corn Sallad*, must be growing in a Garden, because it helps to make up a Sallad in the *Winter*."

—Benjamin Townsend,
The Complete Seedsman (1726)

The Williamsburg Gardener's Assistant

The obstacle to germinating corn salad. Often the most difficult thing about growing corn salad is getting it to germinate. The seed, unless stored under ideal conditions, has a short viability, and old seed often will disappoint. Even fresh seed can be slow to germinate. As recorded in *The Practical Gardener* (1778): "It lies a great while in the ground, and takes the first growth slowly; if the seed be kept till spring it is a great chance whether it succeeds, but if sown fresh at this time of year [August], however long it lies in the ground, you need not fear its coming up."

Planting and harvesting corn salad. The method of sowing the seed is similar to spinach. As explained by

John Rutter in 1767: "Level the surface, and scatter on the seeds . . . pretty thick. When the plants appear, weed the ground, and take up some where they rise too close. They should be left at four inches distance." Like spinach, the seeds germinate better in a continuously moist soil.

In Williamsburg, we sow the seed in early September and harvest the leaves while young. As described by Samuel Fullmer in 1795, corn salad is "a wholesome sallad-herb while young . . . but strong tasted when old; and is estimable for its hardy growth to stand the Winter's frost . . . when other sallad-herbs are scarce." It will grow throughout winter in most areas of the country and can be used for a spring salad before it runs to seed.

Frosted corn salad

SMALL SALAD ESSENTIALS

PLANTING The main crop of garden cresses, mustard, and corn salad is sown in early fall, when the goldenrod blooms. Successive sowings can be made in fall in middle and southern states. Sow again in early spring and through summer months. In the South, sow nasturtium in late summer, when phlox and asters bloom. In the North, sow nasturtium in spring, when the lilacs and dogwoods bloom.

SPACING Small salads are, indeed, small plants and are sown thickly in rows or plots. Rows may be spaced 1 foot apart, and plants are usually thinned as required for the table. Nasturtium may be grown as a ground cover or trained on walls.

FOR BEST GROWTH Garden cress, mustard, and corn salad grow best in a cool soil in the fall and spring garden. A rich, moist soil provides for quick growth and better flavor. Nasturtium likes it not too hot and not too cold.

HARVESTING For garden cress, mustard, and corn salad, entire plants or individual leaves may be harvested. Nasturtium leaves, flowers, and seeds are harvested as required.

TO SAVE PURE SEED As there are few varieties of these greens, crossing is not usually a problem. All are insect pollinated, so may cross with other varieties up to 1 mile.

COLLECTING AND STORING SEED All except nasturtium quickly run to seed in hot weather. Garden cresses, mustard, and corn salad produce small seed capsules that shatter quickly, so must be diligently gathered. They will often reseed. Nasturtium produces large, three-part seed clusters that are collected when they turn from green to brown.

SEED VIABILITY Garden cress, mustard, and corn salad seed is viable for 3 to 4 years, and nasturtium seed for up to 7 years.

Seed Varieties

Varieties listed in 18th-century Virginia

- Garden cress: **'Double Peppergrass'** (*Lepidium* varieties)

- Winter cress: **'Scurvy Grass'**, round leaved (*Barbarea* sp.)

- Watercress

- Nasturtium

- White mustard

- Corn salad

Heirloom varieties for the modern gardener

The small salads have changed very little over the centuries.

- Garden cress: Both curled and flat-leaf varieties

- Winter cress: Often gathered wild and called "creasy greens"

- Watercress: Seldom grown in gardens

- Nasturtium: Both bush and climbing

- White mustard: Not to be confused with mustard greens from Asia

- Corn salad: Now called mâche, comes in several varieties with slightly different leaf shapes

CHAPTER 4
of
Root Crops

The root crops known to colonial Virginians originated in various places around the world. Radishes and skirrets came from Asia, parsnip and salsify from Europe, carrots from the Near East. The beetroot was developed, or at least perfected, in Germany from the chard or white beet. Jerusalem artichokes are native to North America, while both the white and sweet potato originated in South America. Root crops, as a group, have been a staple food for societies throughout time.

Some roots, such as radish, carrot, turnip, and parsnip, were cultivated in the kitchen gardens of all classes of people. They became staple vegetables because of their easy culture, keeping ability, and nutritional value. Other roots, such as salsify, scorzonera, and Jerusalem artichoke, were much more subject to individual taste. The sweet potato was already known to Virginia natives when the colonists arrived at Jamestown in 1607. The white potato did not become an American staple until the second half of the 18th century. The skirret fell out of fashion in the early 18th century just as the beet came into fashion. The Jerusalem artichoke enjoyed a brief period of popularity early in the 17th century, fell out of favor in the 18th, and was rediscovered in the 19th. Many of these crops were as important for feeding livestock as they were for feeding people.

A letter from George Divers to Thomas Jefferson in 1809 gives an idea of one man's preferences for several of the root crops. "I sow 200 feet each of parsnip and beet. 320 feet each salsafy and carrots . . . which is a very ample provision for my table and indeed more than sufficient."

CARROT

Daucus carota

Americans were slow to appreciate the culinary pleasures of the carrot. In 1867, Peter Henderson wrote of carrots in *Gardening for Profit*: "This may be classed more as a crop of the farm than of the garden, as a far larger area is grown for the food of horses and cattle than for culinary purposes." In 1787, George Washington wrote to Benjamin Fitzhugh Grymes: "I am convinced that in a proper Soil, the culture of Carrots will be found very advantageous for feeding the farm horses, and every species of Stock. . . . I am inclined to think that the rows of Carrots will yield five, 8, or I do not know but 10, bushels of Carrots for every one of Corn."

The Carrot and Its Kinds

Carrots have probably been used since prehistoric times for medicinal properties that are found, primarily, in the seeds. The wild carrot of Europe is the common Queen Anne's lace, which long ago made the transatlantic trip to become a common roadside weed in this country. Queen Anne's lace produces a small, white, generally branched root of no culinary value. The modern carrot evolved from the purple carrot, native to Afghanistan. From Afghanistan it spread to the Mediterranean basin, where it was adopted by the ancient Egyptians. A tomb painting from around 2000 BCE shows what appears to be a purple carrot.

The early history of the carrot in Europe is difficult to trace, because both the carrot and the parsnip were named *pastinaca* by the Romans, a generic term for any long single root. This probably derives from the Latin verb *pastinare*, "to dig up." In the 1st century CE, Pliny the Elder, in his *Natural History*, described a root "that bears the same resemblance to a parsnip, which our people call the Gallic parsnip, but the Greeks . . . call *daucos*," and it is from the Greek that we get the modern genus name for the carrot, *Daucus*. Caelius Apicius, who wrote a book on cookery titled *De re coquinaria* in 230 CE, called it "Carotæ," and this was the origin for the English *carrot*. The carrot was likely introduced into the rest of Europe by Roman legions.

Carrot; purple carrot

'Long Orange' carrot; 'Horn' carrot

The Purple Carrot in Ancient Europe

The oldest surviving English herbal, the *Leech Book of Bald* (*læce* in Old English means "healer"), compiled between 924 and 946 CE, contains many references to carrot as an ingredient in medicinal concoctions. It is not clear whether this was the Queen Anne's lace or the purple Afghan carrot.

The earliest reference to the carrot as a culinary plant in Europe, outside of Rome, comes from Moorish Spain, where Ibn Sayyār al-Warrāq produced a cookbook circa 950 CE that included carrots. The purple carrot was recorded in France and Germany by the 13th century, and in England, William Turner recorded in 1548: "Pastinaca is called . . . in englishe a Carot. . . . Carettes growe in al countreis in plentie."

A Preference for Orange

The yellow carrot appeared as a mutant of the purple carrot, and by the end of the 16th century, there is evidence to suggest that it was more common than the purple. John Gerard wrote in *The Herball* (1597): "The roote is long, thicke and single, of a faire yellow colour, pleasant to be eaten, and very sweete in taste.

There is another kinde hereof like to the former in all partes, and differeth from it onely in the colour of the roote, which in this is not yellow, but of a blackish red colour."

Purple carrots have an orange or yellow core and are predisposed to produce orange variants. There is pictorial evidence for orange carrots as early as 512 CE, but these early examples were apparently not stable varieties. It was not until the 18th century that a recognized variety of carrot, known as the 'Long Orange', was developed in the Netherlands. Popular legend has it that the Dutch developed the orange carrot as a tribute to the House of Orange, the royal standard of the Dutch monarchy. It is more likely that the orange carrot was favored over the purple because it did not give the brownish coloration to soups and stews that the purple one did.

It was from the 'Long Orange' that all other varieties of carrots were developed. By 1740, the 'Early Horn' carrot was developed in Holland. This was a shorter, stubbier root developed in the Dutch town of Hoorn. It became the most popular carrot of the 18th century, both in England and North America.

"Carrots . . . are of two sortes, the Orange and white, the former being generally used, tho' the latter is much the sweetest kind."

—John Randolph, *A Treatise on Gardening* (1793)

The Williamsburg Gardener's Assistant

What soil is necessary for the successful raising of carrots. For all of the root crops, but most particularly for carrots, the gardener must prepare a deep, light soil that is free of stones, to bring carrots to perfection. The method is best explained by John Hill in 1757: "Dig up a good Piece of Ground for Carrots and Parsnips, turn it up two Spades Depth, and break it well: it will greatly assist this Crop to dig in a good Quantity of old and thoroughly rotted Dung [compost] mix'd with Sand, and to blend them very carefully together. Nothing but very old Dung [compost] will do for this; for if such as is newer should be used, the Carrots will be ill-tasted and Worm-eaten. . . . with this Assistance the Carrots will not fail to grow with a strong, single, and strait Root, without splitting or shooting sideways; and they will be tender and well tasted. More depends upon this Management than would easily be thought: there is no other Way to bring this excellent Root to its full Perfection."

Preparing ground

Several methods for the sowing of carrots. Carrots may be sown in rows, or they may be broadcast. The method of broadcast sowing is also explained by Hill: "Let the Surface of this Piece of Ground be leveled; then mix with the Seeds a good Quantity of Sand; and chusing a calm Day, scatter them as equally as possible over the Ground. This Care will prevent their rising in the usual irregular Manner in Clusters in some Places, with great Vacancies between."

Hill continued: "When all the Seed is on, tread over the Ground, and then rake it in. Observe when they come up; for the Weeds will rise with them. As soon as they have a little Strength, let them be thin'd and clear'd from the Weeds that are among them. . . . the Plants should be left at about five Inches Distance."

Thinning carrots is an onerous task, but the gardener can employ a method described in *Adam's Luxury, and Eve's Cookery* (1744), which with a little practice will greatly lessen the need for thinning: "You may . . . sow at the same time a few Radishes, which will be drawn off presently and not hurt the Carrots." By mixing the radish and carrot seed together with a little sand, the seeds will be evenly distributed in the row. The greatest lesson a gardener can learn in the sowing of this, and many other types of seed, is restraint in the quantity of seeds sown. Most gardeners tend to sow their seed too thickly and then spend hours thinning vegetable plants, when a little more optimism at planting time would have lessened the need for thinning. Perhaps William Shakespeare said it best when he wrote in *Henry IV*, part 1: "More then a little, is by much too much."

Harvesting the radishes will serve to thin the carrots. We perform a second thinning when the roots are less than ½ inch in diameter at their tops, and we begin the main harvest when they reach ¾ inch in diameter.

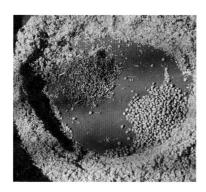

(Top) Sand, radish, and carrot seeding mix; sowing mix; raking in seeds; (bottom) radish and carrot seedlings; harvesting radishes; carrots pulled for thinning

Seed Varieties

Varieties listed in 18th-century Virginia

♦ **'Short Orange'** and **'Early'** carrots, probably **'Horn'** carrots

♦ **'Long Orange'**

Heirloom varieties for the modern gardener

♦ **'Danvers Half Long'**: A 19th-century carrot similar to the 'Horn' carrot

♦ **'James Scarlet'**, **'St. Valery'**: Longer varieties, similar to original 'Long Orange'

CARROT ESSENTIALS

PLANTING Sow carrot seed in early spring, when the daffodils bloom, for the early summer crop. A second sowing can be made when the dogwoods and lilacs bloom, for a late season harvest. In the southern and middle states, a third sowing can be made in late summer, when the phlox and asters bloom, for an early winter harvest.

SPACING Sow seeds in rows, or broadcast in bands, ¼ inch deep in rows 12 to 18 inches apart, and thin plants to stand 3 to 5 inches asunder.

FOR BEST GROWTH Carrots require a deep loose soil to form well-shaped roots. Lime is beneficial in acidic soils.

HARVESTING For most varieties, individual roots can be pulled after they grow to a ¾-inch diameter at the top. Grasp the foliage at its base and pull straight up. If the entire row is to be harvested, a spading fork can be used to loosen the soil.

TO SAVE PURE SEED Varieties must be separated by half a mile. Carrots will also cross with Queen Anne's lace, which often makes saving pure seed difficult.

COLLECTING AND STORING SEED Carrots are biennials that must pass through a winter season to flower and set seed. In northern climates, clip the foliage back to 1 inch, dig the roots, and store in sawdust in a cool space for winter. Seeds are harvested as the seedheads begin to brown. Refrigerate in airtight containers.

SEED VIABILITY 3 years

"There is another variety called the horn-carrot, differing in the *form* of its root, the lower part terminating in a round, abrupt manner, and not tapering off gradually, like the others."

—Bernard McMahon, *The American Gardener's Calendar* (1806)

RADISH

Raphanus sativus

The radish appears to have originated in China and moved west to the Middle East. Once there, it met with a mixed reception. In Rome, Pliny the Elder recorded in his *Natural History* (circa 77 CE): "Radishes are flatulent to a remarkable degree, and are productive of eructations [belching]; hence it is that they are looked upon as an aliment only fit for low-bred people." The Greeks had a very different opinion. As further noted by Pliny: "Such, too, is the frivolity of the Greeks, that, in the temple of Apollo at Delphi, it is said, the radish is so greatly preferred to all other articles of diet, as to be represented there in gold, the beet in silver, and the rape in lead."

Radish flowers

The Radish and Its Early Usage

The Roman author Lucius Columella named the radish *radicula*, from the Latin *radix*, or root, and from this we get the English *radish*. After the Roman period, the radish became one of the most common of all root crops in Europe. In 1577, Thomas Hill wrote in *The Gardener's Labyrinth*: "The Garden Radish with us, is better knowen, than I with pen can utter." Its earliest use seems to be medicinal, rather than culinary. Leonhart Fuchs, who published *De Historia Stirpium* in 1542, believed the practice of consuming uncooked radishes to be downright dangerous: "I am surprised at the doctors, as well as ignorant laymen, who at dinner eat them raw to aid digestion. . . . no one can follow their example without injury."

The Ancient Forms of Radish

The oldest varieties of radish were long rooted, like a fat carrot, and generally white. Some of these radishes grew to tremendous size. Thomas Hill wrote in *The Gardener's Labyrinth* (1577): "In Germanye hath sometymes bin seene a Radish, which grew in compasse so big as an infants middle." This quote came almost verbatim from Pliny's description of a large radish in his *Natural History* in the 1st century CE.

The turnip-rooted radish was probably introduced into England in the second half of the 16th century. William Turner wrote in the *Names of Herbes* (1548): "There are two kindes of radice, the one is the commune radice wyth the longe roote. . . . The other kynde hath a rounde roote lyke a rape. . . . The former kynde groweth communely in Englande, but I have sene the seconde kynde no where els savynge only in high Almany [Germany]." The black-rooted radish also reached England in the 16th century. Henry Lyte's 1578 English translation, *The New*

Herball, of Rembert Dodoens's *Cruydeboeck* (1554), mentions "[The radish] with the blacke roote whiche of late yeeres hath ben brought into Englande, and now beginneth also to ware common."

The Evolution of the Red Radish

The trend toward a redder radish with smaller leaves, or what later became known as the short-topped radish, began with the red-topped varieties of the ordinary long white radish. John Evelyn wrote in *The Compleat Gard'ner,* the 1693 translation of Jean de La Quintinye's 1690 French work, that seed should be saved only from those plants "that have the *Reddest* roots and fewest leaves."

By the 18th century, the red-rooted form of the long radish was the most common spring radish. The 'Spanish' or 'Turnip' radish was the most common variety for the winter crop. John Randolph recorded these two varieties in 18th-century Williamsburg: "Scarlet or Salmon, London short topped &c. [etc.]" as well as "a Turnep Radish, being very like one, called in England the round rooted radish."

By the end of the century, the smaller-rooted radishes began to appear out of Italy. Philip Miller wrote in *The Gardeners Dictionary* (1754): "The small round-rooted Radish is not very common in *England*; but in many Parts of *Italy* it is the only Sort cultivated." These modern-looking radishes reached the colonies by the second half of the 18th century. Robert Squibb recorded the "small round" radish in *The Gardener's Calendar for South-Carolina, Georgia, and North-Carolina* in 1787.

The long scarlet radish remained the premier radish throughout the 19th century, until it was replaced by small round radishes in the 20th century.

> "If any anoynteth the hands circumspectly with the juyce of the Radish, he may after handle Scorpions or any other venomouse thing, without daunger."
>
> —Thomas Hill,
>   *The Gardener's Labyrinth* (1577)

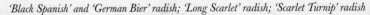

'Black Spanish' and 'German Bier' radish; 'Long Scarlet' radish; 'Scarlet Turnip' radish

The Williamsburg Gardener's Assistant

The easiest culture of radishes. Radishes are among the easiest vegetables to grow in the garden. They are not overly particular of soil type, although the long-rooted radish requires a lighter soil, as explained by Batty Langley in 1728: "All kind of Radishes love a sandy Loam, that they may freely strike down with their Roots."

In Williamsburg, we sow our radishes as advised by John Abercrombie in *The Garden Vade Mecum* (1790): "For general crops of radishes, begin sowing . . . about the middle or latter end of February, and continued in March . . . once a fortnight or three weeks. . . . If they are too thick, thin them somewhat regular, two or three inches distance." As spring radishes are quick to germinate and soon ready for the table, sowing them every 2 or 3 weeks will supply a continuous harvest until hot weather arrives and renders them rank and coarse. The gardener must promote the quickest growth to produce a crisp, mild radish. To achieve this, the crop must never lack for water.

The radish as a companion crop. Radishes may be sown in rows or broadcast in beds, and they make an excellent companion to plantings of longer-season root crops. Richard Bradley described the radish in 1718 as "a *Root* which might be sown promiscuously among other Roots." The radishes are harvested long before roots such as carrots, beets, or parsnips are ready, and they serve to space these larger roots when they are pulled from among them.

The proper time to harvest radish in root and pod. It has long been believed that radishes are at their best when harvested before noon, as explained in *Modern Eden* (1767): "To eat them in perfection, they must be pulled about ten o'clock in the morning, and laid in a cool cellar till the time of dinner; for this way they keep their spirited taste, and that agreeable firmness: whereas, if they be taken out of the ground

(Top) Thinned radishes; (bottom) radish flowers and pods

at noon, the sun will have exhausted, and rendered them poor and flimsy." This is particularly true if the weather is hot and dry.

In Williamsburg, we always allow one row of radishes to shoot up to flower and set its pods. The pods, when gathered while green and tender, are crisp and well flavored. They are even better when pickled. One variety, known as the 'Rat-Tailed Radish', has been developed specifically for this purpose.

Radishes for the winter season. In the first 2 weeks of September, we sow both the 'German Bier' radish, which is much like the 18th-century 'White Turnip' radish, and the 'Black Spanish' radish. These are both large radishes, often 4 inches in diameter. John Abercrombie advised in 1790: "The black Spanish turnep-rooted radish, growing very large, like a middling turnep, is commonly cultivated for Winter, being very hardy, and of a strong warm flavour. . . . thinning the plants in their young growth six to eight or ten inches distance." The 'German Bier', in particular, is a very spicy radish. From this fall planting we are able to harvest radishes all winter long.

RADISH ESSENTIALS

PLANTING Spring radishes may be sown as soon as the ground thaws and the early daffodils bloom, and successively until the dogwoods and lilacs bloom. In the middle and southern states, radishes (particularly the larger-rooted varieties) can be sown again in early fall, when the goldenrod blooms.

SPACING Sow seed ½ inch deep in rows 1 to 2 feet apart, or broadcast in bands. Thin plants to stand 2 inches asunder for the smaller varieties, 6 inches apart for the larger types.

FOR BEST GROWTH Radishes require a cool season for best flavor and texture. Maintain adequate moisture for rapid growth and finest quality.

HARVESTING Harvest spring radishes while they are still small. Larger roots quickly become woody. Large winter radishes are sweeter after a frost.

TO SAVE PURE SEED Separate varieties by half a mile.

COLLECTING AND STORING SEED Radish seed stalks will grow to about 3 feet tall and may need support. Harvest entire seed stalks when pods turn from green to brown. Refrigerate seed in airtight containers.

SEED VIABILITY 5 years

Seed Varieties

Varieties listed in 18th-century Virginia

♦ **'Scarlet', 'Salmon', 'Short-topped':** All long-rooted radishes

♦ **'Rose':** May be ancestor of 'Early Rose'; a short, blunt radish

♦ **'Black Turnip', 'White Spanish', 'Black Spanish', 'Purple Turnip':** Large radishes primarily used for the winter crop

Heirloom varieties for the modern gardener

♦ **'Long Scarlet':** Long-rooted radish

♦ **'Black Spanish':** Relatively unchanged over hundreds of years; round and long

♦ **'German Bier':** Likely similar to 'White Spanish' radish

♦ **'Early Rose':** Short, blunt radish

PARSNIP
Pastinaca sativa

The Roman emperor Tiberius, who ruled between 14 and 37 CE, exacted an annual tribute of a root that he was particularly fond of from a fortress at Gelduba on the Rhine River in what is now Germany. Pliny called the root *siser* in his *Natural History,* leading Rudolf Jakob Camerarius to identify it as the skirret (*Sium sisarum)* in 1586. However, Pliny almost certainly took his name from the Greek *sisar* or *sisarum,* meaning parsnip. Pliny also commented on the superiority of this root when grown in the colder German climate, which further suggests that this mystery root was actually the parsnip. Gardeners have long known, as John Randolph recorded in 18th-century Williamsburg, that parsnips "are not sweet till bit by the frosts."

The Origin of the Garden Parsnip

The wild parsnip is native to Europe and Western Asia. DNA analysis indicates that the domesticated parsnip originated on the Italian peninsula. From there it moved to northern Europe, where its extreme cold-hardiness made it a staple vegetable.

Parsnips were first recorded in England in Aelfric's Latin vocabulary compiled in 995 CE. In 1548, William Turner wrote in *The Names of Herbes* that: "Persnepes, and skirwortes are commune in Englande." After this time, parsnips are recorded in all garden books that list vegetables.

A Curious Sweetness

Noted agriculturalist John Worlidge described parsnips in *Systema horti-culturae* (1683) as "a delicate sweet food." However, the curious, almost nutty, sweetness of parsnips is not relished by all palates. As Rev. William Hanbury recorded in *A Complete Body of Planting and Gardening* (1773), "It is exceeding wholesome; but is possessed of such a physical sweetness, that very few relish it." Twenty years later, John Abercrombie gave a much more favorable rating in *The Garden Vade Mecum* (1790): "THE parsnep is. . . . very deserving of principal culture in every garden, in considerable supplies, being a very good and profitable root in a family." Profitable or not, this difference of opinion over the desirability of the parsnip still continues to this day.

'Hollow Crown' parsnip

The Kinds of Parsnip

Unlike carrots and radishes, the parsnip never developed distinctly different varieties. There is occasional mention of a shorter, fatter parsnip—called the swelling parsnip or pine parsnip—but most authors list only the common parsnip.

By the 19th century, several varieties of parsnip were advertised, but according to Peter Henderson in *Gardening for Profit* (1867), "A number of varieties of Parsnips are enumerated in seed lists, but the distinctions, as far as I have seen, are hardly worth a difference in name." The hollow-crown parsnip, developed in England in the 1820s, is the most common type of parsnip grown today, and a mid-19th-century variety named 'The Student' is still one of the best of all parsnip varieties. All of the modern parsnips are smaller than their 18th-century ancestors, which could reach nearly 3 feet in length.

"There is another sort of garden Parsnep, called the Pine Parsnep, that is not common in every Garden. . . . The root is not so long, but thicker at the head and smaller below."

—John Parkinson, *Paradisi in Sole* (1629)

The Williamsburg Gardener's Assistant

The common culture of the parsnip. Many of the root crops have similar cultural requirements. John Rutter explained in 1767: "IN the management of a kitchen-garden, one thing naturally leads the way to another, and he who has seen the culture of carrots will need but short directions for this root." One of the most important differences between parsnips and other roots was pointed out by John Randolph in 18th-century Williamsburg and is recognized by gardeners to this day: "Seed are not to be trusted after a year old." Of all the garden plants that we save seed from, parsnip seed is among the shortest lived. It is critical, therefore, that your seed be fresh.

Parsnips also prefer a somewhat richer ground than do carrots, for their season of growth is much longer. Like carrots, they demand a deep, light soil to produce well-formed roots.

Sowing and thinning of parsnips. Parsnip seed germinates best in a cool soil. In Williamsburg, we sow the seeds in the middle of March and manage them as advised by Richard Bradley in 1718: "The *Seeds* of it are sown in *March,* and will come up in about three Weeks time; when they have been above ground about a Month, they must be [thinned], leaving the space of about five or six Inches between the Plants. A skilful *Gardener* will sow *Radishes* among them, which in about forty Days may be drawn off." As with pulling from among carrots, pulling the radishes will serve to thin the parsnips and extract a greater use from your garden space.

Robert Edmeades similarly suggested sowing carrots with parsnips, as explained in *The Gentleman and Lady's Gardener* (1776): "Mix about one third of Carrot and two thirds of Parsnep-seed, and sow it at the end

Thinning parsnips

of February. . . . When the plants appear . . . and when about four inches high . . . leave the Parsneps at about ten inches or a foot asunder, with a few Carrots interspersed amongst them. . . . Draw off the Carrots as you have occasion for them . . . and when they are all taken away, give the ground a good deep hoeing, which will be of great use to the Parsneps."

The benefits of caterpillars and frost. Once the parsnips are established and the leaves are fully grown, little other care is required. In fall in Williamsburg, the caterpillars of the black swallowtail butterfly appear; we move them from the parsley and fennel plants to the parsnips, as they do no harm to the parsnip roots and provide a pretty ornament for the garden.

When the first hard frosts arrive, the parsnips will be fit to harvest. After this time, the parsnips can be harvested as needed throughout the winter months. For plants in colder climes, a straw mulch to keep frost from going deep into the ground will help the gardener in the digging of them. As they are deep rooted, a fork will be of assistance in loosening the ground.

Black swallowtail caterpillars; harvesting parsnips

Seed Varieties

Varieties listed in 18th-century Virginia

♦ **'Parsnip'**: There was generally only one variety of parsnip listed by period sources.

Heirloom varieties for the modern gardener

♦ **'The Student'**, **'Hollow Crown'**: Similar to 18th-century variety, but smaller and more refined

♦ **'Half Long Guernsey'**: A short variety, perhaps similar to the pine parsnip listed by English authors

PARSNIP ESSENTIALS

PLANTING Parsnip seed needs a cool soil to germinate, so seed is sown in early spring when the daffodils bloom.

SPACING Sow parsnip seed ½ inch deep in rows 18 to 24 inches apart, then thin to 4 inches asunder.

FOR BEST GROWTH Parsnips must be grown in a deep, loose, rock-free soil to develop well-formed roots. Maintain even moisture, particularly while plants are young.

HARVESTING Roots are much sweeter after a frost and can be left in the ground over winter in most areas of the country. Mulch the ground to keep it from freezing for as long as possible. The soil must be loosened with a fork or spade to prevent the root from breaking while harvesting.

TO SAVE PURE SEED Separate varieties by 1 mile. Wild parsnips are found in some parts of the country and will cross with cultivated forms.

COLLECTING AND STORING SEED Parsnips must pass through a winter to form flowers and seed. Seed is held in umbels that should be cut once the seeds begin to brown. Parsnips can become a garden weed if left to seed themselves.

SEED VIABILITY 1 year

TURNIP

Brassica rapa

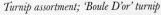

In 18th-century England and America, the turnip was as important for feeding livestock as it was for feeding people. It was such a significant part of the English economy that the development of varieties suitable for agriculture was sponsored by the English monarch, George II. This was the likely origin of the 'Hanover' turnip, George II being of the House of Hanover. Why it took so long to realize the turnip's potential was a puzzle to Philip Miller in 1754: "It is not many Years since the Practice of sowing Turneps, for feeding of Cattle, has been of general Use: how it happen'd that this Improvement should have been so long neglected in every Part of *Europe,* is not easy to determine."

The Most Ancient of Roots

The turnip seems to have arisen from its wild progenitor somewhere between Afghanistan and the Mediterranean basin in prehistoric times. Nearly all the ancient languages of the Middle East have a word for turnip in their vocabularies. In the 1st century CE, Pliny described long turnips, flat turnips, and round turnips. The ancient garden turnips could grow to be quite large. Thomas Hill recorded in *The Gardener's Labyrinth* (1577) that he had seen turnips weighing 30 and 40 pounds "to the admiration of many."

In 1597, John Gerard wrote in *The Herball:* "There be sundrie sorts of Turneps . . . some with round rootes

Turnip assortment; 'Boule D'or' turnip

globe fashion; other ovall or peare fashion; some great; and some of a smaller sorte." Turnips also came in several colors, as Parkinson recorded in *Paradisi in Sole* (1629): "There are divers sorts of Turneps, as white, yellow, and red."

The Navew or French Turnip

Parkinson's yellow turnip was very likely the navew, which in later years was called the French turnip. This was a small root of the *Brassica napus* species and was stronger flavored than the common turnip. According to James Justice in *The Scots Gardiners Director* (1754), it was used only for soups and was "neither fit to be eaten raw or boiled." The best-flavored of all turnips, according to John Gerard in 1597, was the small white turnip, which he assured, "is much sweeter in tast, as my selfe have often prooved."

The Arrival of the Purple-Top Turnip

By the 18th century, the purple-top turnip, familiar to modern gardeners, had appeared, while the other, coarser varieties of turnips began to disappear as table food. Philip Miller wrote in 1754: "The yellow Sort, and that with long Roots, were formerly more cultivated than at present; for it is now very rare to see either of these brought to the Markets."

The turnip was one of the first European vegetables introduced into America. Jacques Cartier recorded planting turnips in Canada in 1541. Turnips were planted by Virginia colonists in 1609 and in Massachusetts in the 1620s. By the 18th century, turnips were the most important root crop for feeding both people and cattle. The turnip remained an important part of the American diet until the 19th century, when the white potato replaced it as the primary starchy root.

The Swedish Turnip

The rutabaga or Swedish turnip is a result of a cross between the turnip and the cabbage, which may have occurred in Europe as early as the Middle Ages. The Swedish turnip differs from the turnip in having smooth rather than somewhat bristly foliage, and generally yellow rather than white flesh.

Rutabaga or Swedish turnip appears to have been unknown in the American colonies until very late in the 18th century. Peter Kalm, during his travels in America, recorded on March 27, 1749: "Nobody around here had ever heard of *rutabagas* or Swedish turnips."

Thomas Jefferson was one of the first Americans to grow the rutabaga. In a 1795 letter to John Taylor he wrote: "I enclose you a few seed of the *Rutabaga,* or Swedish winter turnep. this is the plant which the English Government thought of value enough to be procured at public expense from Sweden, cultivated and dispersed. a mr. Strickland, an English gentleman from Yorkshire, lately here, left a few seeds with me, of which I impart to you. he tells me it has such advantage over the common turnep that it is spreading rapidly over England & will become their chief turnep."

Purple-top turnip

The Williamsburg Gardener's Assistant

The proper season and situation for turnips. Turnips do well in a sandy—even gravelly—soil, and many gardeners claim that their flavor is superior in a poorer ground. In Williamsburg, the primary season for sowing turnips is in August and September; farther to the north and west, turnips are sown in July. A small crop can be sown in early spring. The 'White Dutch' turnip (probably similar to the modern 'White Egg' turnip) was the premier 18th-century spring turnip, as

'White Egg' turnip

described by James Justice in 1771: "THE first ['White Dutch' turnip] is chiefly used in this country for early crops, and for eating raw in *May* and *June,* of which many are very fond. To have them very early is a great ambition amongst gardeners."

The danger to spring-sown turnips is that they are much more prone to bolting, especially if exposed to freezing weather when young, or if the weather turns hot and dry as they mature. The fall crop is, by far, the best and most reliable.

The right ordering of turnips. While their culture is not difficult, some attention to detail will ensure a better crop. As explained by John Rutter in 1767: "NO root rewards the gardener's care better than the turnep; for its excellence depends more than all others upon culture, and will be proportioned in goodness to the attention shewn it in its growth."

Rutter continued: "The manner of sowing should be this: draw lines across the bed at one foot distance, and make a trench with a hoe along each line; then drop in the seeds along these trenches not

Seed Varieties

Varieties listed in 18th-century Virginia

- ◆ **'Large English', 'Norfolk', 'Early Hanover', 'Large Field', 'Stewart's', 'Cambell's', 'Norway', 'Reynold's':** Large, often long-rooted varieties used for feeding livestock

- ◆ **'Early Dutch', 'White Round':** Early season turnips, either white or yellow; often used as spring turnips

- ◆ **'Red Ring', 'Round Red', 'Purple':** Today known as purple-top turnip

- ◆ **'Early Green':** Perhaps similar to 'Gilfeather'

Heirloom varieties for the modern gardener

- ◆ **'Tankard':** General term for cattle-feeding turnips

- ◆ **'White Egg', 'Snowball', 'Golden Ball':** Early season turnips

- ◆ **'Gilfeather':** Green turnip

- ◆ **'Purple Milan'**

too thick; draw the mould [fine organic soil] over the seeds, and give a gentle watering. The next morning lay some soot over the whole length of each trench; and for the future water over that. If rain does not fall, they should be watered carefully every other day."

Two methods to defend against the flea beetle. Gardeners often spread soot over their turnip rows to ward off the flea beetle, which can be devastating to the young seedlings. The 18th-century gardener had a number of elaborate recipes for combating this pest. John Rutter described one in 1767: "Steep the seed in the following liquor: Boil a good quantity of tobacco stalks in water till it is very strong of them; then stir into this some aloes, soot, and flour of brimstone [sulfur]. Put in the seeds, and let them lie eighteen hours; then draw off the liquor, and sow them with the ingredients. . . . The ingredients used in steeping will give no taste to the roots; they only promote the first growth, and keep off the fly. When the rough leaves are come, the danger of this enemy is over."

Turnip greens

The necessity and rewards of thinning turnips. To have well-formed roots, it is necessary to thin the turnips to stand at least 4 inches apart. This is particularly true for the 'White Egg' turnip, which is the least tolerant of overcrowding and will often not form a root at all if not thinned. Many people are fond of turnip greens. The young greens produced by thinning are the finest of the season.

TURNIP ESSENTIALS

PLANTING Sow seed in fall when the goldenrod blooms, and in spring when daffodils are in full bloom.

SPACING Sow seed ½ inch deep in rows 18 inches apart. Thin turnips to 4 inches asunder.

FOR BEST GROWTH Fall turnips provide the largest and sweetest crop; spring turnips are liable to bolt if exposed to prolonged cold snaps. Maintain evenly moist soil; turnips grown in dry soils develop woody cores.

HARVESTING Harvest turnip greens when the leaves are 4 to 6 inches high. Harvest roots when 3 inches in diameter. Roots and greens harvested after a frost are sweeter.

TO SAVE PURE SEED Isolate varieties of turnip by 1 mile, as well as from Chinese cabbage and broccoli raab.

COLLECTING AND STORING SEED Turnips are biennial plants that must pass through a winter season to form flowers and seed. Turnips will overwinter with the help of mulch in most areas of the country. In colder regions, they must be dug and stored for winter and replanted in spring. Seed stalks are typically 3 feet tall and may need staking. Seedpods shatter soon after ripening, so must be harvested as they come ripe. Refrigerate seed in airtight containers.

SEED VIABILITY 5 years

BEET

Beta vulgaris var. *esculenta*

The beet, in its chard form, has been known for thousands of years; the red beetroot is a relatively recent introduction. It was first recorded in Europe by Leonhart Fuchs, who wrote in *De Historia Stirpium* (1542) that it was "cultivated almost everywhere in Germany." This seems only fitting for a country that also gave us the giant fodder beet, or *mangel wurzel,* and the sugar beet. The earliest English description of the red beetroot names it the "Romaine beete," suggesting that this is yet another innovation of the Italians, Europe's consummate vegetable gardeners.

The Beetroot and Its Kinds

Beetroot was known in England by the early 17th century. John Parkinson wrote in *Paradisi in Sole* (1629): "The Romane red Beete . . . is both for leafe and roote the most excellent Beete of all others." These were beets with long thick roots rather than the familiar round roots of the modern beet.

The preferred beet in the 17th and early 18th centuries had red leaves as well as red roots. John Evelyn in *The Compleat Gard'ner* (1693) wrote they "are the best that have the *Reddest* substance and the *Reddest* Tops."

The Modern Beetroot

By 1754, Philip Miller was able to list four varieties of beetroot in *The Gardeners Dictionary*. He also wrote that there was a type of the common red beet "which has been introduced lately into the Kitchen-gardens with a short Top, and green Leaves, with a very red Root: this is preferred to the common red Beet." These short-top varieties had rounder roots and would have looked very much like the modern beet.

Beetroot was known in colonial Virginia but was far less common than carrots, radishes, turnips, or parsnips. This was a reflection of the colonists' English cousins' lack of enthusiasm for the beetroot. By the 19th century, however, the beet had become one of the most popular roots in America. William Cobbett wrote in *The American Gardener* (1821): "This vegetable, which is little used in England, is here in as common use as carrots are there."

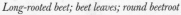

Long-rooted beet; beet leaves; round beetroot

The Williamsburg Gardener's Assistant

The time and manner of sowing beetroot. As is true for nearly all root crops, beets prefer a light soil. They are relatively frost-hardy and may be sown in early spring. In Williamsburg, we largely follow the advice found in *The Young Gardener's Best Companion* (1795): "It is propagated by seed sowed annually in March or April, in an open quarter of rich ground to remain; sowed either broad-cast, and raked in, or in shallow drills a foot asunder, and not more then an inch deep." We generally sow the seeds somewhat shallower than this, for they are prone to poor germination if buried too deeply and are impeded by soils that tend to crust over after a rain.

The thinning and care of beetroots. After the seeds germinate, they must be thinned. As explained by John Abercrombie in 1790: "When the plants are come up with leaves an inch or two broad, they must be thinned and cleared from weeds." This thinning provides one of the best greens of the year. The small beetroots removed during thinning may be boiled together with the leaves for a spring delicacy. The remaining beets should stand at least 4 inches apart to develop their full size.

Beets are weak-rooted plants that are easily stunted by weed competition or by tillage that disturbs the root zone as the beets are forming. Weeds must be pulled by hand while still small, and the young beetroots must not be allowed to suffer drought.

For a continual harvest of roots and greens, seeds can be sown every 3 or 4 weeks until early summer. It is particularly important that the later sowings are in a moist ground, and some shade would not be amiss.

Beet seedlings; thinned beets

BEET ESSENTIALS

PLANTING Begin sowing beets when the crocuses fade and the daffodils open, and for successive crops, resow every 3 or 4 weeks until early summer and water well. In the middle and southern states, beets can be sown again, when the phlox and asters bloom, for a fall crop.

SPACING Plant seeds ½ inch deep in rows 12 to 18 inches apart. Thin to stand 4 inches asunder.

FOR BEST GROWTH Beets are shallow-rooted vegetables that will not stand competition from weeds or each other. Hand weeding and timely thinning are critical to success.

HARVESTING Beet thinnings make an excellent salad green when used with both the tops and the tiny beets still attached. Begin pulling roots, with tops, when they are 1½ inches in diameter and harvest all before they are larger than 3 inches.

TO SAVE PURE SEED Beets are wind pollinated and will cross with chard. Pollen can travel up to 5 miles. Isolation cages give the surest results.

COLLECTING AND STORING SEED Beet is a biennial that must pass through a winter season to flower and set seed. In cold climates, beets are dug in fall. Foliage and roots are trimmed and stored in damp sand in a cool dark place. Beet seeds are actually clusters of seed that may be broken apart, but this often reduces their germination percentage. Refrigerate seed in airtight containers.

SEED VIABILITY 6 years

Seed Varieties

Varieties listed in 18th-century Virginia

♦ **'Red'**: Used to distinguish what we call beets from chard, which was called "White" beetroot.

Heirloom varieties for the modern gardener

♦ **'Cylindra', 'Crapaudine'**: Long roots typical of ancient varieties of beetroot

♦ **'Bull's Blood'**: Round red root with dark red leaves

♦ **'Early Blood Turnip', 'Early Wonder'**: Round red root, green leaves

♦ **'Chioggia'**: Red beet with distinctive concentric white rings in flesh

"The Roots of the *Red Beet,* pared into thin Slices and Circles, are by the *French* and *Italians* contriv'd into curious Figures to adorn their *Sallets.*"

—John Evelyn, *Acetaria: A Discourse of Sallets* (1699)

POTATO
Solanum tuberosum

The potato reached England late in the 16th century, but it took another 100 years to become common at the English table. In 1629, John Parkinson regarded it as "not altogether so pleasant" in comparison to the sweet potato. In 1707, John Mortimer observed, "The . . . Root is very near the nature of the *Jerusalem Artichoak,* which is not so good or wholesme. . . . and prove good Food for Swine." However, 20 years later, the English had so enthusiastically embraced this versatile root that Batty Langley was able to write, "To describe Potatoes would be a needless Work, seeing that they are now very well known by most (if not every) Person in *England.*"

The New World Potato

The potato is a native of South America, and wild forms are still found in Peru, Chile, Bolivia, and Ecuador. It was probably on the high Andean plateau of Bolivia and Peru that the potato was first domesticated. It became the highland staple crop, while corn dominated the lowlands. The first European record of the potato came from a Spanish raiding party at the headwaters of the Rio Magdalena River in Colombia in 1537. The Spanish found stores of maize, beans, and what they originally called truffles. The Spanish introduced the potato into Europe, calling it *papa,* taken from the Quechua (Andean) word for potato. The English, in a case of mistaken identity, called it *potato* from the West Indian word for the sweet potato, *batata.*

Its Arrival in the British Isles

There are many legends about how the potato was introduced into the British Isles. The only point that

Red potato flowers; potato foliage

nearly everyone agrees on is that it was first introduced into Ireland. One account claims that Sir John
Hawkins found potatoes in Santa Fe de Bogata in
1565 and returned with them to Ireland. Another has
it that Sir Francis Drake, after sacking Cartagena in
1586, made a present of potatoes to Sir Walter
Raleigh for his Irish estates. Raleigh may have
planted them before this at Youghall, Ireland, in
1585. Not to be outdone, Sir Robert Southwell, president of the Royal Society, recorded in the December
13, 1693, minutes that it was actually his father who
received the potatoes from Raleigh and planted them
on *his* Irish estate. A local Irish legend has it that
ships from the Spanish Armada foundered off the
coast of Ireland in 1588 with potatoes onboard, which
were collected by the Irish peasants and planted in
the counties of Kerry and Cork.

White potato flower

Its Embrace by the Irish

Regardless of how it arrived, the potato became the
primary staple in the Irish diet, partly as a result of
war. During the Irish civil war in the middle of the
17th century, English troops under Oliver Cromwell
ransacked the countryside, stealing or burning the
wheat and rye and driving off the livestock. The
potato crop was largely spared, partly because the
English were not familiar with the potato and partly
because the potatoes were, conveniently, underground.
Faced with famine, the Irish turned to the potato,
which until the potato blight arrived two centuries
later, was ideally suited to the cool Irish climate and
provided more calories per acre than did wheat.

The Potato Comes to England

The white potato was first described in England in
The Herball, or Generall Historie of Plantes, published by
John Gerard in 1597. This mammoth tome included
descriptions of almost 2,000 plants. Of all these
plants, Gerard chose the flower of the potato to be
pictured in his portrait in this work. Despite this
early attention, the potato remained obscure and
largely unregarded by the English until the 18th century. Once accepted, however, it quickly became an
important agricultural staple. In 1727, Stephen Switzer recorded that the potato "is propagated by the
Irish, and from them . . . by us here in *England*. . . .
The great produce and profit that arises from these
roots, cause many fields in and about *London* . . . to be
planted with them."

The Potato in North America

There are almost as many legends about how the
potato reached North America as there are for it
reaching the British Isles. Much of the confusion originated with Gerard, who referred to the white potato
as "Potatoes of Virginia" in the 1597 *Herball*. This
mistake was propagated by later writers such as Jacob
Bobart, who continued Robert Morison's *Plantarum
historiae universalis Oxoniensis* (1699) after his death.
Bobart's Latin text had been translated to say that the
potato "from Virginia called Openauck or Apenauk,
it was brought into England and thence it was scat-
tered throughout Europe." "Openauk" was a native

root described by Thomas Hariot, a member of the 1585 expedition to Roanoke Island, but Hariot's "Openauk" was almost certainly the groundnut or cinnamon vine (*Apios americana*).

The confusion over the origin of the white potato lasted into the 19th century, when Thomas Jefferson attempted to set the story straight in an 1809 letter to a Mr. Spafford: "In page 186 [*General Geography,* by Spafford,] you say the potato is a native of the United States. I presume you speak of the Irish potato. I have inquired much into the question, and think I can assure you that plant is not a native of North America. . . . The most probable account I have been able to collect is, that a vessel of Sir Walter Raleigh's, returning from Guiana, put into the west of Ireland in distress, having on board some potatoes which they called earth-apples. That the season of the year,

and circumstance of their being already sprouted, induced them to give them all out there, and they were no more heard or thought of, till they had been spread considerably into that island, whence they were carried over into England, and therefore called the Irish potato. From England they came to the United States, bringing their name with them."

The first documented introduction of the white potato into North America does not come until 1719, when it was introduced into Londonderry, New Hampshire, by Irish immigrants. It caught on quickly. Thirty years later, a student of Carolus Linnaeus named Peter Kalm traveled between Philadelphia and Canada and recorded: "*Potatoes* are planted by almost everyone." By the American Revolution, the white potato replaced the sweet potato as the most commonly grown potato in North America.

The Williamsburg Gardener's Assistant

The season and situation for potatoes. Potatoes are planted 2 to 3 weeks before the last average frost date, for while the roots prefer a cooler soil, the tops will not withstand temperatures below 28°F. In Williamsburg, we plant potatoes in the second week of March. This planting is harvested before potato beetles become a concern later in summer.

Potatoes do best in a light, well-drained soil. As John Abercrombie directed in 1790: "They should have a lightish rich mellow ground; or if of a sandy loamy nature, it will be an advantage . . . if some lightish or moderately rotted dung [compost] is digged or plowed in." They are heavy feeders, so the richer the soil, the more plentiful the harvest.

What remedies are available for a heavy soil. If one is burdened with a heavy soil, the authors of *Adam's Luxury, and Eve's Cookery* (1744) advise: "Dig out a Trench a Foot or fourteen Inches wide, and about eight or ten Inches deep, shaking into the Trench some old dry Thatch, the Bottoms and Tops of a Hay-Stack, or any other such like stuff. Then being provided with Potatoes, which, were I to chuse, should not be small ones, as is by some recommended, but the larger ones cut into two or three Pieces; for these having longer Eyes or Buds to them, will produce stronger Stalks and of consequence larger Roots."

When the trench is prepared, press the seed potatoes into the ground with an eye facing upwards. Cover the potatoes with straw to the top of the trench, and then cover the whole with the soil taken from the trench and square it up handsomely. This method will provide large, well-formed roots that are easily harvested.

To cut or not to cut potatoes for planting. Some gardeners prefer to plant whole seed potatoes, while

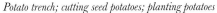

Potato trench; cutting seed potatoes; planting potatoes

others prefer to cut the seed potatoes into pieces with at least one eye in each piece. The conventional wisdom is that whole potatoes with many eyes will produce more but smaller potatoes, while potatoes planted from pieces with only one or two eyes will produce fewer but larger potatoes.

If "new" potatoes are desired, they should be dug when the plants' flowers appear. For baking potatoes, the tubers are dug after their foliage begins to decay. We prefer a fork over a spade for harvesting potatoes, as less damage is done to them.

(Top) Lumper potato; potato foliage; (bottom) digging potatoes in straw and soil

POTATO ESSENTIALS

PLANTING Plant seed potatoes when the early daffodils bloom. Successive plantings may be made until the dogwoods and lilacs bloom. Either plant small seed potatoes whole, or cut pieces that contain at least two strong eyes from larger potatoes.

SPACING Plant potatoes at least 3 inches deep and 10 to 12 inches apart, in rows 2 feet asunder. Potatoes planted in straw are placed 6 inches deep. In warmer climates, a deeper planting in straw will keep seed potatoes cooler, which is important for tuber formation.

FOR BEST GROWTH Potatoes must have a well-drained soil to prosper. In poorly drained sites, the straw method is preferable. For shallow plantings, earth up plants as they grow, to prevent sunscald and "greening" of potatoes that appear aboveground.

HARVESTING Harvest "new" potatoes when flowers first appear on the plants. Red potatoes are most commonly used as new potatoes. Harvest for baking potatoes when the plants' foliage decays. Loosen the ground with a fork to make pulling easier.

TO SAVE POTATOES For propagation, potatoes are usually saved as tubers, rather than seeds. We have had good success by washing the potatoes, thoroughly drying them, and then wrapping individual potatoes in paper and storing them in a refrigerator's vegetable bin. To prevent propagation of tuber-borne disease, we plant these potatoes in sterile pots and harvest shoots when 6 to 8 inches tall, cutting them off 2 inches above the potting medium. These shoots can then be rooted in a sterile medium to produce disease-free tubers.

Seed Varieties

Varieties listed in 18th-century Virginia

- ◆ **'Irish'**, probably **'Northward'**, **'White Irish'**: Tan skins
- ◆ **'Red'**: Red skins
- ◆ **'Blue'**: Blue skins

Heirloom varieties for the modern gardener

- ◆ **'Garnet Chili'**, **'Early Rose'**, **'Beauty of Hebron'**: Red- to pink-skinned potatoes
- ◆ **'Blue Christie'**: Blue-skinned potato
- ◆ **'Lumper'**, **'Ash-Leaved Kidney'**, **'Champion of Vermont'**, **'Irish Cobbler'**, **'Green Mountain'**, **'Yellow Fin'**: Tan-skinned potatoes

"We have potatoes, white & red (I mean those you call Spanish ones) as for the Virginia kind, I have not seen it in this country, nor can I hear any news of it, though it be common in your European Gardens."

—Rev. John Banister, *Natural History of Virginia 1678–1692*

SWEET POTATO
Ipomoea batatas

The sweet potato is a far richer, more luscious tuber than the white potato, and it was probably for this reason that it acquired an early reputation for provoking lust. John Gerard recorded in *The Herball* (1597) that sweet potatoes were known to "procure bodily lust, and that with greedinesse." It was, therefore, almost certainly the sweet potato that the shameless Falstaff refers to in his pursuit of Mistress Ford in Shakespeare's *The Merry Wives of Windsor* (1623): "Let the skie raine Potatoes . . . haile-kissing Comfits."

The First Potato to Cross Two Oceans

The sweet potato is a native of South America and may have been the first New World vegetable to cross the ocean–although, in this case, it was the Pacific and not the Atlantic. There is a growing body of evidence to suggest that seafarers from Polynesia made it to the New World long before Columbus and returned with sweet potatoes. A legend among the Maori people of New Zealand relates that the sweet potato first arrived on log boats.

The sweet potato and white potato were hopelessly confused by English botanists and garden writers beginning with Gerard. His 1597 *Herball* listed the white potato as "Virginia Potatoes" and the sweet potato as "Skyrrits of Peru." John Parkinson renamed the sweet potato as "The Spanish kinde" in 1629, and this is the name used by most authors after that time.

The sweet potato was far better known in 17th-century England than was the white potato, but it could not be grown in most parts of England and had to be shipped from Spain and Portugal. By the 18th century, tastes were beginning to change. Philip Miller wrote in *The Gardeners Dictionary* (1754) that the sweet potato was, "by some Persons greatly esteemed; tho' in general they are not so well liked as the common Potato, being too sweet and luscious for most Palates."

An Early Arrival in North America

In the North American colonies, Robert Beverley listed the sweet potato as one of the plants "our Natives had originally amongst them" in his *The History and Present State of Virginia* (1705). It is likely that the sweet potato was brought to Virginia by Spanish explorers or possibly through trade among native tribes. Beverley also attempted to clear up the confusion between the white potato and sweet potato by writing: "I take these Kinds to be the same with those, which are represented in the Herbals, to be *Spanish* Potatoes. I am sure, those call'd *English* or *Irish* Potatoes are nothing like these, either in Shape, Colour, or Taste."

Before the arrival of the white potato in Virginia in the middle of the 18th century, sweet potatoes were grown on a large scale. Francis Michel, a Swiss traveler who visited Tidewater, Virginia, in 1702, recorded: "There are potatoes in great quantities." Thirty years later, William Hugh Grove recorded: "Their Potatoes are . . . of the Barmudas Kind . . . they are Either White or red & Comonly rosted they are Sweet & over luscious best in a pye." Sweet potato pie remains one of the finest products of the Virginia garden.

Sweet potato vines

The Williamsburg Gardener's Assistant

The season and manner of sweet potato propagation. Sweet potatoes are tropical plants and must have a warm soil and long season to thrive. They are planted in the garden once the nighttime temperature is consistently above 60°F and require 100 to 140 days to form mature tubers.

Sweet potatoes are planted from slips raised from mature roots. To produce your own slips, lay several sweet potatoes on their side in a warm hotbed and cover with about 2 inches of sand or very fine com-

post. The temperature of the rooting medium should be maintained between 70° and 80°F and kept continually moist. As the slips appear, cover with another inch of sand or compost.

In about 6 weeks, the slips will be 6 or 8 inches long and ready to pull. Remove them from the potato with a twisting motion and take them directly to the garden for planting. The soil for sweet potatoes should be well composted but not overly fertilized. A too rich soil will produce abundant vines and very

(Top) Planting potatoes in hotbed; young sweet potato foliage; mature slips in hotbed; (bottom) removing slips from potato; planting slips; digging potatoes

poor roots. We plant sweet potatoes on ridges thrown up to about 8 inches high. This promotes the warming of the soil and prevents the roots from becoming waterlogged if the weather turns rainy.

Planting the sweet potato slips. Plant the slips 1 to 1½ feet apart on ridges 3 to 4 feet apart and water them well to set the roots. Sweet potatoes produce very large plants, but are often slow to establish, especially if the weather remains cool. Keep your beds well weeded until the vines cover the ground, and they will then exclude the weeds by virtue of their very dense growth.

As the season progresses, keep the plants moist, but be careful not to overwater them, or the roots will be long and stringy. Cease watering altogether in the last month before harvest. The potatoes will be ready to be dug when the foliage begins to yellow or before the first hard frosts arrive. A light frost will not damage the roots, but the roots must be removed as soon as frost has touched the leaves.

Care should be taken when the roots are dug, as they bruise easily and this will greatly reduce their storage life.

To fully develop the sweetness of the potatoes and to increase their storage life, the potatoes must be cured for 10 days at 80° to 85°F with high humidity.

SWEET POTATO ESSENTIALS

PLANTING Plant sweet potatoes in late spring, when the dogwood and lilac drop their blooms and nighttime temperatures are above 60°F.

SPACING Sweet potato slips are best planted on ridges 6 to 8 inches high with slips 12 to 18 inches apart, and 3 to 4 feet between ridges.

FOR BEST GROWTH Sweet potatoes require a long warm season to prosper. Water frequently after planting to establish slips and also during extended dry periods in midsummer. Once established and after the vines

have covered the ground, they require little care. Plants grown in ridges will be easier to harvest.

HARVESTING Stop watering 4 weeks before harvest. Care must be taken that they are not bruised when harvested.

TO SAVE SWEET POTATOES Sweet potatoes are propagated by slips grown from mature tubers. Start the slips in hotbeds 1 month before planting. Store tubers for next year's slips in a root cellar, buried in sawdust, and ensure that they do not touch.

Seed Varieties

Varieties listed in 18th-century Virginia

- **'Spanish':** A somewhat more slender root than the modern sweet potato
- **'Bermuda':** The 'Bermuda' sweet potato eventually came to mean a blunter variety; this may be an ancestor of it.

Heirloom varieties for the modern gardener

- **'Bermuda Pink', 'Arkansas Red', 'Hayman', 'Southern Queen',** and many others

JERUSALEM ARTICHOKE

Helianthus tuberosus

The Jerusalem artichoke is not from Jerusalem and is not an artichoke. In 1605, Samuel de Champlain noted it growing along the coast of Massachusetts and described it as having "the taste of an artichoke." The name stuck. The origin of "Jerusalem" is not as clear. Most think it a corruption of *girasole*, the Italian word for the annual sunflower. However, the first English use of the name "Artichocks of *Jerusalem*" was recorded in Tobias Venner's *Via recta ad vitam longam* in 1622, and the Italians did not adopt *girasole* for the sunflower until 1666, so the etymology of "Jerusalem" for the Jerusalem artichoke remains a mystery.

A Vegetable of North America

The Jerusalem artichoke, a member of the sunflower genus, is one of the few vegetables native to North America. Asa Gray, the great 19th-century American botanist, postulated in *A Flora of North America* (1838–1843) that the Jerusalem artichoke originated west of

Jerusalem artichoke flowers; Jerusalem artichokes

the Mississippi River and was carried east through Indian trade.

John Parkinson gave it the name "Potatos of Canada" in *Paradisi in Sole* (1629) and wrote: "We in England, from some ignorant and idle head, have called them Artichokes of Jerusalem, only because the roote, being boyled, is in taste like the bottome of an Artichoke head . . . the French brought them first from Canada into these parts . . . from one roote, being set in the Spring, there hath been forty or more taken up againe."

It is nearly certain that it was the French who first brought this root to Europe, likely as a part of the 1607 Pierre Dugua, Sieur de Mons, expedition to Port Royal, Nova Scotia. From France, the Jerusalem artichoke was introduced into England. As recorded by Sir J.D. Hooker in the July 1897 edition of *Curtis's Botanical Magazine*: "In the year 1617 Mr. John Goodyer of Maple Durham, Hampshire, received two small roots of it from Mr. Franquevill of London, which being planted, enabled him before 1621 'to store Hampshire.'"

A Potato Fit for a Queen

This propensity for rapid propagation, which enabled Goodyer "to store Hampshire" in such short order, is perhaps the Jerusalem artichoke's most notable attribute. By 1629, John Parkinson recorded in *Paradisi in Sole*: "The Potato's of Canada are by reason of their great increasing, growne to be so common here with us at London, that even the most vulgar begin to despise them, whereas when they were first received among us, they were dainties for a Queene." This

may be in reference to an inventory of household purchases for James I in 1619 that included potato at the very high price of one shilling per pound.

Service for Man and Beast

In Virginia, Rev. John Banister recorded in his *Natural History of Virginia 1678–1692* that "the Batatas Canadensis, or Jerusalem Artichokes are little esteemed of here." The objection to this root by colonial Virginians was explained by John Randolph in *A Treatise on Gardening* (1793): "Some admire them, but they are of a flatulent nature, and are apt to cause commotions in the belly."

The Jerusalem artichoke did find use as livestock feed. George Washington was one of the first to experiment with it. He inquired of Clement Biddle on December 5, 1786: "Are the Artichoke of Jerusalem to be had in the neighborhood of Philada? Could as much of the root, or the seed, be got as would stock an acre? I want to bring it in with my other experiments for the benefit of stock." Thomas Jefferson also tried the experiment and recorded in an 1817 letter to Tristran Dalton: "With respect to field culture of vegetables for cattle, instead of the carrot and potato recommended by yourself and the magazine, and the beet by others, we find the Jerusalem artichoke best for winter."

In the middle of the 19th century, a couple of improved varieties of Jerusalem artichoke were developed. They enjoyed another brief period of popularity, but it has generally remained one of the more obscure root crops. It is only occasionally found at market today, often under the name of sunchoke.

"The Jerusalem Artichoke is . . . very subject to trouble the belly by their windy quality, which hath brought them almost into disuse."

—Philip Miller, *The Gardeners Dictionary* (1768)

The Williamsburg Gardener's Assistant

What space is needed to accommodate Jerusalem artichokes. The Jerusalem artichoke is a large plant that should be planted where you intend it to remain. It spreads rapidly by the edible tubers and is not easily removed once it is established. The flower stems will grow to 8 feet tall or taller, so a northern quarter of the garden where it will not cast shade over other plants is generally best. Once a location is found where the plants can be conveniently contained, they will reward you with a profusion of yellow sunflowers in early autumn followed by a bountiful harvest of roots in late fall.

Jerusalem artichokes will grow in most areas of the United States, though they suffer in the southernmost states, particularly in dry weather. They are tolerant of most soils but prefer a lighter soil and are much easier to dig in a sandy situation.

Means of propagation for Jerusalem artichokes. Their propagation and management are very easy. As explained in *Adam's Luxury, and Eve's Cookery* (1744): "It is propagated by the Roots in the same Manner as you do Potatoes, cutting the large Roots and preserving a Bud or 2 to each Piece, and planting them in Rows with Setting-sticks about 18 Inches asunder, and two Foot Row from Row. . . . They will grow in almost any Soil or Situation, being very hardy: It will therefore be proper to plant them in some remote Corner of your Garden, for when they are once establish'd in a piece of Ground, they are not without difficulty to be eradicated."

Larger-size tubers will give better results. They should be planted 3 to 5 inches deep. Little else is required, as weeds are seldom a problem, but if it should turn very dry in late summer when the tubers

Planting and harvesting Jerusalem artichokes

are forming, some irrigation will improve the size and quality of the roots.

What annual maintenance is required for Jerusalem artichokes. To produce the largest roots, however, the bed must be dug annually. Plantings that are left unharvested quickly become overcrowded and produce only small roots. Wait until the roots have gone through a couple of frosts, and then follow the advice found in *The Garden Vade Mecum* (1790): "It will be proper, about November, when the stalks decay, to dig up a quantity, and lay them in sand under cover, to be ready for use as wanted in Winter." We find that a spading fork is most suited to this work and that the soil should be turned twice to discover the most roots. As soon as the roots are harvested, select those that are to be replanted and put them in the ground 3 to 5 inches deep and about 12 inches asunder.

JERUSALEM ARTICHOKE ESSENTIALS

PLANTING Jerusalem artichokes are replanted after harvest in fall from existing beds. New beds can be started in spring when the daffodils bloom.

SPACING Plant tubers with at least two or three prominent buds, 3 to 5 inches deep, on 12- to 18-inch centers, or in rows 3 feet asunder.

FOR BEST GROWTH Jerusalem artichokes do not grow well in the Deep South. From the middle states northward, they are among the easiest plants to grow and can be invasive. Supplemental irrigation during drought will give better roots.

HARVESTING Harvest after the first frost and after the foliage has died, for ease of access and for sweeter roots. Take care to remove all the roots that you can find before replanting.

SAVING JERUSALEM ARTICHOKES Jerusalem artichokes are usually propagated from tubers, replanted after harvest.

Seed Varieties
Heirloom varieties for the modern gardener

There are few varieties of Jerusalem artichokes, and because they are almost always propagated vegetatively, seed sources have not been developed as they have been for other crops. The most notable differences among varieties are in skin color. These varieties are often difficult to find; Jerusalem artichokes are often sold simply as *H. tuberosa*.

♦ **'Mammoth French White':** Has white skin

♦ **'Smooth Garnet':** Has red to purple skin

♦ **'Golden Nugget':** Has yellow skin

SALSIFY and SCORZONERA

Tragopogon porrifolius and *Scorzonera hispanica*

These are two of the more obscure roots in the kitchen garden. Salsify seems to have fallen in and out of favor over the centuries. Scorzonera has long been considered a Spanish root and never achieved prominence in the English diet. In 1867, Peter Henderson described salsify in *Gardening for Profit* in a manner that suggests it had earlier disappeared from the American garden but was being rediscovered: "This vegetable is coming rapidly into general use. . . . As this vegetable will be unknown to many, I will state that it is used in various ways, but generally boiled, or stewed, like Parsnips or Carrots. . . . has a decided flavor of the Oyster." Of scorzonera, he says: "It is not . . . so generally esteemed as the Oyster Plant."

An Obscure and Admired Root

Salsify was never a particularly important root in the English diet, but has always had its admirers. It is a European native of ancient cultivation, recorded by the Greek writer Theophrastus in the 3rd century BCE and by nearly all writers on agriculture and gardening after that time.

There are several species of *Tragopogon* native to Europe that go by the name of goatsbeard. The yellow-flowered *T. pratensis* was the first species used as a culinary plant, both for its roots and its young stems that are eaten like asparagus. The purple-flowered *T. porrifolius* was apparently developed in Italy and introduced into England sometime in the 16th century.

Salsify and scorzonera; salsify flower

Gerard described both species in the 1597 *Herball*, calling the yellow-flowered form "Go to bed at noone" because the flowers are open in the morning and close at about noon. He recognized the purple-flowered form as an imported root. Gerard wrote: "[It] groweth not wilde in England that I coulde ever see or heare of" but observed that it "is sowen in gardens . . . almost every where" and that it is "a most pleasant meate and wholsome, in delicate taste farre surpassing either Parsnep or Carrot."

The Viper's Grass, a Cheerful Root

A similar root, scorzonera, was domesticated in Spain at an early date and introduced into the rest of Europe in the late 17th century. Switzer, in *The Practical Kitchen Gardiner* (1727), wrote: "THE *Scorzonera* (by original a *Spaniard*) has of late met with great entertainment at the tables of the curious. . . .

Scorzonera

The *Scorzonera* has its name from a viper or serpent, called in *Spain Scorzo*." This plant also went by the name of viper's grass in England and was occasionally known as black salsify. It is given a good recommendation from almost all English authors of the 18th century, despite its general obscurity among the general population. Batty Langley wrote in 1728, "The Root being eaten, causes chearfulness." John Rutter wrote in 1767, "THIS is a root not unlike the salsafie, but more delicate." Despite such testimonials, scorzonera was never a well-known root in England or her colonies.

Salsify was somewhat better known than scorzonera, but still was not universally accepted. Philip Miller observed in *The Gardeners Dictionary* (1754): "[Salsify] was formerly more in Esteem than at present; this was brought from *Italy,* and cultivated in Gardens for Kitchen-use, the Roots being by some People greatly valued: but of late there is but little cultivated for the Markets."

The Oyster Root Comes to America

The only 18th-century Virginia references to salsify come from two Williamsburg gardeners, John Randolph and Joseph Prentis. Thomas Jefferson, who probably grew more exotic vegetables than any Virginia gardener, encouraged its cultivation in an 1812 letter to Charles Clay: "I do not remember to have seen Salsafia in your garden, & yet it is one of the best roots for the winter. Some call it oyster plant."

Bernard McMahon, a Philadelphia nurseryman, described it favorably in *The American Gardener's Calendar* (1806): "The salsafy is estimable both for its roots as above, and for the young shoots rising in the spring from year-old plants, being gathered while green and tender, are good to boil and eat in the manner of asparagus. . . . Some have carried their fondness for it so far, as to call it a vegetable oyster."

Here as in England, public enthusiasm for salsify never caught on, and it remains in obscurity even to this day.

The Williamsburg Gardener's Assistant

Salsify allows the easiest culture. The cultivation of salsify and scorzonera is very similar to the cultivation of the carrot. All are long, slender roots better formed in a light soil. The seeds are sown in early spring. As advised by John Abercrombie in 1790: "Sow the seed . . . in March and April in an open situation, either broad-cast, or in small drills six or eight inches distance; and when the plants are up two or three inches, thin them half a foot apart."

Both salsify and scorzonera produce clumps of grasslike leaves. Scorzonera leaves are thicker and darker green than salsify's. Both plants are of the easiest culture. Water as required over the course of the summer, and the roots will be ready for harvest after the weather has cooled. In Williamsburg, we follow the advice of *The Gentleman and Lady's Gardener*

(1776): "In the Autumn when the leaves begin to decay, they [the roots] will be fit for use, and will continue good till they begin shoot in the Spring." Like that of many root crops, their flavor is improved by frost. Salsify roots are long and slender and somewhat brittle, so the ground must be thoroughly loosened before they are pulled, or else they are easily broken.

Salsify gives a second season of harvest and a blooming bonus. We always leave a few plants of salsify in the ground to overwinter. As recommended by *The Young Gardener's Best Companion* (1795), "The young shoots of its seed-stalks in Spring, when but a few inches high, while crisp and tender, are also good to boil like asparagus." In Williamsburg, the shoots

Scorzonera foliage; digging salsify

are harvested in early April and are, indeed, very tasty. After the shoots are harvested, salsify will shoot up to form very attractive purple flowers that are worth reserving a spot for in the garden. After the flowers are spent, they will form large, dandelion-like seedheads. If the seedheads are not removed, you will find salsify sprouting in odd corners about the garden the following spring.

Scorzonera is harvested in a similar manner to salsify, but the roots are even longer and quite brittle. Use a spade to trench the ground and extract the roots. Unlike salsify, all the plants are harvested before spring, as described by Robert Edmeades in 1776: "As soon as the leaves begin to decay, the roots are arrived at their full growth, and may be taken up for use, but if any are left in the ground till February, they will then begin to push forth their flower-stems, and will be unfit for eating."

(Top) Salsify shoots; salsify flowers; (bottom) salsify seedhead; digging scorzonera root

SALSIFY AND SCORZONERA ESSENTIALS

PLANTING Sow salsify and scorzonera in early spring when the daffodils bloom.

SPACING Sow seed ½ inch deep in rows 12 to 18 inches asunder; after germination, thin seedlings to stand 2 to 3 inches apart.

FOR BEST GROWTH Salsify and scorzonera require a deep, loose, stone-free soil to produce well-shaped roots. Salsify is more sensitive to drought than other roots crops and will form better roots in an evenly moist soil.

HARVESTING Both salsify and scorzonera are sweeter after a frost and can be left in the garden for a successive harvest over the winter months. The roots are brittle, so the soil must be loosened with a fork before they are pulled.

TO SAVE PURE SEED There are very few varieties of salsify and scorzonera, so crossing is generally not a problem. They will not cross with each other or the closely related wild goatsbeard. Separation of varieties by half a mile will ensure purity.

COLLECTING AND STORING SEED Both are biennials that must pass through a winter season to flower and set seed. Both produce fluffy, dandelion-like seedheads that must be harvested frequently to prevent them from sailing away on the wind. Some seeds invariably escape; and salsify seedlings, in particular, are often found sprouting in the odd corners of the garden and even in the garden next door! Refrigerate seed in airtight containers.

SEED VIABILITY Salsify seed is viable for 4 years, scorzonera seed for 2.

Seed Varieties

Varieties listed in 18th-century Virginia
Salsify varieties are not listed other than by flower color in European sources.

Heirloom varieties for the modern gardener
- ‘Mammoth Sandwich Island’: The only variety carried by seed houses

"The salsafy is estimable both for its roots as above, and for the young shoots rising in the spring from year-old plants, being gathered while green and tender, are good to boil and eat in the manner of asparagus. . . . Some have carried their fondness for it so far, as to call it a vegetable oyster."

—Bernard McMahon, *The American Gardener's Calendar* (1806)

SKIRRET

Sium sisarum

Throughout history, the skirret has been blessed and cursed with the highest recommendation and the lowest popularity of any of the root crops. In 1727, Stephen Switzer wrote, "THE skirret, *sisarum,* (says Mr. *Evelyn*) is hot and moist, corroborating and good for the stomach, exceeding nourishing, wholesome and delicate, and of all the root-kind not subject to be windy. . . . Mr. *Evelyn* tells us also, that this excellent root is seldom eaten raw, but being boil'd, stew'd, roasted under embers, bak'd in pies, whole, sliced, or in pulp, is agreeable to all palates." Almost a decade earlier, Richard Bradley observed in *New Improvements* (1718): "THE *Skirret* has a very agreeable Root, altho' it is propagated but in few *Gardens.*" Its obscurity persists today.

A Root of Mysterious Origin

The skirret is a curious little root of mysterious origins. It probably originated in central Asia and migrated from there to Germany as early as 1100 CE. It was first illustrated in Germany by Leonhart Fuchs in 1542. Olivier des Serres recorded in 1600 that the skirret was introduced into France from Germany. However, in 1548, William Turner wrote in the *The Names of Herbes,* "Persnepes, and skirwortes are commune in Englande," suggesting it had been known in the British Isles for some time before this.

In a much older English record, Roger, the gardener to the Archbishop of Canterbury at Lambeth Palace, included a penny's worth of skirret in a 1321 to 1322 inventory. Skirrets were also listed by Friar Henry Daniel in *De re Herbaria* in 1375, but in both cases these references could be to the carrot.

Skirret's Brief Period of Fame

Skirrets were fairly well known in 17th-century England, although John Parkinson wrote of them in a way that suggests he was promoting them to an uninformed garden public in 1629: "Any way that men please to use them, they may finde their taste to be very pleasant, far beyond any Parsnep, as all agree that taste them."

The roots relapsed into obscurity during the 18th century, a mystery to Philip Miller, who wrote in *The Gardeners Dictionary* (1754): "This is one of the wholsomest and most nourishing Roots that is cultivated in Gardens; and yet it is at present very rare to meet with it in the Gardens near *London*: what may have been the Cause of its not being more commonly cultivated, I can't imagine."

Skirrets are equally scarce but not altogether absent from the Virginia record. In 1774, James Wilson, gardener at the College of William and Mary in Williamsburg, offered skirret seed for sale.

The Williamsburg Gardener's Assistant

The propagation and culture of skirrets. Skirrets can be started from seed or from root divisions. For seed, we follow the advice found in *Adam's Luxury, and Eve's Cookery* (1744): "The Season for sowing of this Seed is in the Middle of *February,* in a piece of good rich Ground that is pretty moist." Of all the roots crops known to colonial Virginians, the skirret is most tolerant of wet soils, and many people agree that the roots are larger and sweeter in a moist situation. It is also desirable that the ground be light and friable, as the roots will be much longer. A well-composted ground is the best recipe for a light moisture-retentive soil.

Most prefer to propagate skirrets by slips, or offsets from the mother plants. As described by Richard Bradley in *New Improvements* (1718): "In *March,* when the Leaves begin to put forth, take them out of the Ground and part them into as many Slips as you can take off with *Roots*; but be sure let only the fresh springing *Fibers* remain on them, and not any of the old *Roots*; then prepare *Drills* about four or five Inches deep, to plant them in five or six Inches a-part, and keep them well water'd." You will find that some of the plants will have only slender fibrous roots. These should be discarded, reserving only the largest to be planted for the ensuing season.

They are ready for harvest in early autumn. As described in *The Garden Vade Mecum* in 1790: "In September or October, the roots may be taken up as wanted . . . to use all Winter and Spring, till they begin to shoot." In Williamsburg, where the ground seldom freezes, a light mulch is all that is required to keep them. In colder climes, a heavier mulch will be needed for survival and for easier digging over the winter months.

Separate skirrets with roots; skirret roots

SKIRRET ESSENTIALS

PLANTING Skirret seed is sown ½-inch deep in spring in the middle and northern states when the daffodils bloom. In the South, they may also be sown in late summer when the phlox and asters bloom. Plants sown in starter pots and transplanted to the garden are most reliable. Seeds often take 4 weeks to germinate.

SPACING Thin seedlings or set transplants 6 inches apart in rows 18 inches asunder.

FOR BEST GROWTH Skirrets need a continuously moist soil and will tolerate wet conditions better than any other root crop. It grows best in full sun in the middle and northern states, prefers some shade in the South, and is more shade tolerant than most vegetables in all areas. It is a perennial plant in the middle and southern states, though a light layer of mulch or compost will better preserve them for the winter.

HARVESTING Pull the roots after the first frost in fall.

TO SAVE PURE SEED Skirret can be propagated from root divisions in the middle and southern states. There is only one variety, so crossing is not a problem.

COLLECTING AND STORING SEED Seeds are formed in round flower heads, called umbels, very similar to those of carrots. Gather as the seed capsules dry and refrigerate in airtight containers.

SEED VIABILITY 10 years

Seed Varieties

Varieties listed in 18th-century Virginia

♦ **'Skirret'**: Single variety; rarely grown in colonial Virginia

Heirloom varieties for the modern gardener

♦ **'Skirret'**: Single variety; can be difficult to find these seeds

"Most commonly not a finger thicke, they are sweet, white, good to be eaten, and most pleasant in taste."

—John Gerard, *The Herball* (1597)

CHAPTER 5
Of the
Onion Family

The onion and its relatives—leeks, shallots, garlic, and chives—are among the most ancient and important vegetables known to humankind. In *Acetaria* (1699), John Evelyn recorded the often repeated legend that 90 tons of gold were spent on onions in building the pyramids. The ancient Egyptians were famous for their fondness of onions, leeks, and garlic to the point of deifying them. King Ramses IV, who died in 1160 BCE and was buried in the Valley of the Kings, was entombed with onions covering his eye sockets. To the Egyptians, the concentric rings of the onion bulb signified eternal life.

After the Jews escaped into the wilderness with Moses, they lamented in the Book of Numbers (11:5): "We remember the fish, which we did eat in Egypt freely; the cucumbers, and the melons, and the leeks, and the onions, and the garlick." Greek athletes consumed onion juice and rubbed themselves down with onions in preparation for the Olympic Games. The Romans held them in such high regard that onions were grown in special beds called *cepinae*.

Onions were brought to England with the Roman legions and were quickly adopted both for their culinary and medicinal properties. Nicholas Culpeper's *The English Physician* (1652) recorded one of many medicinal uses: "The juyce of Onions is good for either scalding, or burning . . . and used with Vineger, taketh away all Blemishes." Onions were among the first European vegetables transported to the New World, and both onions and leeks were common components of the colonial Virginia garden. Shallots and chives were uncommon, and the 'Welsh' onion never was adopted by the American colonists. Garlic was used to treat the bite of the mad dog and to take away corns on the feet but was seldom brought to the colonial table.

Prior to Linnaean taxonomy, the onion family was spread over four genera. The bulb onion, shallot, and 'Welsh' onion were placed in the *Cepa* genus. Garlic was a member of the *Allium* genus, leeks were listed as *Porrum,* and chives were classed as *Schoenoprasum,* their current species name. Today, all of these plants are included in the *Allium* genus.

ONION

Allium cepa

Onions have always been an important staple and one of the few luxuries at the tables of the poor. The Scottish politician Sir John Sinclair wrote, "It is a well known fact, that a Highlander, with a few raw onions in his pocket, and a crust of bread, or some oat-cake, can travel to an almost incredible extent for two or three days together." In North America, onions were quickly established as an essential element in the kitchen garden. Robert Buist, author of *The Family Kitchen Gardener* (1847), declared: "The Onion crop is an interesting portion of gardening to every good housewife. She is ever solicitous that it should be full and certain."

An Ancient and Useful Bulb

The garden onion has been cultivated for so long that its wild progenitor is lost, but it likely arose from one or more species of wild onion in central Asia. The genus name, *Allium*, comes from the Celtic *all*, meaning pungent, and the species name, *Cepa*, derives from the Roman name for the onion, *cepae*. The common name, *onion*, comes from the Latin *unio*, or one, signifying that the bulb is a single unit.

The onion probably came to England with Roman invaders, and references to onions and the other *Alliums* are often found in medieval account books. Henry de Lacy, Earl of Lincoln in Holbourne, listed onions and the tithe paid for them in the 1295–96 yearly reckoning: "Of 4s. $1\frac{1}{4}$ d [4 shillings, $1\frac{1}{4}$ pence] for onions and garlick sold, the tithe being deducted."

The Ancient Varieties of Onions

The ancient Greek and Roman writers listed several varieties of onions with characteristics that changed very little over the next thousand years. Dioscorides wrote in the *De Materia Medica* (circa 64 CE): "The long onion is sharper than the round, the red more than the white." In 1773, Rev. William Hanbury recorded in *A Complete Body of Planting and Gardening* that the long onion, known as the "Strasburg" (Strasbough), "is an excellent Onion for keeping." The "Spanish" onion was either round or flat and was much sweeter, and the "Blood-red is the most beautiful . . . but it is a strong Onion, and inferior in flavour to the other sorts."

Hanbury also listed several other onions that were developed in the 18th century, including the "Portugal" onion, "very mild and sweet," and the "Silver-skinned" onion, which "is seldom raised, tho' it is very mild." While varieties have changed and improved over time, onions can still be classed into the three general groups of sweet, storage, and red onions. Today the 'Portugal' onion is often used as a pearl onion for pickling.

The Medicinal Virtues of the Onion

Historically, onions have been nearly as important for their medicinal properties as they have been for their culinary use. Thomas Hill wrote in 1577: "Onions mayntayne health, cure ulcers, remove spottes in the body, profitte the eares runnyng . . . open piles, cleare the eyes, remove the pin and web . . . recover the hears [hairs] shed away, the biting of a madde dogge, &c [etc.]." However, moderation is a virtue in all things and particularly with onions. As Hill went on to explain, "Onions often used, engender evill humours, procure thirste, swellings, windinesse, headeache [and] cause to become foolyshe."

The Onion in North America

The only notable American *Allium* of culinary use is the wild garlic or ramp (*A. tricoccum*). It is a pungent leeklike plant that is still gathered in the mountains

"That the kinds of *Onions* worth the *Gardiner's* Care is the *Spanish Onion,* which is generally very large, and sweet; and the *Strasbourg* [Strasbough] *Onion,* which is more mordicant, and keeps much longer than the former."

—Batty Langley, *New Principles of Gardening* (1728)

of Virginia and other areas of Appalachia. In 1624, Father Theodat Gabriel Sagard observed this onion among the Huron Indians and wrote that they "have also little onions, named *Anonque,* which put out only two leaves . . . they smell of garlic. . . . the savages. . . . eat them baked in ashes when quite ripe . . . but never in soup."

The onion family was of minor importance to the Native Americans. Thomas Hariot observed in *A Briefe and True Report of the New Found Land of Virginia* (1585): "There are also *Leekes* differing little from ours in England that grow in many places of the countrey, of which, when we came in places where, wee gathered and eate many, but the naturall inhabitants never."

Onions were among the first vegetables introduced into Virginia by the English colonists in the 17th century, and by the 18th century, Virginia planters were exporting onions to British colonies in the West Indies. In 1752, the *Merry Fellows* left the James River for New Providence in the Bahamas with 15 bushels of onions. The following year, a ship named *Providence* embarked for Jamaica with two hogsheads [casks] of onions aboard.

Onion; red onion

The Williamsburg Gardener's Assistant

The types of onions and when they are sown. Onions are categorized as short-day and long-day varieties. Long-day varieties require day lengths of 14 to 16 hours to form bulbs, while short-day varieties will bulb with day lengths of 10 to 12 hours. Long-day varieties are grown from Virginia north (or from latitude 36°N), while short-day varieties are grown south of Virginia. In the middle states, short-day varieties can be grown for an early crop and long-day varieties will produce the later crop. There are some newer varieties classed as intermediate that will form bulbs with day lengths between 12 and 14 hours, which are suited for the middle states (latitudes 32° to 40°N).

Today, gardeners often start their onion crop with sets, or small onion bulbs, purchased from a garden shop. The propagation of onions from sets was a 19th-century American innovation. The 18th-century gardener would have raised the crop from seed. Sets are not always reliable for the production of bulb onions, as the gardener has no control over the origin or growing conditions under which the sets were formed. Sets larger than about $1/2$ inch in diameter will often bolt and should be used for scallions, or green onions. The smaller sets are reserved for bulbs.

What care is required in the seeding of onions. Onions are weak-rooted plants that require a moist, fertile soil but one that does not stay waterlogged. Walter Nicol observed in 1798: "It requires a strong rich loam to produce it in perfection; but in wet seasons we frequently see good crops raised in light land." In Williamsburg, in order to provide a rich soil that does not stay wet, we plant our onions on ridges raised 5 or 6 inches.

Once the ground is prepared for spring sowing, we follow the instructions given by John Randolph in 18th-century Williamsburg: "The [onions] should be sown in February, the first open weather or beginning of March . . . and in about six weeks your Onions will be up, and ought to be [weeded]. The rows should be

Onion seedlings; scallions; bulb exposed for curing

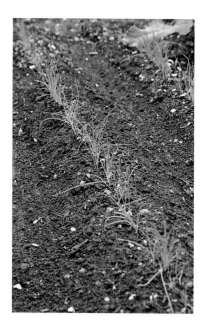  

about 12 or 18 inches asunder if sowed in drills [rows], which is the best method, and the plants should be drawn to be about 5 or 6 inches apart. This may be no loss, because they will serve with young sallad in the spring." What Randolph was referring to is the use of the onion thinnings as scallions, or green onions. They are, indeed, a spring treat.

Raising onion transplants for an early harvest. In Williamsburg, an earlier harvest can be had by raising transplants. The seeds are sown around the first of October and will survive all but the harshest winters for an onion crop in June. In the northern states, where spring-seeded onions may not have time to fully ripen, transplants will ensure the harvest. To raise spring transplants in the North, sow the seed in a hotbed or conservatory 8 to 10 weeks before the last frost date. If the seedlings grow tall and lanky, trim the foliage back to 4 inches. When the transplants are about half the thickness of a pencil, they will be ready to be moved into the garden. Set them with a dibble 1 to 1½ inches deep and 4 to 6 inches apart. In the South, the seedlings that have overwintered can be transplanted in March or thinned for scallions and left in place to form bulbs.

What steps are necessary for harvesting and curing onions? As the bulbs approach their full size, the soil should be pulled away to expose about ⅓ of the bulb. This will help the bulb and neck cure. The onions will be ready for harvest when most of the leaves have fallen down. All 18th-century garden works recommend that onion leaves be broken down before this, to encourage the formation of a larger bulb. This advice is occasionally repeated today, but we now know this does more harm than good.

When the onions are ready to harvest, loosen the soil under the bulbs with a spade, and as advised by John Rutter in 1767, "Lay them upon the two next alleys to harden, and turn them every day." We cure the onions under a hedge that shades them from the hottest sun, and within 5 to 7 days they will be sufficiently cured to be stored indoors. If the weather should turn rainy, bring them into an airy shed and dry them on shelves. For storage, John Randolph advises: "You are then to rub off all the earth and take care to remove all that are any ways decayed, and the sound ones laid as thin as possible in some room or garret . . . and at least once a month look over them, to see if any of them are decayed, for if any are so, they will

Onions ready for harvest; harvested onions; onions laid out for curing

effect the rest . . . and probably ruin the whole crop." Sweet onions will keep up to 3 months in a cool, dry place. The more pungent varieties will keep for another month.

ONION ESSENTIALS

PLANTING Plant sets 2 weeks before the last frost, as the daffodils begin to fade. Sow seed outdoors in spring after danger of frost and soil temperature is above 50°F. Seed for transplants can be sown 4 weeks earlier. In the South, seeds can also be sown in early autumn.

SPACING Onions started from seed are sown thickly, ½ inch deep, and thinned to provide scallions. Space onions for bulbs 4 to 6 inches apart in rows 12 to 18 inches asunder.

FOR BEST GROWTH The best onions are formed when the plants grow under cool conditions before their bulbs begin to form and attain the best form on raised beds or furrows. Onions are best adapted to lighter soils. Keep the ground clear of weeds and maintain constant moisture.

HARVESTING Pull the soil away from the bulbs several weeks before harvest to expose ⅓ of the bulb. Harvest when foliage falls over and allow to cure for 1 week.

TO SAVE PURE SEED Separate varieties by 1 mile.

COLLECTING AND STORING SEED Onions are biennials and must pass through a winter season to flower and set seed. In the North, the best bulbs are stored over winter in a cool cellar or individually wrapped in paper and stored in the vegetable bin of the refrigerator. In the South, the bulbs can be left to overwinter in the ground. Onion seed capsules shatter easily and are best harvested by bending the seedhead over into a paper sack as it dries and shaking the seeds into the bag.

SEED VIABILITY 1 to 2 years

Seed Varieties

Varieties listed in 18th-century Virginia

- **'White Spanish', 'Portugal'**: Pale, straw-colored skin, large round to flattened onion
- **'Silver Skin'**: A class of onions with very white, papery skin, mild flavored, poor keepers, often used for pickling
- **'Madeira'**: Very large, oval, tender with reddish brown skin
- **'Deptford'** and **'Strasburg'**: Round to oblong, brownish red skin, pungent, good keepers
- **'Red'**: Very pungent; considered poorest variety in the 18th century

Heirloom varieties for the modern gardener

- **'Jaune Paille des Vertus'**: Similar to 'Spanish' onion of 18th century; good keeper
- **'Paris Silverskin'**
- **'Australian Brown'**: Oval, pungent, keeps well, similar to 18th-century 'Strasburg'
- **'Red Wethersfield'**: Early 19th-century 'Red', superior to 18th-century 'Reds'

LEEK

Allium ampeloprasum var. *porrum*

Legend has it that in 640 CE, King Cadwaladr of Gwynedd, last of the Briton kings to rule the British Isles, met the invading Saxon army on a battlefield in ancient Wales. As neither army wore uniforms, chaos reigned. Then Cadwaladr ordered his troops to stick leeks into their bonnets to distinguish themselves from the Saxon foe. Order was restored and the Saxons were defeated. It was, alas, a temporary victory, and the Saxons eventually overran the island. The wizard Merlin prophesized that one day Cadwaladr would return to drive the Saxons from the land, but before Cadwaladr was able to muster his reincarnation, the Normans arrived in 1066 and performed the service themselves.

The Origin of the Garden Leek

The garden leek was developed from the wild European leek (*A. ampeloprasum*) that is found throughout Europe and Asia. There is evidence that the Egyptians were cultivating leeks as early as 3200 BCE. Pliny recorded in 1st-century Rome that the best leeks came from Egypt. He also recorded the often repeated story of the Emperor Nero who, "to improve his voice, used to eat leeks and oil every month, upon stated days, abstaining from every other kind of food." The ancient culinary leek was not very different from the wild forms such as the 'Yorktown' onion that today grows along the Colonial Parkway between Yorktown and Jamestown in Virginia. The ancient leek had very narrow leaves and was grown for chives, or *cives,* rather than for the swollen stem of the modern leek.

It has long been held that leeks were first introduced into the British Isles in Wales by way of the Phoenician tin trade. Leeks became an extremely important part of the medieval Anglo Saxon kitchen

Leek; 'Yorktown' onion

garden, which was called the *Leek-garden* and the gardener the *Leek-ward.* The gardener to King Edward I was charged in 1290 to provide coleworts from fall to spring and leeks throughout spring.

The Types of Leeks and Their Properties

All of the 16th- and early 17th-century garden writers identified two types of leek: the "set" and the "unset" leek. A set leek was one that was transplanted from a seedbed, while the unset leek was not. But according to Johnson in the 1633 edition of Gerard's *Herball,* "both these grow of the same seed, and they differ onely in culture." As late as 1727, Stephen Switzer identified a variety of leek as "transplanted leek." Leeks are very hardy plants that will persist in the garden for many years. Leeks that are not transplanted or set will continue to divide, producing smaller and smaller stems. Lifting the clumps of unset leeks, then dividing them and spacing them out in the garden, will bring about the thicker stems of the set leek.

By the middle of the 18th century, better varieties of leek began to emerge, selected for the larger stems

Flag leek

typical of the modern leek. One of the first was called the 'London' leek. Philip Miller listed two types of leek in the 1754 *Gardeners Dictionary*: the "Broad-leav'd Leek, commonly call'd the *London* Leek" and the "common Leek." He also observed, "The two Sorts here mention'd are by many Persons affirm'd to be the same, both of them rising from the same Seed: but this is what the Gardeners near *London* will not believe; for they never sow Seeds of the latter, if they can procure those of the first Sort, there being a great Difference in the Size of the Head, or principal Part of the Leek." Apparently, the 'London' leek was an improvement over the common leek, but not a dramatic improvement.

The modern leek is known as a flag leek and was developed late in the 18th century. It differed from the old 'London' leek in the size of the stem and the arrangement of leaves around the stem. Robert Buist described the two types in *The Family Kitchen Gardener* in 1847, writing that the 'London' leek had leaves spaced evenly around the stem, while the 'Scotch' or flag leek carried its leaves "on two sides of the plant only, flag-like."

The 'Scotch' leek that Buist wrote of was probably what is known today as the 'Musselburgh' leek, named for Musselburgh, Scotland, where Dutch immigrants developed the first flag leeks late in the 18th century. This quickly became the preeminent variety, and as noted by Walter Nicol in 1798, "The true Scotch Leek is to be preferred."

"Leeks . . . of Vertue Prolifick . . . The *Welch,* who eat them much, are observ'd to be very fruitful."

—John Evelyn, *Acetaria* (1699)

The Williamsburg Gardener's Assistant

Raising the "set" or transplanted leek. Leeks require a long season to fully develop their stems, so they must be started early in the year in a hotbed or conservatory. In Williamsburg, we sow the seeds on a hotbed in January, and they are ready to be transplanted to the garden by April. To set them in the garden, we follow the advice given by John Abercrombie in 1790: "Prune the long weak tops of the leaves, and the root fibres, and plant them by dibble, in rows a foot apart, by six inches in the row, inserting them down to the leaves, with the neck part mostly into the ground, to be long and white." Modern gardeners sometimes dig a trench to set the leeks into rather than using a dibble to make individual holes.

What diligence is necessary in the raising of leeks. The best leeks are produced in a fertile soil. As explained by Walter Nicol in 1798, "This is a hardy vegetable, and does well on most kinds of garden land, but is produced in greatest abundance on a strong loam. The ground should always be manured [composted]." It is equally important that leeks are well watered if the season should prove dry.

Gardeners have long trimmed the tops of leeks in the belief that this will produce a larger stem. *The Scotch Forcing and Kitchen Gardener* advised: "*Top* the leaves three or four different times in the course of the season, which makes them put forth new heart leaves, and consequently swell the stalk to a much greater size than they otherwise would." This, like the similar abuse recommended for onion foliage, has not proved to be true in the experience of modern gardeners, though we sometimes trim the longest leaves should they fall onto the ground.

To make leek stems white and sweet. As the leeks enlarge in midsummer, earth should be drawn up around the stems to blanch them. Once the lower stems reach 1 inch in diameter, you can begin to harvest. Except in far northern states, leeks can be left in the garden, with a straw mulch, over winter

Leeks in hotbed; trimming transplants; planting leeks

(Top) Earthing leeks; digging leeks; (bottom) leek flower

and pulled as required for the kitchen. Whether you save seeds or not, it is worthwhile leaving a few leeks in the garden to flower the following spring. The large round purple blooms are highly ornamental and a fascination for visitors to our garden in Williamsburg.

"The orators of old, such as *Cato, Tully,* and the like, never went to the bar on any long harangue, or solemn debate, till they had eaten good store of the boil'd leek."

—Stephen Switzer,
The Practical Kitchen Gardiner (1727)

LEEK ESSENTIALS

PLANTING Leeks are long-season plants and must be started from seed early in the year. Sow the seeds in a hotbed before the snowdrops and the crocuses bloom.

SPACING Set leek transplants 4 to 6 inches deep, 6 inches apart, in rows 18 to 24 inches asunder.

FOR BEST GROWTH Leeks adapt to all but a heavy wet soil. They perform best in a rich soil that is well drained but that is not allowed to dry out. Earth up the stem several times over the season to blanch the stalk.

HARVESTING Begin harvesting leeks when the stems are at least 1 inch in diameter. In the middle and southern states, leeks can be left in the ground over winter.

TO SAVE PURE SEED Leeks do not cross with other members of the onion family. Separate leek varieties by 1 mile.

COLLECTING AND STORING SEED Leeks must pass through a winter season to produce flowers and seed. Flower stems will often grow over 4 feet tall and generally require staking. The seed capsules do not shatter as quickly as onions, so may be left on the plant and harvested when dry. Refrigerate seed in airtight containers.

SEED VIABILITY 2 years

Seed Varieties

Varieties listed in 18th-century Virginia

♦ **Leek** and '**London Leek**': Primitive leeks, inferior to the flag leeks

Heirloom varieties for the modern gardener

♦ '**Giant Musselburgh**': A flag leek

'WELSH' ONION

Allium fistulosum

The 'Welsh' onion is not from Wales or even from Europe; it originated from wild onion populations in Central Asia. It was first imported into England in the 16th century with the old German name of *welsche*, meaning foreign. The confusion over names continued into the 18th century. Philip Miller puzzled in the 1754 edition of *The Gardeners Dictionary*: "The Ciboule, and the Scallion, I believe to be the same, although by most Authors they are made two distinct

'Welsh' onion flowers

Species; and the *Welsh* Onion differs so little from them, as to render it difficult to determine wherein the Difference consists." In fact, the Europeans never did know what to do with the 'Welsh' onion, and all modern varieties are also of Asian descent.

A Confusion about Scallions

Gardeners have been growing onions for their leaves since at least the Roman era. Pliny recorded in his *Natural History*: "The scallion has hardly any head at all, only a long neck, and consequently it all goes to leaf, and it is cut back several times, like common leek." Pliny's scallion was a nonbulbing onion similar to a chive, or green onion, and likely the same as *Chibols (siuolli siue cepule)* that John de Garlandes recorded in Paris around 1220. In England, "Chibolles" were listed in William Langland's *Piers Plowman* (1362) and Andrew Boorde's *The breviary of helthe* (1547).

In 1727, Stephen Switzer described in *The Practical Kitchen Gardiner* "what we call chibouls, or by some scallions." Forty years later, John Rutter wrote, "*Of Welch Onions*. THESE are stronger than the common onions; and are properly what authors call chiboule." All this would seem to say that a scallion is a *chiboule* is a 'Welsh' onion. However, the general consensus is that the 'Welsh' onion was not introduced into England from Germany until the 16th century, so the scallion of Pliny and later authors was clearly a similar but different onion.

The ancient scallion disappeared late in the 18th century. Miller wrote in the 1768 edition of *The Gardeners Dictionary*, "The Scallion, or Escallion, is a sort of Onion which never forms any bulbs at the roots, and is chiefly used in the spring for green Onions . . . but this sort of Onion, how much soever in use formerly, is

Newly transplanted 'Welsh' onions

now so scarce as to be known to few people, and is rarely to be met with." Of the 'Welsh' onion, he wrote that it is an extremely cold-hardy plant that will grow through winter and "by March will be fit to draw for young Onions, and are, in the markets, more valued than any other sort at that season."

The cold-hardiness of the 'Welsh' onion is its most notable and valuable feature, making it available when other onions are not. Philip Miller explained in 1754, "Their being so hardy as to resist the severest of our Winters, and being green, and fit for Use so early in the Spring, renders them worthy a Place in all good Kitchen-gardens." The 'Welsh' onion was a very strong onion. Miller described it as "much stronger than the common Onion in Taste, approaching nearer to Garlick." Modern varieties of *A. fistulosum* are typically mild flavored.

A Rarity in the New World

The 'Welsh' onion was, at best, a curiosity in the 18th-century Virginia garden and never was adopted by American gardeners as a common garden plant. In 1865, Fearing Burr wrote in *The Field and Garden Vegetables of America*: "The Welsh Onions are of little value, except in cold latitudes; and are rarely found in the vegetable gardens of this country." Almost all scallions found at the modern market are varieties of *A. fistulosum* but come from Asian, rather than European 'Welsh' onion stock, and are commonly known today as the Japanese bunching onion.

"Sow some beds of Welch Onions, which bid defiance
to the most rigorous frost."

—John Abercrombie, *The Universal Gardener and Botanist* (1778)

The Williamsburg Gardener's Assistant

By what method the 'Welsh' onion is propagated. The 'Welsh' onion is a very adaptable perennial onion that is usually propagated by division. As explained by Philip Miller in 1732: "This Sort is easily propagated by parting the Roots, either in *Spring* or *Autumn* . . . These Roots should be planted three or four together in a Hole, at about six Inches Distance every Way . . . which in a short time will multiply exceedingly, and will grow upon almost any Soil and in any Situation."

Dividing and earthing up 'Welsh' onions

It can also be propagated from seed, and the plants that overwinter will reliably produce an abundance of seed in late spring. The seed can be replanted or stored for a fall sowing. As explained in *The Complete Seedsman* (1726), "You may sow it in *March* or in *September*, to draw in the *Winter.*"

The plants that grow over summer will go dormant in August. As explained by John Rutter in 1767: "When they die to the ground in autumn, sift over the bed half an inch of mould. They will appear again in February, and be fit to draw very soon. This is a method of rendering them fine, and is a secret among the best gardeners." In Williamsburg, we commonly mulch the stems several inches deep in midwinter to preserve them and to whiten them, which makes the stems somewhat milder.

The hardy little 'Welsh' onion is best suited for the middle and northern states, as it suffers in the long hot season in the South.

'WELSH' ONION ESSENTIALS

PLANTING Propagate from divisions or from seed. Sow seed in spring when the dogwood and lilac bloom, or in late summer when the phlox and asters bloom.

SPACING Set divisions or thin seedlings to 4 inches apart in rows 1 foot asunder.

FOR BEST GROWTH The 'Welsh' is a very adaptable onion that prefers a light soil but will tolerate a heavier, wetter soil. It prefers full sun but will tolerate some shade.

HARVESTING Harvest from divisions in late winter or early spring when other onions are not available.

TO SAVE PURE SEED Separate varieties by 1 mile. It will occasionally cross with *A. cepa.*

COLLECTING AND STORING SEED Like all *Alliums,* it is a biennial and requires a winter season to flower and set seed. The seedheads retain their seeds fairly well and are easily harvested.

SEED VIABILITY 2 years

Seed Varieties

Varieties listed in 18th-century Virginia
- ◆ **'Welsh'** or **'Ciboule'**

Heirloom varieties for the modern gardener
Old varieties of **'Welsh'** onion are available from collectors. The **Japanese bunching onion** is the form available from seed catalogs.

"Welch [Welsh] Onion . . . merits culture only to draw as young green onions."

—John Abercrombie, *The Universal Gardener and Botanist* (1797)

SHALLOT

Allium cepa var. *aggregatum*

It was long thought that the terms *"Askolonion krommoon"* of Theophrastus (372–288 BCE) and *"cepae Ascalonia"* of Pliny (23–79 CE), named for the town of Ascalon in ancient Judaea, described the shallot. Ascalon also gave rise to the term *scallion* via the Anglo-Norman *scalun*, the Old French *escalogne,* and the Latin *Ascalonia.* The result was more than 1,000 years of confusion between the shallot and the scallion in garden literature. In 18th-century Williamsburg, John Randolph recorded in *A Treatise on Gardening*: *"Cepa ascalonica, from asca[l]on, a city in India."* While Ascalon is not in India, recent evidence suggests that the shallot originated in central Asia and traveled to the Middle East by way of India.

The Classification of the Shallot

Throughout most of history, the shallot was classified as a distinct species of onion, *A. ascalonicum.* This classification was based on the works of Theophrastus and Pliny. In 1956, the shallot was reclassified as a member of the bulb onion species, *A. cepa* var. *aggregatum.* This includes several varieties of shallots and the potato onion, all under the general grouping of multiplier onions. Multipliers are onions that are generally propagated vegetatively, or one bulb producing many secondary bulbs. The French gray shallot, 'Grise de la Drôme', is the exception. This unique shallot was introduced into France by Crusaders returning from Palestine and appears to have

evolved from another Central Asia species of onion, *A. oschaninii*.

Because of the confusion between shallots and scallions in the historic record, it is difficult to document shallots prior to the 16th century. The *Capitulare de Villis* prepared for King Charlemagne around 800 CE lists *"ascalonicas"* with chives, onions, leeks, and garlic and is a possible reference to shallots.

The Shallot in England

Henry Phillips, in *History of Cultivated Vegetables* (1822), gives 1548 as the date of the shallot's introduction into England. William Turner described a "holleke" in 1551 that sounds very much like a shallot: "If ye take one of the cluster of[f], wher as there are a dosene together, and set it in harvest in the grounde alone, that one shall bryng you out a dosen." Thomas Hill in *The Gardener's Labyrinth* (1577) described a "Scalion" that may be a shallot. If these are, indeed, references to the shallot, it was apparently of limited distribution until late in the next century. John Worlidge did not list shallots in the 1675 edition of *Systema Agriculturæ,* but by the time his *Systema horti-culturae* was published in 1683, he recorded, "Eschalots are now from *France* become an *English* Condiment." In the same year, Leonard Meager recorded in *The English Gardener*: "Shelot is set in a manner as Sives or Garlick . . . and is said not to offend by the smell."

By the 18th century, the shallot was well known by English gardeners. Batty Langley recorded in *New Principles of Gardening* (1728): "Eschalots, or Shallots, being of the same Family with the Garlicks . . . are of great Use in Sauces, and therefore a Kitchen Garden ought not to be without them. . . . a Border of four Feet wide, and about thirty five or forty Feet long is sufficient for a very large Family."

The Shallot in North America

It is not certain when the shallot first came to North America. The confusion over names was transplanted from Europe to the New World, making identification difficult. In 1756, Martha Logan, a

'Old White' shallot

South Carolina gardener, listed "scallions" in her "Directions for Managing a Kitchen-Garden Every Month of the Year" almanac article, and that may be a reference to shallots. Jefferson recorded planting "shalots" in 1794. However, shallots never became a common garden onion in this country. Robert Buist, a Philadelphia nurseryman, recorded in *The Family Kitchen Gardener* (1847): "Though it has been two hundred years in cultivation, very little of the article is used in this country, unless by the French."

"Called . . . by some . . . *Scalions,* but more commonly *Eschalots,* or according to some *Shalots.*"

—Richard Bradley,
Dictionarium Botanicum (1728)

The Williamsburg Gardener's Assistant

By what means the shallot is propagated. Shallots, as Benjamin Townsend instructed in 1726, "are to be raised by the Root; for they encrease plentifully." Plant the bulbs with the pointed end up, with its tip just under the soil line. They can be planted in late fall or early spring.

In Williamsburg, we plant shallots in October on small ridges about 1 foot apart. In our experience, they are of relatively easy care, but Walter Nicol cautioned in 1798, "SHALLOTS Are a precarious crop, being equally subject to injury by too much drought or wet." By growing them on ridges, the bulbs will stay dry should the weather turn wet, and can be thoroughly watered by flooding the trenches if the weather stays dry.

When a shallot is a scallion. Part of the confusion between the shallot and the scallion is that the foliage of shallots has long been used for scallions, or green onions. Fall-planted shallots will produce leaves that may be harvested for use as scallions over winter. As explained in *Modern Eden* (1767): "They are what used to be called scallions, and are very fine."

What precautions are necessary for raising shallots. *The Scotch Forcing and Kitchen Gardener* (1798) explained: "Keep clean of weeds, and whenever any of the plants begin to canker and become maggoty, pull them up; as otherwise the whole will be quickly affected." The onion maggot can be a serious pest of shallots, as well as of other onions, and infected plants must be quickly removed before pupae are deposited in the soil. A contributor to the *Country Gentleman* periodical in November 1886 professed that an elixir made from the mashed stems and leaves of burdock and sprinkled around the base of the plants would destroy the maggots.

How to know when shallots are ripe. As the bulbs begin to swell in spring, they will often form aboveground and should not be buried. Exposure to the sun as they reach maturity assists in curing them.

Planting shallots; harvesting shallots for scallions; harvesting shallots

In Williamsburg, the shallot bulbs are ready for harvest by the first of June. John Abercrombie explained in 1778: "The bulbs will have attained their full growth, as will be determined by the withering of the leaves." Once the lower leaves have turned yellow, loosen the ground with a spading fork and remove the shallots. In Williamsburg, we hang them in a tent, out of the sun and weather, to cure.

Most 18th-century garden writers agree with James Justice, who advised in *The British Gardener's New Director* (1771) that after harvest, "their large heads are the best for use, but for planting, take their smallest single cloves, with good bottoms for pushing out their fibres." Many modern gardeners recommend the same method of harvesting the larger bulbs for use and replanting the smaller bulbs. But other gardeners feel this will, over time, breed a smaller

Curing shallots

variety of shallot. Of the bulbs destined for the kitchen, the larger shallots are better keepers, so the smallest bulbs should be used first.

SHALLOT ESSENTIALS

PLANTING Plant bulbs in fall when the leaves color, or in spring when the daffodils fade.

SPACING Plant bulbs no more than 2 inches deep, spaced 4 to 6 inches apart in rows 12 to 18 inches asunder.

FOR BEST GROWTH Shallots prefer a cool, moist soil. Exposure to the sun in the last month before harvest helps the bulbs to cure.

HARVESTING Harvest scallions when the foliage yellows.

SAVING BULBS FOR REPLANTING The bulbs intended for replanting should be placed on racks or shelves in a cool, dry room, out of the sun, and cured for a week or two. The shriveled foliage can then be removed and the roots trimmed. Keep the shallots on shelves or in netted bags until wanted.

Seed Varieties

Varieties listed in 18th-century Virginia
Varieties were not specified.

Heirloom varieties for the modern gardener
- ♦ **'Old German Red'**
- ♦ **'French Gray'**: Considered by some to be the "true" shallot

GARLIC

Allium sativum

The English have never been garlic eaters. In 1699, John Evelyn proclaimed: "Tho' both . . . *Spaniards* and *Italians*, and the more Southern People, [eat garlic], with almost every thing . . . we absolutely forbid it entrance into our *Salleting*, by reason of its intolerable Rankness. . . . To be sure, 'tis not for Ladies Palats, nor those who court them." The English carried this prejudice to North America. In 1851, Peter Adam Schenck recorded in *The Gardener's Text-Book*, published in New York: "Among all classes of society in the southern parts of Europe, it enters into the composition of nearly every dish for the table. In England and the United States, however, it is by no means a favorite, as its strong, nauseating smell is repulsive to our more *refined* taste."

The Origin of the Garlic Bulb

Garlic and its many varieties originated from one or more wild species of onion in Central Asia. *A. longicuspis*, a very close relative and possible parent, may have been used and disseminated by nomadic populations between China and the Near East in prehistoric times. The Egyptians were famous for their love of garlic, and clay sculptures of garlic have been found in the tombs of El Mahasna dating from 3200 BCE. These depictions appear to be of a hardneck garlic, which botanists believe was the original form of all garlic.

Garlic and Its Types

Garlic is divided between hardneck and softneck types. The primary difference is that hardneck vari-

eties produce flower stalks called scapes that terminate in round seedheads (actually clusters of bulbils). Softneck varieties do not produce scapes. 'Rocambole' garlic (*A. sativum* var. *ophioscorodon*) is the most ancient of the hardneck forms. It develops a single rank of relatively large cloves around a central stem that produces the hard neck. The cloves range in color from white to a russet brown and have much thinner skins than the softneck varieties, making them easier for the cook to prepare. They typically are stronger flavored, as well.

It is believed that the softneck varieties arose from a hardneck garlic at a very early date. Softneck garlic, as the name implies, has thinner bulb stems that can be fashioned into the familiar garlic braid. The bulb of softneck garlic is usually larger than 'Rocambole' and composed of an outer rank of cloves that surrounds an inner rank of much smaller cloves, all wrapped in several layers of skin. Pliny the Elder described a garlic in his *Natural History* (circa 77 CE) that may have been a softneck variety: "The external coat consists of membranes of remarkable fineness, which are universally discarded when the vegetable is used; the inner part being formed by the union of several cloves, each of which has also a separate coat of its own."

He also described a garlic variety called "*ulpicum*" that "holds a high rank among the dishes of the country people, particularly in Africa, and it is larger than garlic." This is a possible reference to great-headed, or elephant, garlic (actually a leek).

The Uses of Garlic

Garlic is listed in English garden works as both a culinary and medicinal root. William Turner wrote in *A New Herball* (1551): "Garlyke is not onlye good meat but also good medicine." Its medicinal properties are legion, or as Nicholas Culpeper explained in *The English Physician* (1652), "This was anciently accounted the poor man's Treacle, it being a remedy for all diseases or hurts." Of its curative properties, one of the most bizarre was recounted by Thomas Hill in *The Gardener's Labyrinth* (1577): "In his tyme hapned a husbandeman to sleepe open mouthed in the field by a hey cocke, caste up in the harvest tyme, which when he had unwittily suffered an Adder to creepe into his body, wyth the eating . . . of Garlike heads, [he] was . . . delivered."

Long life is often attributed to the consumption of garlic. Stephen Switzer testified in 1727: "A gentleman, a neighbour too . . . arrived to near an hundred and twenty years of age, without any other physic, or extraordinary diet, than that of roasted garlick." He also provided the well-known caution, "Those that so eat [garlic] ought as it were to exclude and divest themselves from the world, and all human society, as least for a time."

When garlic was used as a culinary plant in England, 'Rocambole' was the preferred type. Switzer explained: "The roccambo, or *Spanish* garlick, a kind . . . differing from any of these before-mentioned; is not so much as mention'd in any of our books of plants that I have seen, and therefore may be suppose'd to be brought from Spain. . . . A finer plant the garden does not produce, for all uses where eschallots or garlick are used."

Garlic in the New World

There are no references to garlic in the early records of Virginia, but it may have been introduced as one of the unnamed herbs listed by the colonists. In Virginia, as in England, its primary use seems to have been as a medicine. In a December 1769 edition of the *Virginia Gazette,* there is an article entitled "A celebrated *CURE* for the bite of a *MAD DOG*" that includes a recipe using 3 ounces of garlic along with several other ingredients. In January 1773, the *Virginia Gazette* provided another use for garlic: "A remedy for corns on the feet. ROAST a clove of garlic on a live coal, or in hot ashes; apply it to the corn, and fasten it on with a piece of cloth, the moment of going to bed." After 3 or 4 nights, it will "leave the part as clean and smooth as if it had never been attacked with any disorder."

The Williamsburg Gardener's Assistant

What season garlic is planted in. Garlic is best when planted in fall, although in the far northern states, it is sometimes planted in early spring. The hardneck varieties, which are much more cold-tolerant, are preferred in the northern states. 'Rocambole' does not grow well in the Deep South. In Williamsburg, we plant garlic cloves in October, in the fashion explained by John Abercrombie in 1790: "Having some large bulbs of garlick, divide them into separate cloves, or smaller bulbs, which then plant in beds, in rows lengthways, six to nine inches asunder." The larger, outer cloves produce the best bulbs. In the southern states, the cloves are planted 1 or 2 inches deep. In northern states, they can be planted up to 4 inches deep.

We plant the cloves about 2 inches deep, in ridges 5 or 6 inches tall. Planting on ridges ensures that the bulbs will stay dry in a wet season, and it ensures that the roots will stay continually moist in a dry season, from water collected in the valleys between the ridges. Planting on ridges also makes it easier to draw the soil away from the bulbs to cure them before harvest. Space the rows 18 inches apart.

The growth of garlic's root and leaves. In the southern and middle states, the leaves will appear aboveground about 2 weeks from sowing and the foliage will stay green throughout winter. In northern climates, the cloves will grow roots in fall, but the leaves will not appear until spring. In the northern states, a straw mulch is beneficial, especially in winters with little snow, to prevent the bulbs from heaving from the ground.

Tying garlic leaves and cutting scapes. The leaves will start growing rapidly with the first warm weather in spring, and provided that the soil is well enriched with compost, little else is necessary. William Hanbury recorded in *A Complete Body of Planting and Gardening* (1773): "Nothing need be done except keeping them clean from weeds until the beginning of June, at which time the leaves should be tied in knots; and this will cause the bulbs to grow larger, by preventing the plants from running to seed." Most 18th-century authors repeat this dubious advice, while indicating that the hardneck form, which pro-

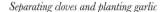

Separating cloves and planting garlic

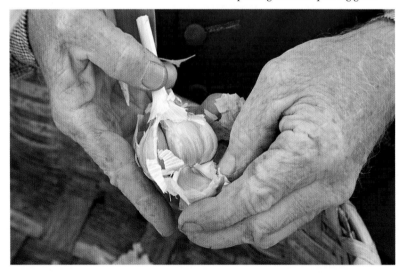

duces scapes, was the most common garlic of the century, as the softneck garlics rarely form scapes.

Today, no one recommends that the leaves should be tied in knots, but modern gardeners do debate the value of cutting the flower stalks, or scapes, on hardneck garlic. Some feel a larger bulb is produced when the scape is cut, and some feel the resulting bulb stores better if the scape is not cut. For many, the deciding factor is the delicate flavor scapes have when cut young and put into a stir-fry.

How to know when to harvest garlic. The garlic will be ready for harvest, advised Benjamin Townsend in 1726, "when the Leaves and Stalks are dry, or turn'd Yellow." For softneck varieties, in particular, you will have a better-shaped bulb if the garlic is dug when the bottom leaves turn yellow and while the upper leaves are still green. Garlic bulbs that are left in the ground until the entire plant is brown often separate between the cloves and tend to produce stronger-flavored bulbs. To pull the garlic, we first loosen the ground

(Top) Newly sprouted garlic; garlic leaves in winter; garlic ready for harvest; (bottom) harvesting garlic; garlic hung for curing

next to the bulbs with a spading fork, and they are then easily removed. After the garlic bulbs are harvested, they are immediately taken to an open shed where we tie them in clumps of four or five and hang them to cure. From this harvest, we select the largest, best-formed bulbs for planting in fall.

Of the types of garlic, the softneck variety known as 'Silverskin' will keep in storage the longest, while 'Rocambole' has the shortest storage life. They should be used by the cook accordingly.

GARLIC ESSENTIALS

PLANTING Garlic is best planted in fall after the autumn equinox. An early spring planting can be made in the North when the daffodils bloom.

SPACING Plant cloves 2 to 4 inches deep (deeper in the North), 6 to 9 inches apart, in rows 18 inches asunder.

FOR BEST GROWTH Garlic needs a fairly rich soil and prefers its roots to be moist and its bulb to be dry. Growing in raised beds or on ridges meets these requirements nicely.

HARVESTING Harvest when the lower leaves yellow for best-formed bulbs. Bulbs that are left in the ground for too long start to separate between the cloves.

SAVING BULBS FOR REPLANTING Pull the bulbs after the lower leaves have turned yellow and hang in a cool, dry shed. Save the largest and best-looking bulbs for replanting.

Seed Varieties

Varieties listed in 18th-century Virginia

Individual varieties were not specified.

Heirloom varieties for the modern gardener

♦ **'Romanian Red'** and **'German White'** (Porcelain types, with a white covering and very few but very large cloves)

♦ **'German Red'** and **'Purple Italian'** ('Rocambole' types): Hardneck varieties

♦ **'Siciliano'**, **'Early Red Italian'** (Artichoke type, with fewer but larger cloves and a milder flavor)

♦ **'Silver White'** ('Silverskin' type): Softneck varieties

"It being well boyled in salt broth, is often eaten of them that have strong stomackes, will not brooke in a weake and tender stomacke."

—John Parkinson, *Paradisi in Sole* (1629)

CHIVE

Allium schoenoprasum

The dainty little chive is found in rich nooks and sunny crevices of soil throughout the Northern Hemisphere and is the only member of the onion family native to both the Old World and the New World. It has almost certainly been collected from the wild since prehistoric times and has come down through history relatively unchanged and unremarked upon. Unlike the showier members of this group, chives were just right the way nature made them. Stephen Switzer recorded the fondness felt by many gardeners for this plant in *The Practical Kitchen Gardiner* (1727): "To the . . . kitchen bulbs, may be added *cives,* one of the prettiest little kind of onion or permanent garlick, or rattle-leek, that our gardens are furnish'd with."

Out of the Wild

There is no clear reference to the chive by Greek or Roman writers, likely a result of the chive's preference for more northern latitudes. There is evidence for the chive in Chinese cooking from around 3000 BCE, and Marco Polo has long been credited with its introduction to European cooks. It is more likely that it was adopted by different groups of people at different times from wild populations.

The first English reference to chives comes in *De re Herbaria,* written by Friar Henry Daniel in 1375. He recorded that it was a: "Herb common among us. It groweth not but set. It keepeth himself in ground over winter . . . in his top but one flower, red purple, shape most like the top of 'Sowkle' [clover] save more fair, and no seed but dwineth away. We call it Chives."

The chive has long been compared to the leek, and similar medicinal properties have been ascribed to both. John Gerard wrote in *The Herball* (1597) that

chives "ingender hotte and grosse vapours, and are hurtfull to the eyes and braine. They cause troublesome dreames, and worke all the effects, that the Leeke doth."

Chives in the English Garden

By the 18th century, chives were a common component in all well-appointed English gardens. In 1773, William Hanbury recorded, "They are very common, afford an excellent potherb for the housewife, and are in great esteem in spring-sallads." As to their flavor and the quantity necessary for a family, we have the advice of Batty Langley in *New Principles of Gardening* (1728): "Their Taste is between an Onion and a Leek, and are by many called the Leekrush. . . . That a Border about three Feet and half in breadth (which will receive seven Rows) and twenty five or thirty Feet in length, is fully sufficient to serve a very large Family."

Chives are not listed among the vegetables brought by the first colonists to Virginia and do not appear in any 18th-century Virginia diary. The only Virginia listings for chives come in Randolph's *A Treatise on Gardening,* published in Richmond in 1793 and probably written in Williamsburg in the 1760s. As this treatise often simply relates advice found in the English work, *The Gardeners Dictionary,* it does not provide definitive evidence for the presence of chives in colonial Virginia. The only other reference comes from a 1730s Virginian work entitled *Natural History* of undetermined authorship. After the 18th century, chives are listed in all garden works, including *The American Gardener* (1804) and *The American Gardener's Calendar* (1806), and by Jefferson in 1812. All culinary chives in cultivation today originated from European imports.

Williamsburg Gardener's Assistant

The best situation for the best chive harvest. Chives are a perennial herb that will grow in sun or part shade in most types of soils. In the southern states, Batty Langley's advice in *New Principles of Gardening* (1728) is appropriate: "They delight in the Shade, and love a light rich Land." In Williamsburg, we grow chives where they receive full sun until mid-afternoon and are then in the shade during the hottest part of the day.

They are harvested as needed by the kitchen, and as Langley explained: "The oftener Chives are cut, the finer their Leaves come, and consequently more agreeable in Sallets." Cut the leaves down to about 1 inch above the soil. In late spring, the flowers appear and are as well flavored as the leaves and perhaps a little sweeter. They are easily broken apart and make a pretty garnish on salads and sauces and sprinkled over baked potatoes.

What skill is required to propagate the chive. To propagate chives, we follow the advice found in *The Complete Seedsman* (1726): "The way to encrease them, is to divide the Root very early in the *Spring*, or in *July* or *August*." They should be lifted and separated every 3 years or so, to keep the planting in good shape. To grow from seed, plant the seed in a well-prepared bed as early in spring as the ground can be worked.

Once up, thin the seedlings to 4 inches asunder. Chives are small plants that make a pretty and useful border on the edge of beds or along walkways and sidewalks.

In the North, the plants will lose their leaves in winter months and reappear as soon as the weather warms in spring. In Williamsburg, chives remain evergreen during mild winters, though the leaves fall down and are of little use to the cook.

Dividing and planting chives

CHIVE ESSENTIALS

PLANTING Chives are most easily propagated by dividing existing clumps. Sow seed in early spring in well-tilled soil.

SPACING Space new plants 4 inches apart. Chives make a tidy little border plant.

FOR BEST GROWTH Very adaptable plants, chives are shade tolerant and do best in a moist soil.

HARVESTING Regular harvesting promotes regrowth and better-quality foliage. Cut leaves to 1 inch above the soil.

TO SAVE PURE SEED Chives do not cross with any other *Allium* species, and the common chive is generally the only one available. There are a few varieties of chives that are seldom seen, one with red flowers and one with white. Separate these varieties from common chives by 1 mile.

COLLECTING AND STORING SEED Collect seedheads when fully dry and shake into a paper bag. Store in airtight containers. Refrigerate to prolong viability.

SEED VIABILITY 3 years

CHAPTER 6

of

Cucumbers and *Melons*

In 1845, Jane Loudon wrote in *The Lady's Country Companion*: "I would not advise you to grow *cucumbers* or *melons*; but, should you feel inclined to try your skill, you have only to have a hotbed." The ability to produce quality cucumbers and melons was a measure of the skill of the 18th-century English gardener. This is because both plants came from much warmer climates.

Melons are thought to have originated in eastern Africa, south of the Sahara and north of the equator. Primitive cultivars are still grown in Sudan that look much like the depictions of melons found in the remains of ancient Egypt. Melons were the *qishu'im* lamented by the Israelites as one of the lost luxuries of Egypt. These were long, slender melons used in the immature stage and probably similar to the *chate* variety of *Cucumis melo*, known today as the 'Egyptian' or hairy cucumber. Several forms of melon were known in ancient Rome, including the even longer snake melon (*C. melo* var. *flexuosus*).

The modern cucumber originated from *C. sativus* var. *hardwickii* in the foothills of the Himalayas. It was domesticated 3,000 years ago in India but was slow to make its way to Europe, and was first illustrated in Italy in the 14th century. The small pickling cucumber, known as the gherkin, was identified by 18th-century garden writers as a native of the West Indies, Jamaica in particular. It has since been shown to be a native of Africa and was probably introduced into the Caribbean with the slave trade.

Watermelons originated in the Kalahari Desert of southern Africa. The African explorer David Livingstone wrote that the natives and several kinds of wild animals eagerly devoured the wild fruit. Watermelons were being cultivated in the Nile Valley by 2000 BCE but were too tender for the English climate, even with the advantage of hotbeds.

CUCUMBER
Cucumis sativus

The cucumber has not always been considered a healthful fruit. A 1616 edition of *The Countrey Farme* averred: "The use of Cucumbers is altogether hurtfull." An entry in Samuel Pepys's diary on August 22, 1663, reads: "Mr. Newburne . . . is dead of eating Cowcoumbers, of which the other day I heard another, I think Sir Nich. Crisps son." By the end of the century, opinions were changing, as attested to by John Evelyn in 1699: "The *Cucumber* it self, now so universally eaten, being accounted little better than *Poyson*, even within our Memory." Despite Evelyn's optimism, Landon Carter recorded in Virginia on July 24, 1766, his concern for his teenage daughter, Judy: "She does bear ungovernable the whole summer through, eating extravagantly and late at night of cucumbers and all sorts of bilious trash."

Pliny's Cucumber

The common name *cucumber* derives from the Latin *Cucumis*, the genus name for cucumbers and melons. This shared name has made it very hard to distinguish between the two fruits in the historic record. The most famously confusing cucumber story came from the Roman writer Pliny the Elder around 77 CE. His *Natural History* entry for *Cucumis* has long been translated as "the cucumber, a delicacy for which the emperor Tiberius had a remarkable partiality." This story has been repeated for more than 2,000 years as evidence of the Roman love of cucumbers, but recent scholarship has pointed to another passage in Pliny's work that described the cucumber as "covered with a white down, which increases in quantity as the plant gains in size."

Cucumbers are never hairy but young melons are, so it is nearly certain that Pliny's cucumber was actually a melon. There was some skepticism con-

cerning Pliny's cucumber even in the 18th century. Stephen Switzer wrote in 1727: "The encomiums that *Pliny* has given . . . caus'd many to believe that what the antients call'd cucumbers, was in reality our melons." The first pictorial evidence for the cucumber in Europe is found in a manuscript prepared in Pisa around 1335. How the cucumber was introduced into Europe is not known, but it may have been another of the many vegetables introduced through Moorish Spain.

The Cucumber Arrives in England

It was long believed that the cucumber was introduced into England during the reign of King Edward III. This was based on a list of seeds prepared by Roger, the gardener to the Archbishop of Canterbury from 1326 to 1327, which included "concumber & gourde." However, it now seems more likely that this was a reference to a melon. The cucumber was clearly illustrated in Germany by Leonhart Fuchs in 1542 and in England by John Gerard in 1597.

By 1629, the cucumber was well known to the English. John Parkinson described several varieties in *Paradisi in Sole*: "The long greene Cowcumber" and "The short Cowcumber, being short, and of an equall bignesse in the body thereof, and of an unequall bignesse at both ends." The ancient cucumber had a blocky form and black spines sprouting from wartlike eruptions on the skin, much like the modern pickling cucumber. The modern culinary cucumber produces small white spines on a much smoother fruit.

The Historic Varieties of Cucumbers

In the 18th century, these varieties were generally known as the 'Early Prickly' (or 'Short') and the 'Long Prickly' cucumbers. From these two varieties,

(Top) 'Long Prickly' cucumber; 'Short Prickly' cucumber; (bottom) 'Cluster' cucumber; white cucumber

a proliferation of subvarieties emerged. William Cobbett explained in *The English Gardener* (1829): "With regard to sorts, however, people generally save the seed themselves of this plant, or get it from some careful and curious neighbour; and every one sows that which happens to suit his fancy." Nevertheless, several stable varieties emerged that were distinctive from the common 'Prickly' cucumbers.

The 'Cluster' cucumber was first described by Richard Bradley in *Dictionarium Botanicum* (1728) and was listed by most English authors in the 18th century, as well as by Bernard McMahon in this country in *The American Gardener's Calendar* in 1806. This black-spined cucumber, 5 to 6 inches long, has a blunt, angular shape and is a prolific and very early bearer.

The white cucumber was the most prized of all cucumbers. It may be the descendant of the "long Yellow" cucumber listed by John Parkinson in 1629. References to yellow cucumbers began to disappear early in the 18th century and were replaced with the white. In 1728, Richard Bradley listed both a short and a long white cucumber. In the 1754 edition of *The Gardeners Dictionary,* Philip Miller described the white cucumber as "by far the better Fruit, as being less watry, and containing fewer Seeds, is the most common Kind cultivated in *Holland*; for I do not remember to have seen one of our green Sort in any of the Markets in that Country." The white cucumber was not as common as the green, probably because it was more difficult to grow. As Amelia Simmons observed in *American Cookery* (1796), "the white is difficult to raise and tender."

The Cucumber in North America

The cucumber arrived with the first explorers to the Americas. Columbus introduced the cucumber to Haiti in 1494, and cucumber seed was probably aboard the first ships to arrive at Jamestown, Virginia, in 1607. *A True Declaration of the Estate of the Colonie in Virginia*, published in 1610, recorded: "What should I speake of cucumbers, muske melons, pompions, potatoes, parsneps, carrets, turnups, which our gardens yeelded with little art and labour." By the 18th century, the cucumber was a common popular fruit in Virginia. In Williamsburg, John Randolph noted: "Cucumber . . . is esteemed in its season the most refreshing and delecate of all vegetables."

The Gherkin and Its Nativity

The source of the gherkin cucumber (*C. anguria*) was long thought to be the West Indies, first documented in Joseph Pitton de Tournefort's 1694 work, *Eléments de botanique*. The great French biologist Charles Naudin instead suggested an African origin in his 1859 monograph—pointing out that all other members of the cucumber genus were Old World plants—but as no wild African cucumber populations had been found, he left the West Indies origin intact. Alphonse de Candolle speculated in *Origin of Cultivated Plants* (1884) that: "The name *maroon* cucumber, given in the French West India Islands, indicates a plant which has become wild, for this is the meaning of the word *maroon* as applied to the negroes." He also observed that the range of the gherkin in the Western Hemisphere was restricted to coastal areas most influenced by the slave trade, and that no inland gherkin populations had been found. It was not until 1958 that A. D. J. Meeuse finally concluded that the West India gherkin was "a cultigen descended from a non-bitter variant" of the African *C. longipes*.

The first documented occurrence of this little cucumber in North America came in a 1792 advertisement by Minton Collins, who kept a store in Richmond, Virginia. Thomas Jefferson, in an 1813 letter to his brother, Randolph, recommended John Gardiner and David Hepburn's *The American Gardener* (1804) as a guide for his sister to use in the garden and remarked, "She will not find the term Gerkin in the book. it is that by which we distinguish the very small pickling cucumber."

The Williamsburg Gardener's Assistant

The season for planting cucumbers. Cucumbers are robust plants of vigorous growth and require a rich, well-composted soil that retains moisture. As they are native to tropical climes, cucumbers are frost-intolerant and do not thrive until nighttime temperatures remain above 60°F. For this reason, there is little to be gained by setting them out too early in spring. As cautioned by John Randolph in 18th-century Williamsburg: "Altho' many are ambitious of having early fruit, yet it is certain that Cucumbers are not wholesome till the hot weather comes on."

In England, the cucumber was "cultivated in three different Seasons," as explained by Philip Miller in 1754: "The first of which is on Hot-beds under Garden-frames, for early Fruit: the second is under Bell or Hand-glasses, for the middle Crop: and the third is in the common Ground, for a late Crop, or to pickle." In the warmer Virginia climate, hotbeds and bell glasses were not as necessary but were still used to produce an early harvest. Modern gardeners can achieve an earlier harvest by starting the plants indoors, 4 to 5 weeks before they are intended for the garden. Cucumbers resent having their roots disturbed, so are best started in peat or paper pots that can be planted directly into the garden.

Raising cucumbers in hotbeds. In Williamsburg, we plant cucumber seeds within loosely woven baskets, plunged into a hotbed, in early March. Six or seven seeds are planted in each basket, and when they are germinated, we thin them to the best three, evenly spaced one from the other. When the second rough leaves appear, the stems are pinched back to promote branching and to produce a more compact plant for transplantation. They are ready to be placed in the garden after the middle of April. To move the cucumber baskets from the frames, plunge your trowel all around the outer rim of the basket until it is separated from the surrounding soil. The young plants are then carefully moved to

Cucumbers in hotbed; transplanting cucumbers; shading cucumbers

predug holes in shallow hills, hollowed out to hold water around the plant. For the first 5 to 7 days after transplanting, we cover the plants with straw bells during the day. This will prevent the seedlings from wilting, which is extremely debilitating to transplanted cucumbers.

If the seeds are sown directly in the ground, the gardener need only follow the advice found in *The Gentleman and Lady's Gardener*, published in 1776: "Every three feet and half, hollow a place one foot over in the form of a bason, in these put about ten seeds, and when the plants have put forth their rough leaf, pull up all except four of the strongest, and draw the earth up to their stems."

Trellising the cucumbers. John Abercrombie instructed in 1790: "As cucumbers are climbing plants by means of their tendrils, some branchy sticks may be placed to a few, they will readily ascend upon them, and thereby produce their fruit at a distance from the ground, free from spots, and be firm and well-flavoured." We reuse the woven frame that was fashioned to provide protection for the broad beans over winter. The frame is cut in half and then fastened to upright stakes. This provides a very serviceable support. Cucumbers that are allowed to ramble along the ground hide their fruit under their leaves, and the plants are almost always damaged through the process of moving the leaves to find the cucumbers.

Cucumbers require a constant, steady supply of water, as Abercrombie further explained: "Let this crop have necessary supplies of water in dry weather, both in their young and advanced growth, two or three times a week; or every day in very hot weather, in July and August."

The first flowers produced by cucumbers are all male and will not produce fruit, but the female flowers quickly follow and will produce an abundance of fruit in a short time. It is now that the gardener must be diligent in looking over the plants. Fruit will be ripening every day and must be picked while still young and before the seeds become too large within the fruit. Spring planting will provide cucumbers throughout summer in the northern states. In the South, a second planting can be made in early summer for a fall harvest.

Cucumber trellis; flower and fruit

"To have the best Fruit from them, is to let them use the Claspers Nature has given them, and let them run up Sticks."

—Richard Bradley, *Dictionarium Botanicum* (1728)

The ancient practice of soaking cucumber seed. In 1774, Thomas Jefferson experimented with soaking cucumber seeds before planting and recorded: "These were steeped in water from Mar. 31. till this day [Apr. 5] when they were sprouted." Jefferson undoubtedly drew from the ancient tradition of soaking seeds in various mixtures that were thought to sweeten the cucumbers. Pliny recorded in his *Natural History* (77 CE): "We find it stated, also, by the ancient Greek writers, that the cucumber ought to be propagated from seed that has been steeped a couple of days in milk and honey, this method having the effect of rendering them all the sweeter to the taste." This advice was repeated by many authors for the next 1,500 years, with a variety of sweetening solutions. Soaking cucumber seeds is often beneficial, particularly if the weather remains dry. Both melon and cucumber seeds can be slow to germinate in dry soils, so presoaking them will aid germination. The sweetness, however, owes more to the culture of the plant than to the soaking of the seeds.

The curious art of sculpting the fruit. Pliny also recorded the practice of shaping cucumbers by confining the fruit within containers: "The gourd, too, as well as the cucumber, admits of being lengthened to any extent, by the aid of osier [willow] tubes more particularly. Just after the blossom has fallen off, the plant is introduced into these tubes, and as it grows it can be made to assume any form that may be wished, that of a serpent coiled up being the one that is mostly preferred." By the 16th century, Thomas Hill explained how even more fantastic shapes could be produced: "If the Gardener desireth to enjoy Cucumbers, having Romayne letters, strange figures, and skutchings or Armes imbossed on the grene rynde without" then the cucumbers could be grown within clay forms molded to any shape the gardener desired.

The most surprising caution for the raising of cucumbers was provided by Thomas Hill in 1577: "The plantes muche feare the Thunder and Lyghtning" and "if the tender fruites bee not covered over wyth sheetes or thynne Coverlets, when such Tempests or stormes happen, they commonlye after perish and wyther." This caution was repeated by several authors over the next century, but it is now generally accepted that lightning storms are more dangerous to the gardener running about the garden in severe weather than they are to the cucumber plants.

Seed Varieties

Varieties listed in 18th-century Virginia

♦ **'Long Prickly'**, **'Short Prickly'**, **'White'**, **'Gerkin'**

Heirloom varieties for the modern gardener

♦ **'Long Prickly'** or **'Ridge'**: Available from English seed houses

♦ **'Early Fortune'** and **'Longfellow'**: Early 20th-century varieties

♦ **'Russian Pickling'** or **'Everbearing Pickling'**: Similar to 'Short Prickly' of 18th century

♦ **'White Wonder'**

♦ **'West Indian Gherkin'**

CUCUMBER ESSENTIALS

PLANTING Sow seeds in the ground after all danger of frost is over, when the peach and dogwood blossoms fall. For transplants, sow plants indoors or in a hotbed 4 weeks before this.

SPACING Plant on hills 3 to 4 feet apart, or in rows 3 feet apart and 4 feet asunder.

FOR BEST GROWTH Cucumbers need warm weather to thrive and a rich soil that retains water well. They are easiest to care for when trained on supports.

HARVESTING Harvest while the fruit is young and before it yellows. Overripe fruit is bitter.

TO SAVE PURE SEED Separate varieties by ½ mile.

COLLECTING AND STORING SEED To collect seed, allow the cucumber to fully ripen. They will turn yellow and start to soften when ripe. Allow the cucumber to stand for a week or two after harvest and then slice the fruit longitudinally, to facilitate scooping out the seed. Place the seeds in a bowl or tall glass and cover them with water. Allow mixture to ferment in a warm place, out of direct sunlight, for 3 to 5 days. The higher the temperature, the quicker the fermentation. Stir the mixture once or twice a day. Once the seeds have all settled to the bottom of the container, they will be ready for cleaning. Add fresh water to the mixture, stir it around, and after the seeds have resettled to the bottom, pour off the scum and refuse floating on top. Repeat this process until seeds are clean and water is clear. Pour through a paper filter to separate seeds, and allow them to dry thoroughly. Refrigerate dry seed in an airtight container.

SEED VIABILITY 10 years

"Of the Cucumber there is but one real species, but of which are several curious and valuable varieties of the fruit."

—John Abercrombie,
The Universal Gardener and Botanist (1778)

MELON
Cucumis melo

Melons have long been considered by the English to be one of the most delicious and difficult products of the garden. John Parkinson recorded in 1629: "This Countrey hath not had untill of late yeares the skill to nourse them up kindly. . . . They have beene formerly only eaten by great personages, because the fruit was not only delicate but rare." Seventy years later, John Evelyn wrote in *Acetaria* of the melon as "Paragon with the noblest Productions of the Garden. . . . this Fruit was very rarely cultivated in *England,* so as to bring it to Maturity, till Sir *Geo. Gardner* came out of *Spain.* I my self remembring, when an ordinary *Melon* would have been sold for five or six Shillings."

African Origins

The melon has a long history of cultivation in tropical Africa. This has led to the assumption that the ancestor of the modern melon originated south of the Sahara. That melons have been cultivated by humankind for a very long time is suggested by wild populations of these fruits found not only in Africa but also in Asia and even Australia. Some recent DNA analysis suggests that the earliest genesis of melons may actually be in Asia, but it is probable that its introduction into Egypt and from there, into Europe, was out of Africa.

Egyptian depictions of melons from 3,000 years ago show elongated fruits both striped and furrowed. These melons were likely of the *C. melo* var. *chate* group and were consumed in an immature stage in the manner the cucumber is used. By the imperial Roman era, the members of *C. melo* var. *flexuosus*, or snake melons, were probably the most commonly grown melon. These serpentine melons are often called 'Armenian' melons today and can easily reach 3 feet long. Lucius Columella, who died around 70 CE, recorded in *De re Rustica* of *Cucumis:*

Hairy and like a snake with knotted grass
Covered, which on its curving belly lies
Forever coiled.

His description sounds very much like that of an immature snake melon.

A New Type of Cucumber

Pliny recorded that a new type of "cucumber" had recently appeared in Rome: "It is only of late, too, that a cucumber of entirely new shape has been produced in Campania, it having just the form of a quince. It was quite by accident, I am told, that the first one acquired this shape in growing, and it was from the seed of this that all the others have been reproduced. The name given to this variety is 'melopepo.' These last do not grow hanging, but assume their round shape as they lie on the ground. A thing that is very remarkable in them, in addition to their shape, colour, and smell, is the fact that, when ripe, although they do not hang from the stem, they separate from it at the stalk."

This appears to be a description of a primitive muskmelon, judging from its separating from the stem when ripe and its distinctive fragrance. This was not, however, the sweet melon we known today. As Alphonse de Candolle observed in *Origin of Cultivated Plants* (1884): "It was probably of indifferent quality, to judge from the silence or the faint praise of writers in a country [Italy] where *gourmets* were not wanting." The lack of enthusiasm for this fruit in the historic record has led most authors to agree with Candolle.

The Cantaloupe Comes to Europe

Sweet melons originated in southwest Asia in an area encompassing modern-day Iran, Turkey, and southern Russia. Philip Miller described in *The Gardeners*

Dictionary (1754) the introduction of the cantaloupe into Italy and the origin of its name: "This Sort was brought from *Armenia,* on the Confines near *Persia,* where the best Melons in the World grow. . . . This sort of Melon has been long cultivated at *Cantaleupe,* a little District about ten Leagues from *Rome.*" True cantaloupe melons have a much coarser appearance than the familiar muskmelon and are often not recognized as melons by visitors to our garden in Colonial Williamsburg. John Gerard described a melon of this sort in *The Herball* (1597): "The barke or rinde is of an overworne russet greene colour, ribbed and furrowed very deepely, having often chappes or chinkes, and a confused roughnes." Most cantaloupes have deeply furrowed rinds and rough skin.

By the 18th century, so many varieties of melons had been developed that the authors of *Adam's Luxury, and Eve's Cookery* (1744) declared: "TO enumerate all the different Sorts of this Fruit, would be not only endless, but impossible." Even so, the cantaloupe retained its place as the most coveted of all melons, according to *The British Gardener's New Director* (1771): "OF the variety of Melon seeds, which are imported is that of the *Persian* Melon, a fruit far inferior to the *Cantaleupe,* the *Genoa,* or the *Languedoc*; the *Cantaleupe* undoubtedly is preferable to any other."

Cantaloupes and Muskmelons

Cantaloupes are also called rock melons for their thick rinds. Muskmelons typically have thin rinds, are smoother, and usually have a netted skin. A melon of this type was described in John Evelyn's *The Compleat Gard'ner* (1693), a translation of Jean de La Quintinye's 1690 work, as: "not large, but of middling Size, the Rind thin, faintly Embroider'd, and without being Ribb'd or divided along the Sides." In Williamsburg, John Randolph described a "Netted wrought Melon" that was clearly a reference to a muskmelon type. Most of the ancient netted melons were green fleshed.

The true cantaloupe was replaced by the muskmelon in 19th-century gardens. Liberty Hyde Bailey recorded in the 1930 *Hortus* that the muskmelon was: "now widely cult. in many forms in N. Amer., mostly under the erroneous name 'cantaloupe' which is properly applied to a race . . . with hard and scaly or warty rinds and seldom grown with us."

'Pineapple' melon; 'D'Algers' melon; 'Zatta' melon

'Pocket' melons and 'Armenian' melon

The Fragrant Pocket Melon

The pocket melon is a peculiar little fruit of ancient lineage with an interesting relationship to Williamsburg in the 18th century. It is a small melon of the *C. melo* var. *dudaim* group with pretty russet and yellow markings and a disagreeable flavor. It develops a strong, most say pleasant, aroma and hence its use as a perfume when placed in a person's pocket. John Randolph, attorney general for the colony of Virginia, explained that it was also "called by the name of king Charle's Melon, because he used to carry one in his packet."

John Custis was a wealthy Virginia planter who built a garden in Williamsburg that he claimed was "inferior to few if any in Virg[ini]a" in 1734. He was also one of the many gardeners, plant collectors, and botanists who corresponded and exchanged plants and seeds with Peter Collinson, an English merchant and plant collector, who was said to have the largest collection of North American plants in England at his garden at Mill Hill. In response to a letter from Collinson, who lamented the disappearance of the pocket melon from English gardens, Custis wrote in 1737: "The melon which you are desirous of some seeds from its pretty color and scent, has bin very plenty in this country my negros used to make multitudes of

them but finding them unfit to eat; and by most thought a disagreeable smell; left of[f] planting them; and tho I have made a general enquiry to get some of the seeds, can not hear of any."

Collinson was mortified to hear of the inconvenience he had put his friend to in search of the pocket melon and responded the following year: "I am confounded with shame att what you Mention about sending so farr for the sweet smelling Mellon. It gives Mee great uneasiness that you should take so much pains & Trouble about a thing of no Real Value but Curiosity it will make Mee Cautious what I ask for the Future."

In the best tradition of gardeners, though, Custis was determined to find this melon for his friend. He replied later in 1738: "Let me intreat you not so much as to dream that I shall ever think anything a trouble that I can by any means oblige you in; I have at last got some seeds of the sweet smelling Mellon and have planted some which are come up well; I hope to raise some for you but in the mean time have sent you part of the seeds I got from a gentleman's quarter a good distance from me."

This pretty little melon is a prolific bearer, producing dozens of fragrant melons from a single vine. Its small round form, its distinct fragrance, and its disagreeable flavor are probably very much like that of Pliny's "melopepo" "cucumber."

The Amazing Turkey [Turkish] Cucumber

The most remarkable melon in colonial Williamsburg was, again, called a cucumber. In 1737, John Custis wrote to Peter Collinson to report: "The seeds of the long cucumber you sent me; I planted but none came up; I gave my son 3 seeds which all came up; and notwithstanding the excessive drouth he had one more than 3 feet long; to the astonishment of many; severall people rid many miles to see it . . . there are more people begd some of the seed; than 10 cucumbers can afford."

The editor of the local newspaper, *Virginia Gazette*, wrote an article about it in 1737: "There grew, this Summer, in the Garden of Mr. *Daniel Parke Custis,* in *New-Kent* County, a Cucumber, of the *Turkey* or *Morocco* Kind, which measured a Yard in Length, and near 14 Inches round the thickest Part of it. . . . They are ribb'd almost like a Musk-melon, colour'd like a Water-melon; and taste much like the common Cucumber. Several curious Persons have been to view them, the like having never been seen in these Parts before."

The following year, another article appeared in the *Virginia Gazette*, this time in response to an article in a Boston newspaper that appeared to doubt the veracity of the Williamsburg cucumber. The editor, a Mr. Parks, began the story with a quote from the Boston paper: "'Last Week was cut out of a Garden belonging to Capt. *Wells,* of *Cambridge* . . . a Water-Melon, that was in Circumference, both Ways, a Yard and an Eighth Part of a Yard, which weighed 36 Pounds and 10 Ounces. . . . *This Rarity we send to* Virginia, *in Return for their Cucumber.*'"

Parks then elaborated: *"*If the Author of this Paragraph was ingenuous and candid in his Account, we receive his Present very kindly: But if he intended wittily to impose upon us an overgrown imaginary Water-melon, for a real Cucumber, supposing our Account to be false . . . we must beg Leave to assure him, that the Description we gave of that Cucumber was true; and that from the Seed of it, and others of the same Kind, abundance of them have been propagated in several Gentlemens Gardens this Year; particularly in That of Mr. *Thomas Nelson,* Merchant, in *York* Town, who has one in his Garden, which measur'd (this Day) 40 Inches in Length; and has several others 3 Feet long. . . . *As we have undeniable Proofs of the Truth of this Account, we venture to send it to the* Norward, *for Improvement, or Admiration.*"

This "cucumber" was almost certainly what is known today as the 'Armenian' melon. When it is immature, it tastes very much like a cucumber but is a true melon (*C. melo* var. *flexuosum*). We grow the 'Armenian' melon every summer, and to this day, the Turkey [Turkish] cucumber is a source of amazement and admiration to Williamsburg visitors.

The Particular Culture of Melons

The culture of melons provided the inspiration and impetus for the development of many garden devices, such as bell glasses and garden frames, for raising tender fruits and vegetables out of season. The first example of a proto-greenhouse was developed for the Roman emperor Tiberius, so that he could enjoy his beloved *Cucumis* on every day of the year. As recounted by Pliny the Elder: "His kitchen-gardeners had cucumber beds mounted on wheels which they moved out into the sun and then on wintry days withdrew under the cover of frames glazed with transparent stone." These devices would probably have looked very much like our familiar cold frame, on wheels.

The Virginia colonists had the luxury of long hot summers that made the culture of melons relatively easy. This was an astonishment to English visitors, such as William Hugh Grove, who recorded in 1732: "Musk Melons are plentifull Enough but they plant them among their Corn in ye shade & ordinary ground without any Care as our Gardeners use & have not the Advantages of Soyl or Sun & Consequently [not the] high flavor of our Engl Melons." But any Virginian will tell you that quite the opposite is true: Virginia melons are perfectly sweet. It was exactly this type of snobbery that led to the unpleasantness between the colonies and the mother country a few decades later.

The Williamsburg Gardener's Assistant

Aging the melon seed. It was long believed that melon seed needed to be aged for several years to produce the best fruit. James Justice instructed in 1771: "Seed of two or three years old, which has been well kept, is much better than that of the preceding year, and should the seed be soft, keep it in your breeches-pocket for a month or six weeks; by which the superabundant moisture will be better carried off, than in any other way." Batty Langley had a somewhat more elaborate method for aging melon seed: "I took part of the Seed, and caused it to be sewed up in a small Linen Bag, which about the beginning of *August* I put into the Watch Pocket of my Breeches, wherein it remain'd till the end of *December*. . . . the Seed of one Year, which I preserved in my Fob, produced rather a much better Crop, than that which was eight Years old." While melon seed is relatively long lived, modern experience has not demonstrated that older seed produces any better fruit than fresh seed does.

Managing the melon seedlings. We plant melon seed in March on hotbeds for an early and prolonged harvest of this delightful fruit. After the bed is made and the soil temperature settled to near 80°F, the seeds are sown in loosely woven oaken baskets buried in the soil, in the same manner as cucumbers. Six or seven seeds are sown in each basket and then are gently watered in with water heated over the fire to the same or slightly warmer temperature as the bed.

Once the plants are up, thin them to three well-spaced seedlings. A couple of weeks after this, they are pruned as instructed by Robert Edmeades in 1776: "After four leaves appear, pinch off the tops with your finger and thumb, to cause them to throw out side shoots." This also keeps the plants compact, so that they will be easier to transplant the following week. It is important that they are transplanted while still small, as larger plants generally languish after being moved and often never recover.

Making baskets; plunging basket; melons in hotbed

(Top) Removing melon baskets; placing paper frame; (bottom) watering melons; melons on shingles

What skill is required to transplant the melons?
To remove the transplants from the frame, thrust a trowel into the earth of the hotbed all around the rim of each basket, until the melon rootball is detached from the surrounding soil. Using your trowel, carefully remove the melon plants from the hotbed and take them directly to the garden. Place each transplant in a planting hole that has been previously prepared in a shallow basin of soil, and gently firm the soil around the rootball. Water the plants and cover them with a paper frame, as instructed by John Randolph in 18th-century Williamsburg: "The early sowings should be covered with oil paper in preference to glasses." We cover two hills of melons, 4 feet apart, under each frame. The frame will shield them from the wind and sun and should be left over the plants until they resume vigorous growth.

Once the plants are shooting out their runners

and producing flowers, the frames are removed and a shallow canal is constructed around the melon bed. It has long been believed that melons should not be watered directly over the crown of the plant. Robert Edmeades advised in *The Gentleman and Lady's Gardener* (1776): "You must be careful in not giving the plants too much water, and pour it at a distance from the stem." Not only will the shallow canal provide a convenient way of watering the plants in a dry season, it will also serve to draw the water away from the crowns of the plants in wet seasons.

The direct sowing of melon seeds. To sow your melon seeds directly in the garden, throw up hills 4 inches high and about 18 inches in diameter, with their tops shaped like basins. Space the hills 4 or 5 feet apart. Then you may follow the instructions provided by *The American Gardener's Calendar* (1806): "When your hills are all prepared as above, plant in each, towards the centre, eight or nine grains of good melon seed, distant two inches from one another, and cover them about half an inch deep." After the seeds are germinated and well up, select the best three, well separated, and pull the rest.

Summer maintenance of melons. As summer progresses and the melons appear, careful attention must be paid to water. Richard Bradley cautioned in 1718: "Give them gentle Waterings, now and then, if the Earth be extream dry; for *Melons* do not delight in abundance of wet, neither will the *Fruit* be well tasted if the *Plants* are kept too moist." The sweetest melons are formed under dry conditions. If the weather should turn rainy as the fruit is developing, the paper frames are set back over the melon plants, the frames raised up on bricks to allow the vines to run underneath. This will keep water from the crowns of the plants and preserve the sweetness of the melons.

As a precaution against rot, we set the melons upon wooden shingles to keep them off the ground. It

'Valencia' winter melon; 'Prescott Fond Blanc' melon

is important that they are not turned over when performing this task, as they are liable to sunburn if their bottoms are turned up. Judging when the melons are ripe is easy within the tribe of muskmelons, but can be more difficult with other melons. As explained by John Randolph in *A Treatise on Gardening* (1793): "The sign of fruits maturity is the cracking, near the foot stalk; and smelling fragrantly. The Cantaleupe never changes colour, till too ripe. Gather your fruit in a morning before the sun has warmed it . . . and keep those got in the morning in the coolest place."

Harvesting melons by their properties. Muskmelon stems will "slip" or detach from the fruit when the melon is fully ripe. Cantaloupe and winter melons (*C. indorus*), such as honeydew and 'Crenshaw', do not self-detach. Most will change color when ripe, some dramatically, some much more subtly. The only sure predictor for harvesting the perfect cantaloupe or winter melon is the experience of the gardener.

An ancient confusion. It was long believed that growing cucumbers near melons would spoil the flavor of the melon. As claimed by Richard Bradley in *New Improvements of Planting and Gardening* (1718): "For the more certain producing of *Melons* of a right Flavour, let me advise that no *Cucumber Plants* be set near them, [lest] the *Male Dust* of the *Cucumbers* should happen to be carry'd with the *Wind* upon the *Blossoms* of the *Melons,* and perhaps set them for Fruit, which will then certainly give the *Melons,* so produced, the Relish of the *Cucumber.*" This caution is sometimes repeated to this day. In reality, the cucumber, having a different genetic makeup, will not cross with the melon.

MELON ESSENTIALS

PLANTING Sow seeds in spring after the apple blossoms fall, or when soil temperature reaches 65°F.

SPACING Plant on hills 4 to 5 feet apart, or in rows 5 to 6 feet apart with plants 2 feet asunder.

FOR BEST GROWTH Grow in a well-drained soil in full sun. For perfect fruit, the soil must not be too dry or too wet. Water deeply when required, away from the crown of the plant.

HARVESTING Harvest muskmelons when the stems slip from the fruit. Cantaloupes and winter melons are ripe when they change to the color characteristic of their variety.

TO SAVE PURE SEED All types of melons will cross with each other. Separate varieties by ½ mile.

COLLECTING AND STORING SEED Seed is ripe when melons are fit to eat. Scoop seed and seed membrane into a bowl and separate membrane from seed by working the pulp through your fingers. When seeds are free from pulp, add water to float off detached pulp and undeveloped seeds. Good seeds will sink to the bottom. Pour off pulp and hollow seeds, then repeat until good seeds are clean. Pour water through a paper filter to separate out the seeds, then allow them to dry. Refrigerate in airtight containers.

SEED VIABILITY 5 years

Seed Varieties

Varieties listed in 18th-century Virginia

- ♦ **'Fine' cantaloupe, 'Italien', 'Orange and Green Streak'** cantaloupe, **'Zatta Mellon', 'Diarbekr Mellon':** Cantaloupe or rock melon types

- ♦ **'Early Musk-Melon', 'Orange Musk-Melon', 'Netted Wrought Mellon', 'White Netted Melon', 'Green Netted Melon', 'Green Fleshed Mellon', 'Pineapple Melon', 'Roman Melon':** Musk or netted melon types

- ♦ **'Sweet Smelling Mellon', 'Fragrant Melon', 'Portugal Melon'** or **'Pocket Melon':** Small inedible melons used for perfumery

- ♦ **'Turkey Cucumber':** The most ancient form of sweet melon, better known as 'Armenian' melon today

Heirloom varieties for the modern gardener

- ♦ **'Noir de Carmes', 'Prescott Fond Blanc', 'Petit Gris de Rennes', 'Charentais', 'D'Alger':** Cantaloupes

- ♦ **'Ananas D'Amerique', 'Green Nutmeg', 'Jenny Lind',** and many more: Muskmelons

- ♦ **'Queen Anne's Pocket':** Pocket melon

- ♦ **'Armenian':** Snake or serpent melon

WATERMELON

Citrullus lanatus

The watermelon is a native of the Kalahari Desert in southern Africa and is called *tsama* by the native Bushmen. Alphonse de Candolle recorded in *Origin of Cultivated Plants* (1884): "Livingstone saw districts literally covered with it, and the savages and several kinds of wild animals eagerly devoured the wild fruit. They are sometimes, but not always, bitter, and this cannot be detected from the appearance of the fruit. The negroes strike it with an axe, and taste the juice to see whether it is good or bad." While humans cannot tell the difference between sweet and bitter without tasting the melons, antelope can, and choose only the sweet. Consequently, bitter varieties tended to reproduce in situ while sweet varieties were dispersed—courtesy of the antelope—and eventually by the hand of humans.

The Watermelon in the Ancient World

Until recently, the first archaeological evidence for watermelons in northern Africa was a few seeds found in the tomb of Tutankhamen (circa 1330 BCE) in Egypt. The latest evidence for the watermelon in northern Africa has pushed back the intro-

duction date considerably. Seeds from the wild *Citrullus lanatus* have been found at the archaeological site at Uan Muhuggiag in southwest Libya and are 5,000 years old.

The watermelon was apparently unknown to the ancient Greeks and Romans and seems to have entered Europe by way of Moorish Spain. Watermelons were recorded in Spain at Cordoba in 961 and Seville in 1158. The first northern European citation comes from the German theologian Albertus Magnus, who recorded watermelons in the 13th century. Another German, Leonhart Fuchs, illustrated a watermelon in *De Historia Stirpium* in 1542.

An English Rarity

The first description of the watermelon in England is found in Gerard's *Herball* (1597). He called it a "Citrull Cucumber" and described a dark-colored melon with deep furrows. One hundred years later, in 1699, John Evelyn described the watermelon in *Acetaria* as: "large and with black Seeds, exceedingly Cooling, brought us from abroad, and the hotter Climates, where they drink *Water* after eating *Melons.*" The watermelon remained a curiosity in England, primarily because it was difficult to grow in the cool English climate. In the middle of the 18th century, Philip Miller observed watermelons "are cultivated in *Spain, Portugal, Italy,* and most other warm Countries in *Europe*; as also in *Africa, Asia,* and *America*; and are by the Inhabitants of those Countries greatly esteemed for their wholsome cooling Quality; but in *England* they are not so universally esteemed, though some few Persons are very fond of them."

A North American Sensation

The watermelon was introduced into the New World by Spanish and Portuguese sailors at a very early date, probably as a by-product of the African slave trade. No other Old World fruit was so quickly and widely adopted by Native Americans as the watermelon. Master Graves recorded watermelons as abounding in Massachusetts in 1629. Capt. William Hilton observed watermelons being grown by the natives in Florida in 1664. In 1673, Father Marquette recorded watermelons along the Mississippi River. In fact, watermelon culture was so common among Native Americans that many Europeans assumed it was a native American plant. In Virginia, John Banister wrote in 1679: "Water Melons . . . are a large very pleasant & innocent fruit, I have eaten near half a score of them in an afternoon. Most of these I suppose grow naturally somewhere or other in this Continent for the Natives had them before this was a Colony & We from them."

The colonists developed an equal passion for watermelons. Peter Kalm recorded on September 19, 1749, during his travels from Philadelphia to Canada: "*Watermelons* . . . are cultivated in great plenty in the English and French American colonies, and there is hardly a peasant here who has not a field planted with them." In Virginia, Lieut. William Feltman, marching toward Yorktown with the 1st Pennsylvania Regiment, recorded on August 17, 1781: "This evening I had an invitation from Capt. Pierson to assist him in eating two water-melons, which were the best and finest I ever see. This country is full of them; they have large patches of two and three acres of them."

"In the English North American colonies every countryman plants a number of watermelons which are eaten while the people make hay."

—Peter Kalm,
Travels in North America (1748–1749)

The Williamsburg Gardener's Assistant

The season for watermelons. The culture of watermelons is very similar to that for melons and cucumbers. As explained by Bernard McMahon in *The American Gardener's Calendar* (1806): "In order to have water melons in good perfection, you must fix upon a piece of very light, rich, sandy soil; prepare, sow, and manage it, in every respect, as directed for cucumbers and melons, only let the hills be nine or ten feet distant every way." In our small Williamsburg garden, we plant watermelon seed on hills, 4 to 6 feet apart, hollowed out to form basins for ease of watering.

As watermelons were seldom grown in England, English garden books were silent on their culture. As a result, there was no tradition of starting transplants in hotbeds as was often practiced for melons and cucumbers. In Williamsburg, we sow the seed directly in the garden in the last half of April, after all danger of frost is gone. In the northern states with a shorter season, the use of transplants, started indoors 3 to 4 weeks prior to setting out, will provide for a more reliable harvest.

After the plants are up and growing, select the best two or three well-spaced seedlings to grow on. Watermelons, being desert plants, are deep rooted and seldom need watering, unless it is extremely dry. Too much water will often lesson the sweetness of the melons.

How to judge when the watermelon is ripe. Perhaps the most difficult part of growing watermelons is knowing when to harvest them. Watermelons do not ripen after picking, so if you pick an unripe watermelon, it remains an unripe watermelon. Many claim to be able to "hear" the ripeness of melons by thumping them. We have thumped melons, both in the garden and at the market, for decades and have never developed an ear for it. A better method for the tone-deaf is to examine the first little tendril that grows from the leaf axial just beside the fruit. When the tendril turns brown, the melon is very close to ripe. Another method is to look at the melon's underside; when it goes from a light green color to a creamy yellow, it is time to pluck it. At that point, we give it a congratulatory thump.

Watermelon seedlings; watermelon tendril

WATERMELON ESSENTIALS

PLANTING Sow indoors 3 to 4 weeks before planting when the daffodils bloom; or plant directly in the garden after all danger of frost, when the dogwood and peach blossoms fall. Watermelons are sensitive to transplant shock so should be started in peat pots.

SPACING Plant on hills 4 to 6 feet apart or in rows 5 feet apart with plants 4 feet asunder.

FOR BEST GROWTH Watermelons do best in a light, sandy soil. In heavier clays, amend the soil with compost and throw up hills 4 to 6 inches high to grow the plants on.

HARVESTING Harvest after the tendril nearest the fruit turns brown and the underside turns a creamy yellow. For thumpers, a ripe melon will have a dull, hollow sound, an unripe melon, a tinnier, metallic ring.

TO SAVE PURE SEED Separate varieties by $\frac{1}{2}$ mile.

COLLECTING AND STORING SEED Seed is mature when the melon is ripe. Place seed in a colander and rinse thoroughly. Dry seed and refrigerate in airtight containers.

SEED VIABILITY 6 years

Seed Varieties

Varieties listed in 18th-century Virginia

♦ **'Pistoia'** and **'Naples'**: From Pistoia and Naples, Italy. Watermelons are difficult to grow in England, so seed had to come from southern Europe.

Heirloom varieties for the modern gardener

♦ **'Georgia Rattlesnake'**, **'Black Diamond'**, **'Kolb's Gem'**, **'Moon and Stars'**

'Georgia Rattlesnake' watermelon

"There is also a winter or rather water melon, with large black seeds, some of which I have this year reciev'd from *France*."

—Stephen Switzer,
The Practical Kitchen Gardiner (1727)

CHAPTER 7

of
Squash, Pumpkins,
and
Gourds

Squash, pumpkins, and gourds, like melons and cucumbers, are members of the Cucurbitaceae, a large plant family found worldwide but primarily in tropical regions. On the east side of the Atlantic Ocean, the white-flowered bottle gourd, *Lagenaria siceraria,* spread from tropical Africa into the Middle East and India. On the west side of the Atlantic, several species of yellow-flowered *Cucurbita* spread from South and Central America into North America and the Caribbean Islands. In both cases, the first use of the primitive fruits was for their edible seeds. Over time, the bottle gourd was adapted by ancient people to form implements and containers. The New World cucurbits became the third element of the American culinary trinity of corn, beans, and squash.

The Old World gourd found its own way to the New World by floating across the Atlantic Ocean to the Americas, where it was discovered and collected by coastal tribes. In North America, the gourds were used for water and storage containers, floats for fishing lines and for teaching children how to swim, masks, ceremonial rattles, and many other purposes. By the time the first colonists arrived at Jamestown, Virginia, Native Americans had been growing and using gourds for more than 5,000 years.

Going in the other direction, it required the hand of man for pumpkins and squashes to cross the Atlantic, but within 30 years of Columbus's first voyage, New World cucurbits were being grown in southern European gardens. Over time, a uniquely European cucurbit that was typically long, green, and slender was developed. In England, it took the form of the vegetable marrow. The somewhat smaller Italian marrow was returned to America in the form of the ubiquitous zucchini.

PUMPKIN and SQUASH
Cucurbita pepo

This group includes the field pumpkin; the acorn, pattypan, delicata, spaghetti, yellow crookneck, and zucchini squashes; and the ornamental gourds. *C. pepo* is the most diverse of all species of *Cucurbita* and was one of the first New World species domesticated by native populations. The earliest archaeological evidence for *C. pepo* comes from a small cave known as Guila Naquitz in Oaxaca, Mexico. The cave was used by hunter-gatherers between 8000 and 6500 BCE. From Mexico, *C. pepo* spread north, reaching eastern North America by 2700 BCE. Squashes and pumpkins of *C. pepo* were, by far, the most common *Cucurbita* used by both European and American gardeners in the 18th century and are the most common cucurbits in the modern garden.

The Naming of Squash and Pumpkins

The difference between a pumpkin and a squash is purely semantic. The larger, rounder fruit are generally known as pumpkins, while the smaller, generally oblong fruit are known as squash.

The earliest European accounts of *Cucurbita* in North America referred to them as melons, cucumbers, or gourds. In 1535, Jacques Cartier discovered *"gros melons," "concombres,"* and *"courges"* being grown by Native Americans at the village of Hochelega, near modern Montreal, Canada. These were probably pumpkins (*"gros melons"*), summer squash (*"concombres"*), and winter squash (*"courges"*). The Europeans had not yet agreed on a name for the cucurbits, so

Pumpkin; maycock

they simply borrowed French names from fruit they knew from home.

During the 1584–1585 expedition to Roanoke Island, North Carolina, Thomas Hariot recorded: "*Macócqwer*, according to their severall formes called by us, *Pompions*, *Mellions*, and *Gourdes*, because they are of the like formes as those kindes in England." The native *macócqwer* gave rise to the English *maycock*, one of the first names to be applied to the New World cucurbits. This name, which seems to distinguish squash from pumpkins, was used by Capt. John Smith in *A Map of Virginia* (1612): "In May also amongst their corne they plant Pumpeons, and a fruit like unto a muske millen, but lesse and worse, which they call *Macocks*."

The name *squash* was also borrowed from the native language. William Wood recorded in *New Englands Prospect* (1634) that the ground was good for growing a variety of vegetable crops, including "Squonterquashes." In 1672, John Josselyn noted in *New-Englands Rarities Discovered*: "*Squashes*, but more truly *Squontersquashes*, a kind of Mellon, or rather Gourd."

A New World Delicacy Scorned by the Old

Squash was considered by the colonists to be the least of what some natives called the "Three Sisters"—not as important as corn or as glamorous as beans, but still a common fare on American tables. Adriaen van der Donck, a landowner, lawyer, and political activist in what is now New York, recorded in *A Description of the New Netherlands* (1655): "It is a delightful fruit, as well to the eye on account of its fine variety of colours, as to the mouth for its agreeable taste. The ease with which it is cooked renders it a favourite too with the young women." In the Netherlands, squash had a very different reputation. According to van der Donck, the Dutch "generally despised [it] as a mean and unsubstantial article of food." The English back in England were equally unimpressed with squash. As described by Philip Miller in *The Gardeners Dictionary* (1768):

"The fruit are . . . boiled by the inhabitants of America to eat as a sauce with their meat; but in England they are only cultivated by way of curiosity."

A Squash and a Mothering Sunday Cake

The pattypan or scalloped squash was the most commonly grown variety of squash in America and in England. In 1597, John Gerard called it a "buckler," because it was shaped "in a manner flat like unto a shield or buckler." A buckler was a small round shield used to deflect sword strokes in an era before the longbow rendered such small shields obsolete. In *Vienna Codex* (1562), the German herbalist Leonhart Fuchs named it "*Cucumer paniformis*" for its resemblance to a baking pan. From this the French called it *patisson,* which the English translated as pattypan, the name it is most commonly known by today.

In the American colonies, it was known as the simlin (spelled many different ways). This name seems to originate in Beauchamp Plantagenet's work, *A Description of the Province of New Albion* (1648). While exploring

Pattypan squash

the headwaters of the Chesapeake Bay, he noted the natives growing "Symnels." This name derived from the *simnel* cake, a small round cake decorated with balls of almond paste on its outer edge. Also known as the Mothering Sunday cake, it has been prepared in England for Lent since medieval times.

The most striking difference between the simlin and the other *Cucurbita* was its growth habit. Richard Bradley described it in *Dictionarium Botanicum* (1728): "*The Buckler, or Simnel Gourd*. There is a manifest Difference, not only in the Fruit of this Gourd from the rest, but in the manner of growing also, for it groweth upright, with great hollow rough, hairy, crested Stalks, to the Height of three Cubits, and runneth not along on the Ground as the rest." The simlin squash was America's first summer bush squash.

The Names of Squash

There are many different types of squash within the *C. pepo* species, and deciphering them all in the historic record can be a challenge. For example, John Lawson listed in *A New Voyage to Carolina* (1709):

"Pompions yellow and very large, Burmillions, Cashaws, an excellent Fruit boil'd; Squashes, Simnals, Horns, and Gourds; besides many other Species, of less Value, too tedious to name."

"*Pompions*" (pumpkins), "*Cashaws*" (cushaws of *C. argyrosperma*), and "*Simnals*" (pattypans) are readily identifiable. "Burmillions" probably represent bur melons and are likely one of the warted squashes, classified as *C. verucosa* by 18th-century botanists. Philip Miller recorded in *The Gardeners Dictionary* (1763) that this squash was "very common in most parts of America, where it is cultivated as a culinary fruit." "Horns" are possibly summer crookneck squashes, as they are shaped like horns of plenty.

Lawson's "Squashes" and "Gourds" are the most difficult to identify. In most English literature, squash and simlin (pattypan) are synonymous. Lawson listed "Simnals" separately, so by the process of elimination, he may be referring to a winter squash, similar to an acorn squash. In New England, John Josselyn wrote: "the yellow *Squash* called an Apple *Squash*, because like an Apple, and about the bigness

Upright growth of bush squash

Yellow crookneck squash

of a Pome-water, is the best kind." This small round squash may have been similar to the "Macock" described by Capt. John Smith and might represent a type of acorn squash. Acorns are one of the most popular varieties of squash at the modern market, but were seldom listed by colonial gardeners.

Lawson's "Gourd" was certainly a *Cucurbita* rather than a true gourd (*Lagenaria*), as it is listed with the food plants. It was likely a winter squash with a hard gourdlike rind. Squashes that were described as gourds in English literature were often elongated varieties, which could indicate a pear-shaped *C. pepo* or a crookneck squash of *C. moschata*.

The Pumpkin and Its Kinds

The Latin *pepone*, which Pliny used to describe the largest form of *Cucumis* (melon), became the English "Pompion," a name that bounced around between melons, cucumbers, and gourds until finally finding

a permanent home as the New World pumpkin.

The pumpkin was quickly adopted by English colonists in North America, but like the squash, suffered from an image problem back in England. Martha Bradley wrote in *The British Housewife* (1770): "THE Pumpkin is a very ordinary Fruit, and is principally the Food of the Poor." In fact, pumpkins usually did not even make it into the garden. As explained by Philip Miller in 1768, "[The] Pumpkin, is frequently cultivated by the country people in England, who plant them upon their dunghills." Anyone who has ever thrown pumpkin seeds onto a compost pile in fall, to be rewarded by exuberant pumpkin vines in spring, can attest to how well suited this fruit is to growing on piles of rotting organic material.

Pumpkins were introduced into England from the Americas at a very early date. John Gerard described three sorts in *The Herball* (1597): "The great long Pompion," "the great round Pompion," and "the great flat bottom'd Pompion." By the end of the 18th century, the varieties had so proliferated that John Abercrombie was able to list 18, including the common large round-fruited yellow, oval yellow, oblong yellow, whitish fruited, stone-colored, flesh-colored, party-colored, marbled, small round, orange-shaped, pear-shaped, turbinated, hemispherical or semi-globular, egg-shaped, striped roundish, striped egg-shaped, striped turbinated, and striped pear-shaped "Pompion."

'Connecticut' field pumpkin

A New World Wonder

To the North American colonists, the pumpkin was by far the most important variety of *Cucurbita*. Peter Kalm recorded in his journal of 1749: "*Pumpkins of several kinds, oblong, round, flat or compressed, crook-necked, small, etc. are planted in all the English and French colonies. In Canada they fill the chief part of the farmers' kitchen gardens, though the onions are a close second.*" To Native Americans, pumpkins were second in importance, according to Kalm: "They constitute a considerable part of the Indian food; however, the natives plant more squashes than common pumpkins."

For Beer and for Livestock

Landon Carter was an 18th-century planter who lived at Sabine Hall on the Rappahannock River in Virginia. In February of 1775, he wrote a letter to Alexander Purdie, editor of the *Virginia Gazette* in Williamsburg, in response to the suggestion that

'Cushaw' squash

pumpkins be used for making molasses: "Permit me, *Purdie*, to tell the Gentleman who hinted the making molosses, &c. [etc.] from Punckins, as they are called, that the late President Carter [Landon Carter's father] was always fond of a beer made from them, at least 50 years ago." Landon Carter carried on his father's tradition of making beer from pumpkins and called it "Pumperkin."

More important than for making alcoholic beverages, however, was the value of pumpkins for feeding livestock. An 1814 letter written on behalf of Thomas Jefferson to David Gelston provides an example: "The pumpkin being a plant of which he [Jefferson] endeavors every year to raise so many as to maintain all the stock on his farms from the time they come till frost, which is from 2. to 3. months. besides feeding his workhorses, cattle and sheep on them entirely, they furnish the principal fattening for the pork, slaughtered. a more productive kind will therefore be of value."

C. argyrosperma
(formerly *C. mixta*)

The cushaw, striped cushaw, and Tennessee sweet potato squash are included in this group. The wild ancestor of these large squashes is *C. sororia*, a native to the semiarid lowlands throughout much of Mexico and Central America. Evidence for the cultivation of *C. argyrosperma* dating to around 5200 BCE has been found in the Tehuacán Valley in southern Mexico. It is not clear when the variety *callicarpa* (cushaw) reached eastern North America. Accounts by colonial writers suggest it was cultivated by native tribes in pre-contact North America, but no archaeological evidence for *C. argyrosperma* among coastal tribes has been found.

The Various Forms of Pumpkins

Eighteenth-century accounts of crookneck squash or pumpkins are difficult to identify, as they could refer to crookneck varieties of *C. pepo*, *C. argyrosperma*, or

C. moschata. Accounts of crookneck cucurbits in New England by Josselyn and Kalm have generally been interpreted to be varieties of *C. moschata.*

In Virginia, the case for *C. argyrosperma* is stronger. The Rev. John Banister described a likely candidate in his *Natural History of Virginia 1678–1692*: "We plant also Cucumbers & Pompions, the common, & the Indian kind with a long narrow neck, which from them we call a Cushaw." Robert Beverley provided a more complete description of the cushaw pumpkin in *The History and Present State of Virginia*, first published in 1705: "Their *Cushaws* are a kind of Pompion, of a bluish green Colour, streaked with White, when they are fit for Use. They are larger than the Pompions, and have a long narrow Neck." The cushaw is sometimes called the pumpkin squash today. Like the field pumpkin, it is used in its mature stage for pies and breads.

Cushaws have long been associated with Southern gardening and have never been as prevalent in

Cheese pumpkin

the North. Fearing Burr wrote in 1865 of the "Cashaw. Cushaw Pumpkin": "It is not cultivated or generally known in New England or in the northern portions of the United States; for though well suited to Louisiana and other portions of the South, where it is much esteemed, it is evidently too tender for cultivation where the seasons are comparatively short and cool."

Another *C. argyrosperma* pumpkin was described by Thomas Jefferson in a letter to Samuel Vaughan Jr. in 1790: "We have lately had introduced a plant of the Melon species which, from it's external resemblance to the pumpkin, we have called a pumpkin, distinguishing it specifically as the *potatoe-pumpkin*, on account of the extreme resemblance of it's taste to that of the sweet-potatoe. It is as yet but little known, is well esteemed at our tables, and particularly valued by our negroes." The 'Tennessee Sweet Potato' squash descends from Jefferson's "*potatoe-pumpkin*."

C. moschata

Winter (or Canada) crookneck squash, butternut squash, golden cushaw, and the cheese pumpkin are included in this group. The earliest evidence for *C. moschata* was found at Huaca Prieta on the coast of northern Peru and dates to around 2000 BCE. Archaeological evidence for its cultivation was found at Tamaulipas, in northeastern Mexico, from 1400 BCE. This species was one of the most widely grown cucurbits in the New World prior to European contact. Evidence for its cultivation has been found from northern South America through Central America and into southern North America.

A Glorious Sight in the New World

On Columbus's first trip to the New World, he found a village at the eastern end of present-day Cuba that was "planted with many things of the country, as *calabazas*, a glorious sight." Calabash was the European name for the bottle gourd, but Columbus was almost certainly referring to a *Cucurbita*, likely a pumpkin of the *C. moschata* species similar to the cheese pumpkin.

John Gerard classified one of the three pumpkins he listed in *The Herball* (1597) as "*Pepo maximus compressus.* The great flat bottom'd Pompion," which probably refers to a cheese pumpkin, so-called because they are flat like a wheel of cheese. There is no clear description of the cheese pumpkin in colonial Virginia, but Fearing Burr recorded in *The Field and Garden Vegetables of America* (1865): "It was extensively disseminated in the Middle States at the time of the American revolution, and was introduced into certain parts of New England by the soldiers on their return from service."

The winter or Canada crookneck squash is particularly difficult to discern in the historic record. This large squash has a round body and a long curved neck. As a winter squash it is used in its mature state, like pumpkins. Some writers have proposed that the "*courges*" listed by Cartier in 1535 represented winter crooknecks. John Josselyn described a type of squash as "longish like a Gourd" in *New-Englands Rarities Discovered* (1672), but as this is listed among other summer squash, it could be a squash similar to a summer crookneck.

In Pennsylvania, Peter Kalm recorded a "crook-necked" pumpkin in 1749. Kalm always distinguished between squash and pumpkin in his writings, pumpkin indicating a *Cucurbita* used in its mature state. A better description was provided by William Bartram, the Philadelphia nurseryman, in 1786: "Crook neck Pumpkin. . . . They are best eaten after quite ripe & hard when of a deep yellow or orange color &c. [etc.] their exterior shell is piled off, the interior rind is then cut in pieces & stewed in a pot." The Pennsylvania Dutch have a long history of growing this squash, which taken with the above evidence, seems to suggest that at least Kalm and Bartram's *Cucurbita* were winter crooknecks.

C. maxima

The giant or show pumpkin, buttercup squash, banana squash, Hubbard squash, and the turban squash are members of this group. Pumpkins of this species are the world's largest fruit. The earliest known domestication of *C. maxima* was in the Viru Valley of north coastal Peru and dates to around 1800 BCE. It may have originated from wild species of *Cucurbita* found in Argentina and Uruguay. No evidence for *C. maxima* north of the equator has been found prior to European contact.

Giant Pumpkins from Exotic Ports

Members of this species were among the first cucurbits introduced into southern Europe, but they were unknown in the North American colonies until very late in the 18th or early in the 19th century. Sailors returning from South America introduced them into New England. The Hubbard squash was one of the first varieties of *C. maxima* to find its way into American gardens. Fearing Burr described the Hubbard in 1865 as having been introduced to gardeners by: "Mr. J.J.H. Gregory, of Marblehead, Mass., who brought this excellent variety to notice, and . . . states that it was introduced . . . about sixty years since by an elderly man, who followed marketing, from the vicinity of Boston." Today, *C. maxima* is best known for the 1,000-pound giant pumpkins displayed at state fairs across the country.

"The fruit is of different shapes, and in hot counties is boiled and eat by the inhabitants as sauce for their meat."

—William Hanbury, *A Complete Body of Planting and Gardening* (1773)

The Williamsburg Gardener's Assistant

The particular culture of pumpkins and squash. The pumpkins and squash, explained Stephen Switzer in 1727, "require a good deal of water, and the richest soil you can give them." This is particularly true for larger squashes, such as the cushaw, which need ample water to bring them to perfection. In most parts of the country, the seeds for pumpkins and squash may be sown directly in the garden once the weather warms. The summer squashes, such as the pattypan, yellow squash, and the ubiquitous zucchini, are bush squashes and can be grown in the vegetable garden along with other plants. The trailing winter cucurbits, such as the pumpkin and cushaw, need considerable room and are best given a garden of their own. As explained in *The Young Gardener's Best Companion* (1795): "The common pumpion . . . being considerably of the most luxuriant, extensive, and branchy growth, running and spreading themselves amazingly over a surprising compass of ground, producing enormous fruit, should be allowed a capacious space of room to grow."

Dung piles and manure beds. When the weather has warmed, compost your ground and throw up hills, shaped like basins, as described for cucumbers and melon. If you should have the luxury of an unused pile of compost with lots of room around it, you can sow the seeds directly on the pile, as was long practiced in England.

In 1795, Samuel Fullmer described a method for forwarding an early crop: "Dig large holes a spade deep, and two or three feet wide, then filled with hot dung, earthing it six inches deep, and sow the seed therein." English gardeners often used a base of hot manure under their planting hills that would warm the soil, hastening germination and promoting early, vigorous growth. In the warmer climate of Virginia, we prefer to use composted manure for our planting hills. This also avoids any potential health risks from using fresh manure. Sow seven or nine seeds per hill, and after they have germinated, select the two or three best seedlings to remain.

For gardeners in the far North, the plants may be

Inspecting squash and pumpkin vines; pumpkin seedlings

started indoors or in a hotbed. As instructed by Fullmer: "By raising all the sorts in hot-beds, till the plants have three or four leaves, then planted in the open ground, they may be forwarded much sooner to a fruiting state. . . . When the plants have two, three, or four proper leaves, plant them out with balls to their roots." Pumpkins and squash, like all members of the Cucurbitaceae family, are very sensitive to having their roots disturbed, so it is critical that they are transplanted while still small, with an intact rootball. Modern gardeners often use peat pots to ensure this. Once planted, they must be watered thoroughly. Fullmer concluded: "[Give them] water directly, and every dry day till fresh rooted, also plentifully afterwards in all dry weather." If the weather turns hot and windy, a shade or cover for the first week will help preserve them.

An abundance of summer squash. Once summer squash come into flower, they must be inspected daily, for the fruit forms quickly and becomes quickly overripe. Squash that is left too long on the vine produces large seeds in a watery pulp and is greatly infe-

rior. The elongated forms, such as the crooknecks and zucchini, should be harvested when no more than 6 to 8 inches long. For the simlins or pattypans, John Abercrombie advised in 1778 that the fruit should be harvested when "the size of a walnut, or at most not bigger than a hen's egg."

The signs of ripeness in winter squash. The pumpkins and winter squashes—such as acorns, cushaw, delicata, Hubbard, and turbans—are harvested in a mature state, after the seeds have fully formed, so they have a much longer season. All winter squashes can be harvested once the rind has hardened enough so that it resists puncture by your thumbnail. In most cases, the vines will start to die, and the fruit will lose its sheen as it ripens. Pumpkins can usually be harvested anytime after the fruit has turned a uniform, usually orange, color. Cut the fruit with about 4 inches of stem still attached, as this will lengthen storage time. The stems are tough, particularly on the larger varieties, and a sharp knife or secateurs (pruning shears) will greatly facilitate the harvest.

Harvest simlins when size of walnuts.

Two debilitating pests of which the gardener must be aware. In 1804, John Gardiner wrote in *The American Gardener*: "SQUASHES AND SIMBLINS . . . when the plants appear destroy the insects which generally infest the young plants; it may be done by strewing soot, wood ashes or unslacked lime (in powder) over the plants, when wet with dew." Gardiner was likely referring to the squash bug, one of the most difficult pests to control on squashes and pumpkins. Lime or ashes sprinkled on the leaves may provide some control for squash bugs while the insects are still young. As the juvenile squash bugs congregate on the underside of the leaves, a duster or hand bellows will greatly facilitate the application. Squash bugs may also be trapped by laying boards around the plants and destroying the bugs that congregate underneath them. Adult squash bugs overwinter in the garden under debris, so good sanitation will help to limit their population.

The squash vine borer is equally difficult to control. The adult moth lays its eggs on the lower stems, usually within 10 inches of the ground. After the eggs hatch, the larvae tunnel into the stem, leaving a deposit of frass (sawdustlike material) at the opening to the wound. This often goes unnoticed until the vines collapse and it is too late to save the plant. In Virginia, the squash vine borer moth begins flying in the middle of June, so we endeavor to grow as large and robust plants as possible by that time, and we periodically check the stems for damage and scrape off any eggs we discover. We have had some success in preventing damage by coating the lower stems of pumpkin and winter squash plants with beeswax softened with almond oil. Once the stems are completely coated with wax, we add a dusting of lime.

Larvae that have burrowed into the stem can be removed by slitting the stem and spearing the larvae, though this is a tedious process and practiced by few gardeners. For pumpkins and winter squash, covering the prostrate vines with soil at the leaf nodes will encourage secondary rooting. This will, to some degree, compensate for any borer damage done to the stem.

Covering the stems is not possible for the upright

Vines coated with wax and lime

summer squashes, though, so the best strategy for these varieties is to sow multiple crops. Squash sown after the middle of July often escapes damage, as the moth is no longer laying eggs. Remove any infested plants quickly, before more pupae are deposited in the soil. Deep tilling in fall will help to expose any pupae to predation.

Cushaws, cheese pumpkins, and Hubbard squash are not nearly as susceptible to the squash vine borer.

"Commonly known by the title of Pumpkin, is frequently cultivated by the country people in England."

—Philip Miller, *The Gardeners Dictionary* (1768)

GOURD

Lagenaria siceraria

The primary use of the gourd has long been as a container. John Abercrombie recorded in *The Universal Gardener and Botanist* (1778): "Some of which have acquired such a prodigious magnitude, as when scooped, the shell has contained twenty-two gallons of liquid." Other very large gourds described by Richard Bradley in 1728 were "so large that they will cover a Man's Head: these are called Fishermens Gourds in *Italy*, for they are used to catch Ducks." The gourds were fashioned with a head hole in the bottom and two eye holes in the sides. The fisherman would don the gourd, submerge himself in the water, float up to the unsuspecting ducks, and grab them by the legs.

For Food and Utility

The origin of the bottle gourd is not known for certain, but it is presumed to be a native of tropical Africa and Madagascar. The first African documentation for the gourd comes from Egyptian tombs dating to 3500 BCE, but the gourd was almost certainly used by prehistoric people for its edible seeds and, perhaps, as a container. Pliny wrote in the 1st century CE: "The stem is used as an article of food when young, but at a later period it changes its nature, and its qualities become totally different: of late, gourds have come to be used in baths for jugs and pitchers."

In Europe, gourds were used exclusively as containers, but in some parts of Africa and Asia, they were consumed while the fruit was still in an immature stage. Philip Miller wrote in 1768 of the "*Long Gourd*" with white flowers: "In the eastern countries these fruit are very commonly cultivated and sold in the markets for the table, and are a

Bottle gourd

great part of the food of the common people." Elongated forms of the bottle gourd, as well as several other genera of gourds, are popular culinary plants in India today.

Gourds come in many shapes, but they all descend from the bottle gourd. John Gerard described this gourd in *The Herball* (1597): "The fruite . . . are not all of one fashion; for oftentimes they have the forme of flagons, or bottles, with a great large belly, and a small necke." The most common forms of gourds grown today are the dipper, birdhouse, bushel, and basket gourds.

Pots before Pottery

The oldest evidence for gourds in the New World dates to 7200 BCE and comes from caves at Guila Naquitz in the southern Mexican state of Oaxaca. The earliest North American evidence for gourds comes from the Windover Bog site on the Atlantic coast of Florida and dates to around 5300 BCE. The importance of gourds as containers to Native Americans has often been overlooked in the historic record in favor of pottery remains. Gourds, as containers, may very well predate the adoption of pottery. In the Americas, as in Europe, the gourd was used exclusively for implements and containers. Robert Beverley explained in *The History and Present State of Virginia* (1705): "The *Indians* never eat the Gourds, but plant them for other uses."

For Crows, Seeds, and Powder Horns

Gourds were not nearly as important to the English colonists as they were to Native Americans, but Americans, particularly in the backcountry, found uses for them. John Lawson recorded a familiar use in *A New Voyage to Carolina* (1709): "The Planters put Gourds on standing Poles, on purpose for these Fowl to build in, because they are a very Warlike Bird, and beat the Crows from the Plantations." He was almost certainly writing about purple martins, and gourds are used to this day to house these birds. Another use for gourds was recorded by Peter Kalm in 1748: "They are particularly fit for holding seeds which are to be sent over sea; for seeds keep their power of vegetating much longer if they be put in calabashes than by any other means."

The most common use of gourds by the colonists was probably as powder horns. The *Journal of William Calk*, a Kentucky pioneer, recorded this accident in 1775: "I turnd my hors to drive afore me & he got Scard Ran away threw Down the Saddel Bags & Broke three of our powder goards."

Gourd collection

The Williamsburg Gardener's Assistant

The season for gourds. The culture of gourds is very similar to the culture of pumpkins. Gourds are most commonly sown directly in the garden once the weather has warmed and nighttime temperatures are above 60°F. Gourds need a long season to form good thick rinds, so are best adapted to the Southern garden. Peter Kalm recorded while traveling through Pennsylvania in 1748: "They are more difficult to raise than the squashes, for they do not always ripen here except when the weather is very warm." Northern gardeners can forward the season by starting the plants indoors 4 weeks before they are intended to be planted out. Gourds are as sensitive, or more sensitive, than pumpkins and squash to having their roots disturbed during transplanting, so peat or paper pots are advisable.

Hung by the neck until straight. Gourds, wrote Benjamin Townsend in 1726, "are all very rambling, and must be planted where they can run up Props." This is particularly true for the dipper gourd. Dippers that are grown on the ground will have curved necks; to have long straight necks, they must be allowed to hang. We build a simple gourd ladder and allow the dipper vines to run up and over the grape arbor. Birdhouse and bushel gourds can be grown on the ground, but gourds that are allowed to ramble over fences or shrubbery are less likely to be bruised.

Harvesting and curing. Gourds are harvested after the stems that hold them to the vine turn brown. Cut them with about 4 inches of stem. Store the gourds in a dark, well-ventilated place and check them frequently for signs of rot. Most gardeners allow the gourds to dry before they are cut into dippers or bowls. Peter Kalm gave this advice in 1748: "In order to make vessels of them, they are first dried well. The seeds, together with the pulpy and spongy matter in which they lie, are afterwards taken out and thrown away. The shells are scraped very clean within, and then large spoons or ladles, funnels, bowls, dishes and the like may be made of them." When the gourds are fully dry, they are brittle and shatter easily. Most people use a hacksaw or a jigsaw to cut them. We have found that they are easier to cut while they are still green and have had equal success in drying them afterward.

For a natural finish, they are put up to cure without

Dipper gourds on grape arbor; gourd ladder; dipper gourd

any surface cleaning. This makes the gourds slightly more susceptible to rot, but will produce a very pretty mottled rind. For a smoother appearance, Peter Kalm advised: "Some people scrape the outside of them before they are opened, dry them and then clean them within. This makes them as hard as bone." For the smoothest and easiest results, clean the gourds with soap and water and wipe them down with rubbing alcohol before they are put up to cure. Once they are fully dry, a coat of shellac will preserve them.

PUMPKIN, SQUASH, AND GOURD ESSENTIALS

PLANTING Sow seeds for pumpkins, squash, and gourds once the weather has warmed, after the dogwood and peach trees have come to full bloom.

SPACING Plant the larger squash, pumpkins, and gourds on hills spaced at least 6 feet apart. Summer squash can be spaced 4 feet apart. Plant seeds 1 inch deep and thin seedlings to one or two plants per hill. Dipper gourds must have a structure to climb on.

FOR BEST GROWTH All cucurbits, but especially the larger pumpkins, require a rich soil and ample water. A strategy for controlling the damage from squash bugs and vine borers is necessary for success in most parts of the country. Gourds are relatively pest free.

HARVESTING Harvest summer squash while fruit is young and before the seeds expand. Winter squash is harvested as the foliage dies back and the skin hardens. Summer squash should be consumed or frozen within 2 weeks of harvest. Winter squash will keep for months if stored in a dry, cool shed out of the sun. Storage temperatures around 50°F are ideal. Pumpkins and butternuts store for 2 to 3 months; acorns and Hubbards for up to 6 months.

TO SAVE PURE SEED The different species of squash and pumpkins will not cross with each other or with gourds. Squash of the same species must be separated by $\frac{1}{2}$ mile. The different forms of gourds should be separated by $\frac{1}{4}$ to $\frac{1}{2}$ mile.

COLLECTING AND STORING SEED Allow pumpkins and winter squash to cure for 3 or 4 weeks before removing seed. Summer squash, grown for seed, should be allowed to mature and form a tough rind, as is normal for winter squash. Allow to cure for 2 weeks before removing the seed. An ax is a good tool for opening pumpkins, squash, and gourds. (Do not hold the fruit with your fingers, or you may lose them!) Rub the pulp from the seeds and rinse thoroughly. Dry and store in airtight bags under refrigeration.

SEED VIABILITY 6 years for pumpkins, squash, and gourds.

Seed Varieties

Varieties listed in 18th-century Virginia

♦ Squash: **'Cushaw', 'Simlin'**

♦ Pumpkin: **'White', 'Black'**

Heirloom varieties for the modern gardener

♦ Squash: **Cushaw, pattypan, summer crookneck, 'Pennsylvania Dutch' crookneck, 'Fordhook' acorn**

♦ Pumpkin: **'Connecticut'** field, **'Long Island'** cheese, **'Rouge Vif D'Etampes'**

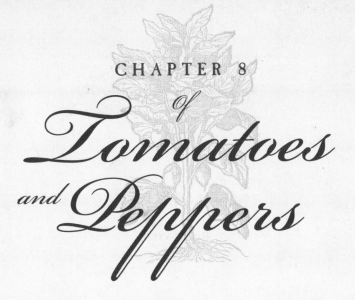

CHAPTER 8
of
Tomatoes
and *Peppers*

The nightshade, or Solanaceae, family has provided two of the most beloved garden plants known to humankind. If an American gardener grows only one plant in a vegetable garden, it will likely be a tomato. The pepper is almost as popular, as its wide array of colors, shapes, and degrees of "heat" makes it not only one of the most useful but also one of the most beautiful plants in the garden.

While both the tomato and pepper were accepted as culinary vegetables by southern Europeans shortly after they were introduced, northern Europeans and the North American colonists were slower to adopt them. The tomato was suspected of harmful effects if imprudently consumed by Englishmen whose stomachs were not suited to their acidic properties. The pepper was apparently just too spicy for Protestant temperaments.

Both the tomato and pepper made circuitous journeys from their home in the New World to the gardens of Europe and back again to North America. The tomato originated in South America, was domesticated in Mexico, and was introduced into southern Europe by Spanish explorers. The tomato was originally used as a sauce in the southern states and was peddled as pills by northern hucksters. It took a Supreme Court decision to decide whether it was a fruit or vegetable. (That august body decided in 1887 that it was a vegetable.) Around 1745, it was introduced to Williamsburg residents as a culinary plant by a Jewish doctor of Portuguese descent. Most varieties of peppers known today had already been developed before the first Europeans arrived in South and Central America. From there, peppers were introduced into Spain and the Near East and from these two centers spread to the rest of Europe. Nathaniel Butler, governor of Bermuda, received pepper seeds from England and shared them with Sir Thomas Gates, governor of Virginia, in 1621.

TOMATO

Lycopersicon lycopersicon

The tomato originated in the highlands of South America, and wild tomato plants are still found in the coastal mountains of Peru, Ecuador, and northern Chile. There is no evidence for its use among the Incas, so it is a mystery how it was transported to Central America, where it was adopted by the Aztecs in present-day Mexico. The wild tomato of South America is a small round fruit, but it was a large lumpy mutant that was found in Mexico by the conquistadors. It was first mentioned by the Franciscan priest Bernardino de Sahagún, who arrived in Mexico in 1529. He wrote that the Aztecs combined tomatoes with chile peppers and ground squash seeds to make a sauce that sounds very much like the world's first salsa.

A Golden Apple That Became the Fruit of Love

The first description of the tomato in Europe was recorded in the 1544 edition of *Commentarii in sex libros Pedacci Dioscoridis* by the Italian herbalist Pietro Andrea Matthioli. His account has been translated as: "Another species [of the Mandrake plant] has been brought to Italy in our time, flattened like the melerose [a type of apple] and segmented, green at first and when ripe of a golden color." He added that it was eaten in the same manner as eggplant, fried in oil with salt and pepper. Matthioli named it "*mala aurea*" or golden apple, suggesting that the first tomatoes introduced into Europe were orange or yellow.

A decade later, Matthioli enlarged his herbal volume and translated the Latin *mala aurea* to the Italian *pomi d'oro*. An illustrated herbaria attributed to Francesco Petrollini that was compiled sometime between 1550 and 1560 labeled the tomato as "*Malus insana, Mandragorae species Poma amoris.*" This citation appears to be the first use of *Poma amoris* or "love apple" as the name of the tomato. *Poma amoris* could simply be a mistaken transcription of Matthioli's *pomi d'oro* or, as was suggested in *Phytologiae hoc est de plantis* (1666), "*Pomum amoris* is so named because amatory powers are attributed to it or because it has a fitting elegance or beauty worthy to command love."

The French named the tomato "*pomme d'amour*," and from this the English called the fruit apples of love or simply love apples. In the second half of the 18th century, "love apple" was replaced by "tomato." As explained by Rev. William Hanbury in *A Complete Body of Planting* (1773): "The names *Love Apples* or *Mad Apples* are now grown useless, especially when talking of the Kitchen Garden produce: The fashionable term to express them is *Tomatoes.*" *Tomato* is a Spanish word and the result of a case of mistaken identity. It was borrowed from the Nahuatl (Aztec) word *tomatl*, which was actually the Aztec word for the husk tomato (*Physalis ixocarpa*).

The Ancient Tomato and Its Kinds

By the middle of the 16th century, the tomato was a well-known ornamental in European botanic gardens. In Germany, several varieties of tomato were described in *Vienna Codex* (1562): "*Malus aurea.* . . . its color usually resembles the color of gold . . . but also occurs in other colors. . . . A second kind . . . is a different color, for instance, red. . . . A third . . . in color saffron, or a whitish yellow, differs even more from the others, and has an oblong fruit."

John Parkinson described a small variety that appears to be a cherry tomato in *Paradisi in Sole* (1629): "The fruite are small, round, yellowish red berries, not much bigger then great grapes." The common tomato, however, was a medium-size lumpy

fruit as described by John Gerard in 1597: "apple of Love. . . . chamfered, uneeven, and bunched out in manie places; of a bright shining redde colour and the bignes of a Goose egge or a large pepin. . . . the whole plant is of a ranke and stinking savour."

For Ornament and Sauce

The tomato was quickly adopted for use as a sauce in Spain and Italy, but was slow to catch on in the rest of Europe. Dr. Jacques Dalechamps, a French physician, wrote in *Historia generalis plantarum* (1587): "This herb is a foreign plant not found at all in this country except in the gardens of a few herbalists. . . . it is dangerous to use them." Olivier de Serres, agronomist to the French monarch Henry IV, wrote in *The Theatre of Agriculture* (1600): "The apples of love are marvelous and golden . . . are used to cover cabinets and arbours, which they grow merrily over. Their fruit is not good to eat: they are only useful in medicine."

The English had a similar opinion. In 1629, John Parkinson recorded: "In the hot Countries where they naturally growe, they are much eaten of the people, to coole and quench the heate and thirst of their hot stomaches." In England, he explained, "Wee onely have them for curiosity in our Gardens, and for the amorous aspect or beauty of the fruit." Opinions changed very little over the next 100 years. In 1728, Richard Bradley wrote that the tomato "makes an agreeable Plant to look at, but the Fruit of most of them is dangerous."

In the middle of the 18th century, the English began to experiment with the tomato as a sauce. The 1758 supplement to Hannah Glasse's *The Art of Cookery* included, for the first time, a recipe for "*To dress Haddocks after the Spanish Way*," meaning in a tomato sauce. Some 20 years later, John Abercrombie stated: "The fruit or apples of these plants are, in some families, much used in soups, and are also often used to pickle, both when they are green, and when ripe." By the end of the century, the *Encyclopædia Britannica* recorded the tomato was "in daily use; being either boiled in soups or broths, or served up boiled as garnishes to flesh-meats."

The Tomato in North America

One of the first examples of the tomato being used as a culinary fruit occurred in Williamsburg, Virginia. Dr. John de Sequeyra arrived in Williamsburg from England around 1745 and may have brought tomato seed with him. A portrait of de Sequeyra currently housed at the Winterthur Museum in Delaware has a note on the back signed by E. Randolph Braxton that reads: "Dr. Secarri . . . was family physician to my grand-father Philip Ludwell Grymes. He first introduced into Williamsburg the custom of eating Tomatos, until then considered more of a flower than vegetable."

De Sequeyra was a Sephardic Jew of Portuguese descent, so he would have been very familiar with the culinary delights of the tomato. In the English work *Eden; or, A Compleat Body of Gardening* (1757), John Hill wrote of the tomato: "Those who are us'd to eat with the *Portuguese Jews* know the Value of it."

The tomato may have been in Williamsburg before Dr. de Sequeyra arrived. Another Williamsburg resident, John Custis, apparently sent an inquiry concerning the tomato to the English plant collector Peter Collinson. The Custis letter is lost, but Collinson replied in 1742 or 1743: "Apples of Love are very much used in Italy to putt when Ripe into their Brooths & soops giving it a pretty Tart Tast. A Lady Just come from Leghorn sayes She thinks it gives an

Agreeagle Tartness & Relish to them & she Likes it Much. They Call it Tamiata. I never yett Try'd the Experiment but I think to do It."

Custis may have observed the tomato being used by his slaves. The tomato was well known in the English West Indies and was probably transported to North America with the slave trade. William Salmon, an English physician, philosopher, and alchemist, recorded in *Botanologia* (1710): "*Of* LOVE APPLES. . . . I have seen them grow in *Carolina*, which is the South-East part of *Florida*." "Florida" during Salmon's journey through the New World was considered by some authors to be everywhere south of Virginia.

The Ascendancy of the Tomato in the American Garden

By the end of the 18th century, the tomato was well established in the Middle Atlantic states and in the

Typical 18th-century tomato shapes

South. Bernard McMahon, a Philadelphia nurseryman, recorded in *The American Gardener's Calendar* (1806): "Tomato, or Love-apple, is much cultivated for its fruit, in soups and sauces, to which it imparts an agreeable acid flavour." In 1828, the English traveler Frances Trollope recorded in Cincinnati: "From June till December, tomatoes (the great luxury of the American table in the opinion of most Europeans) may be found in the highest perfection in the market at about six-pence the peck."

The tomato was a little slower to catch on in New England. In the August 13, 1830, edition of the *New-Bedford Mercury* of Massachusetts, a subscriber wrote that the tomato was "one of the very best plants for the table, and in daily use when in season, over all parts of the country, but New England." By 1847, the tomato had assumed its place as one of the most popular of all kitchen garden plants. Robert Buist recorded that year in *The Family Kitchen Gardener*: "In taking a retrospect of the past eighteen years, there is no vegetable on the catalogue that has obtained such popularity in so short a period. . . . In 1828-9 it was almost detested; in ten years more every variety of pill and panacea was 'extract of Tomato.' It now occupies as great a surface of ground as Cabbage."

"One only seems worth cultivating for the use of the Kitchen Garden, and that is the well known . . . sort, with large, compressed, furrowed fruit."

—Rev. William Hanbury,
A Complete Body of Planting (1773)

The Williamsburg Gardener's Assistant

Methods for the raising of robust tomato transplants in the home. There is relatively little written on the culture of the tomato in 18th-century literature. They were only rarely grown in colonial Virginia and were, at best, garden curiosities in England until late in the century. The 18th-century gardener started tomatoes in frames over hotbeds; the modern gardener often starts tomatoes on windowsills or under grow lights. It is much easier to produce robust, stocky plants in a conservatory or hotbed, but by minding a few simple requirements, good-quality plants can be produced in the home.

The greatest difficulty with windowsill plants is that they tend to grow tall and spindly. To lessen this problem, the plants should be grown in a bright south window and turned every couple of days. You may also try brushing the tops of the plants with your hand several times a day, which has the same effect as wind. Plants produce their structure largely in response to environmental stresses, and by simulating wind you can grow shorter and bushier plants. Plants grown under a fluorescent grow light should have it no more than 6 inches above them, and the light should be left on at least 12 hours a day, with 14 hours being better.

Sowing the seeds and setting the tomato plants. For the earliest crop, tomatoes should be sown indoors or in hotbeds 6 to 8 weeks before the last frost. In Williamsburg, we sow the seed as instructed by *The Universal Gardener* (1778), "in pots, and plunged in a hot-bed." When the plants are 6 to 7 inches tall, and the soil temperature has warmed to over 60°F, they can be transplanted into the garden. Not much is to be gained by setting tomato plants in the garden before the weather warms, as tomatoes will not grow and set fruit until daytime temperatures are over 70°F.

Tomatoes require a deep, rich soil to sustain them throughout summer and into fall, as observed by Philip Miller in *The Gardeners Dictionary* (1754): "When they are planted in a rich moist Soil, they will grow to a prodigious Size, and produce large Quantities of Fruit." Most varieties of tomato will grow quite large and will require some type of support.

Growing tomatoes on a table. Probably the first description of a trellising method in North America is found in Robert Squibb's *The Gardener's Calendar for South-Carolina, Georgia, and North-Carolina* (1787): "Your tomatoes will now begin to run; they, being of a procumbent growth, should have sticks to support them; which should not be very high, but strong and bushy; first let one stick be set in the middle of the hill, then put three or four more round the outside of the plants, to keep them from falling to the ground." In Williamsburg, we train our tomatoes on a horizontal trellis

Tomato seedling in hotbed

similar to Squibb's brush trellis. It is fashioned in the same manner as the winter shelter for the broad beans, being a "table" of interwoven sticks approximately 20 inches high. The tomato plants grow through the sticks and lay across the top of the "table," which renders the tomatoes accessible and easily picked. This has proved to be much more convenient than growing tomatoes vertically on poles or in cages.

An abundance of fruit and fragrance. By midsummer, the vines will be loaded with fruit, and the challenge will be simply keeping up with the harvest. It is then, when the weather is warm and the days are long, that the full sensory pleasure of the tomato may be enjoyed. A vine-ripened tomato is one of the greatest luxuries of the kitchen garden, and the sharp, pungent smell of tomato leaves is the very essence of summer. But not so, apparently, for the 18th-century gardener, as Philip Miller wrote in 1754: "The Plants emit so strong an Effluvium, as renders them unfit to stand near an Habitation, or any Place that is much frequented; for upon their being brush'd by the Cloaths, they send forth a very strong disagreeable Scent." There are few gardeners today who would agree. As you work among your tomatoes, brushing by the plants will aid pollination by shaking pollen onto the flower pistils and thereby increasing fruit set and the number of tomatoes produced.

Tomato table

The end of the tomato season. When August arrives in Williamsburg and temperatures soar into the upper 90s, the tomato harvest slows, and the fruit often softens before it is fully red. At this time of year, a better-quality tomato can be had by picking the fruits while the shoulders (or upper parts) are still green and allowing them to color indoors. Once the weather cools in September, we prune the plants back, and they will produce a fall crop of smaller but still flavorful tomatoes. In Williamsburg, the harvest will continue into early November.

TOMATO ESSENTIALS

PLANTING Sow seeds for tomatoes 6 to 8 weeks before the last frost, or when the last crocuses fade. Once the danger of frost is past, plant the tomatoes in a rich soil. If the plants are leggy, bury the stems up to their first set of leaves.

SPACING The space between plants is determined by their variety and your method of trellising. Staked plants can be placed 2 feet apart; caged plants or tomatoes grown on tables are planted 3 to 4 feet apart.

FOR BEST GROWTH Tomatoes require a constant, even supply of water. Fluctuating levels of moisture, particularly in hot weather, often result in blossom end rot or in cracking.

HARVESTING Tomatoes are best when firm and fully colored. In hot weather, harvest while the shoulders of the tomato are still green and allow the fruit to ripen indoors. Harvest all remaining tomatoes before the last frost for use as pickles or fried tomatoes, or wrap them in paper to ripen over the next 3 or 4 weeks.

TO SAVE PURE SEED Most modern varieties of tomatoes will not cross-pollinate. Some potato-leaved varieties, such as the popular 'Brandywine' tomato, currant tomatoes, and some double-blossom beefsteak varieties, may possibly cross. To ensure purity within these three varieties, separate by $\frac{1}{2}$ mile.

COLLECTING AND STORING SEED Harvest a fully ripe fruit and place in a blender with a metal blade. Blend at slow speed until fruit is entirely mashed. Pour pulp and seed into a tall cup, fill with water, and stir. Place the cup in a warm place to ferment and where it will not be tipped over. This should be done outside, as it *really* stinks. Depending on the temperature, a layer of scum will form on top of the mixture in 3 to 7 days. After a thick layer of scum has formed, spoon it off, add fresh water, and pour off the rotted pulp. The viable seed will sink to the bottom. Add more water, stir, pour off the pulp, and repeat until seed is clean. Pour cleaned seed into a coffee filter and allow to dry. Refrigerate in airtight containers.

SEED VIABILITY 4 to 10 years, depending on variety

Seed Varieties

Varieties listed in 18th-century Virginia
Individual varieties were not specified but usually produced distinctly lobed fruit.

Heirloom varieties for the modern gardener
◆ **'Costoluto Genovese', 'Purple Calabash', 'Brandywine', 'Henderson's Pink Ponderosa',** and many, many more

PEPPER

Capsicum spp.

In his first letter to Ferdinand and Isabella, the Catholic monarchs of the lands that would become Spain, Christopher Columbus noted: "In these islands there are mountains where the cold this winter was very severe, but the people endure it from habit, and with the aid of the meat they eat with very hot spices." The natives called the spice *ají* (*axí*), but the Spanish borrowed the name of an Old World spice and called it *pimiento*, or pepper. Pietro Martire de Anghiera, an Italian cleric at the Spanish court in Barcelona, was present when Columbus returned from his first voyage and noted: "Something may be said about the pepper gathered in the islands and on the continent. . . . but it is not pepper, though it has the same strength and the flavour, and is just as much esteemed."

The Origin of the New World Pepper

The oldest archaeological evidence for the New World pepper comes from cave dwellings in the valley of Tehuacán, Mexico, dating to around 7000 BCE. These remains appear to come from peppers gathered in the wild. The pepper was domesticated between 5200 and 3400 BCE by indigenous tribes and spread throughout South America, Central America, the West Indies, and the southwestern portion of the United States. Gonzalo Oviedo, commander of the castle of Santo Domingo, recorded in *Historia general y natural de las Indias* (1526) what has been translated as: "The Indians everywhere grow it in gardens and farms with much diligence and attention because they eat it continuously with almost all of their food." In Mexico, the Aztecs called the pepper *chiltli*, which was translated by the Spanish as *chilli*, from which the English *chili* derives. The Franciscan friar Bernardino de Sahagún recorded circa 1569 that the food of the Aztec royalty consisted of "frog with green chilis; newt with yellow chili; tadpoles with small chilis . . . maguey grubs with a sauce of small chilis; lobster with red chili, tomatoes, and ground squash seeds."

A Global Crop of Ornament and Use

The New World pepper entered Europe from two different directions. Southern and western Europe acquired the pepper through Spain and the Iberian Peninsula. Central Europe received the pepper from the Ottoman Empire via the Balkan Peninsula. The Turkish Empire probably acquired the pepper during the sieges of the Portuguese colonies of Ormuz, Persia (1513) and/or Diu, India (1538). The Turks introduced the pepper into the Balkans, and from there it was transported to Germany, where it was recorded by Leonhart Fuchs in 1542. He classified it as "*Capsicon*," from the Latin *capsa* or *capsula,* meaning chest or box, alluding to its large seedpods.

Fuchs wrote: "There are some who call it Spanish pepper, others Indian, some even Calcutta." Because of the dual introduction of the pepper into Europe, its origin was confused, and many authors believed it to be a native of India. Gerard proposed in *The Herball* (1597) that the pepper went from India to Spain and from there to England: "These plants are brought from forren countries, as Ginnie, India, and those parts, into Spaine and Italy: from whence wee have received seede for our English gardens." The confusion over the origin of the pepper lasted for centuries. As late as 1865, Fearing Burr wrote in *The Field and Garden Vegetables of America*: "The *Capsicum annuum*, or Common Garden-pepper, is a native of India."

The first reference to the pepper in England comes from Gerard's *Herball* (1597), edited and enlarged by Johnson in 1633. Gerard recorded two forms of the pepper in 1597; Johnson added another dozen fruit forms in 1633. It was possibly in England somewhat earlier. Phillips, in *History of Cultivated Vegetables* (1822), recorded: "Guinea Pepper.–Capsicum. . . . brought to Europe by the Spaniards, and we have accounts of its being cultivated in this country as early as the reign of Edward the Sixth." Edward VI reigned from 1547 to 1553.

The American Guinea Pepper and Its Use

Gerard was the first to call it the "Ginnie" [Guinea] pepper, and this became the most commonly used name for the *Capsicum* pepper in both English and American garden books for the next 300 years. Guinea is a country on the coast of western Africa where the slave trade with the Americas originated. Enslaved Africans quickly adopted the pepper in the New World, which gave rise to its name, as "Guinea"

was nearly synonymous with "African" in common speech. As explained by Charles Bryant in *Flora Diætetica* (1783): "This plant is cultivated greatly in the Caribbee Islands, where the inhabitants, and also the Negroes, use the pods in almost all their soups and sauces, and by reason the slaves are exceedingly fond of them, the whole genus has acquired the name of *Guinea Pepper*." Most authors do not, however, believe that the pepper originated in Africa.

The pepper, like the tomato, was slow to be adopted as a culinary plant by the English. Gerard explained: "In Spaine and sundrie parts of the Indies they do use to dresse their meate therewith, as we do with Calecute pepper: but (faith my Author) it hath in it a malitious qualitie, whereby it is an enimie to the liver & other of the entrails." He also cautioned "that it killeth dogs." A hundred years later, John Evelyn recorded in *Acetaria* (1699): "*Indian Capsicum, superlatively hot and burning, is yet by the Africans*

'Bull Nose' pepper; 'Cayenne' pepper

'Sheepnose Pimento'; 'Scotch Bonnet'

eaten with *Salt* and *Vinegar* by it self, as an usual Condiment; but wou'd be of dangerous consequence with us." However, in a sign that opinions were starting to change, he went on to explain that the pepper "by Art and Mixture is notwithstanding render'd not only safe, but very agreeable in our *Sallet*."

By the 18th century, the pepper was a common ornamental in English gardens and was starting to find its way, with some prudence, into English cuisine. *The Art of Cookery*, by Hannah Glasse, was the most popular English recipe book of the 18th century. In the 1755 edition, there is a recipe that states: "*To dress a* Turtle, *the* West-India *Way*. . . . a little *Cayan* Pepper, and take Care not to put too much." This caution was repeated by many authors. Bradley, in *Dictionarium Botanicum* (1728), observed: "These make a very good Shew in a Garden . . . and when the Pods are full ripe, the Seed within them being clean'd and pounded in a Mortar is very good

to put into Sauces, but 'tis very hot, so that a little of it goes a great way."

The Kinds of Peppers

Almost all of the peppers used by Native Americans and those adopted by Europeans were varieties of *C. annuum*. Bartolomé de las Casas recorded two varieties in *Historia de las Indias* (compiled in 1502, but not published until 1876): One was long and red, likely shaped like a cayenne, and the other was round like a cherry and more pungent. The long pepper would likely be recognized as a cayenne pepper (*C. annuum* var. *annuum*), while the round, hotter pepper was the bird pepper or chiltepin pepper (*C. annuum* var. *glabriusculum*).

The cayenne pepper is named for the capital city of French Guiana on the northern coast of South America. Originally *cayenne* (spelled many ways) referred not to a particular pepper variety but to a preparation of dried pepper generally made from the bird pepper. Philip Miller recorded in the 1754 edition of *The Gardeners Dictionary*: "The Inhabitants of the *West-Indies* make great Use of the Bird-pepper; which they dry, and beat to a Powder, and mix with other Ingredients . . . they send some of these Pepper-pots to *England*, by the Name of Cayan Butter or Pepper-pot; and are by some of the *English* People mightily esteem'd."

The first reference to the milder bell pepper came from Lionel Wafer, an English buccaneer who listed two varieties of peppers in Panama in 1681: "one called *Bell-Pepper*, the other *Bird-Pepper*." Seven years later, Sir Hans Sloane recorded in Jamaica: "I saw them [African slaves] likewise here Preserve, or Pickle Green *Indian*-Bell-Pepper. Before it turns red, this *Capsicum* is cut and cleansed from its Seeds, then has a gentle Boil in Water, and so is put into a Pickle of Lime Juice, Salt and Water, and kept for use." The English commonly used the pepper as a pickle, and of all the varieties used for pickles, the bell pepper was the favorite. John Abercrombie observed of the pepper in 1778: "And for useful purposes, the young or half-grown fruit is esteemed the finest pickle in the world."

There are a few examples of peppers other than *C. annuum* in the historic record. The German *Hortus Eystettensis* (1613) and the English *Florilegium of Alexander Marshal* (circa 1653) include illustrations of an upright pepper that appears to be a variety of *C. frutescens*, very similar to the Tabasco pepper. In the 1754 edition of *The Gardeners Dictionary,* Philip Miller listed a "Bonnet Pepper" that may be a reference to the 'Scotch Bonnet', a *C. chinensis* variety closely related to the habanero pepper. *C. chinense* was named by the 18th-century Dutch botanist Nikolaus Joseph von Jacquin in the mistaken belief that it originated in China. Recently, botanists have concluded that there is no discernible difference between *C. frutescens* and *C. chinense,* and it has been proposed that they be combined under *C. frutescens.*

The Pepper in America

Although the pepper reportedly arrived in North America aboard the ship *Elizabeth* at Jamestown, Virginia, in 1621, there are no references to peppers in 17th-century Virginia documents. It is likely that the pepper was introduced into North America from the West Indies, at many times at many ports, as part of commerce and the slave trade. The earliest reference to the pepper in Virginia comes from Francis Michel, a Swiss traveler in Tidewater, Virginia, from 1701 to 1702. He recorded: "There also grows a sort of red shells, like crab's claws, in which seeds are found which are very strong." In 1732, William Hugh Grove listed "red pepper" among the vegetables found in Virginia. In Williamsburg, John Randolph gave the pepper only a single sentence in *A Treatise on Gardening*, which suggests that it was only a minor part of the Virginia diet: "PEPPER, *Capsicum* . . . shou'd be sown in April, and should be gathered before the pods grow hard for pickles."

Early in the 19th century, Bernard McMahon gave a more optimistic assessment of the nightshade family in *The American Gardener's Calendar* (1806): "The different varieties of the Capsicums, Tomatoes, and Eggplants, being in much estimation for culinary purposes; you should sow some of each kind." McMahon listed the "Red or Guinea," "Long-podded," "Heart-shaped," "Bell," and "Cherry" peppers.

"Its vulgar Name is *Guinea Pepper*. . . . The Fruit is very large, long, thick, and of a glossy Surface. Its Colour is an elegant Scarlet, and it resembles polish'd Coral."

—John Hill, *Eden; or, A Compleat Body of Gardening* (1757)

The Williamsburg Gardener's Assistant

The production of pepper transplants. Because peppers require a long, warm season to mature their fruit, they are almost always set in the garden as transplants. We sow pepper seed on a hotbed in March, as instructed by John Abercrombie in *The Universal Gardener and Botanist* (1778): "The seed may then either be sown on the surface, or in small drills, or in pots, plunging them in the mould, observing in either method to cover it [the seed] about a quarter of an inch deep: the plants will soon appear, observing to give air daily in common with other plants of the bed, by tilting up the light."

The more air you can give the plants in the hotbed frames by raising the window sashes, the better-quality seedlings you will produce. As soon as the weather warms, we take every opportunity to remove the sashes entirely during the day, replacing them at night, until the seedlings are ready to transplant.

When it will be safe to put the peppers in the garden. Peppers do not tolerate cold soils and may be deformed by nighttime temperatures below 55°F, so there is absolutely no benefit to placing pepper plants in the garden too early in spring. After the weather has warmed, with nighttime temperatures consistently over 60°F, the seedlings may be moved from the hotbed frame. Abercrombie recommended the peppers "should be planted out in a rich warm border, in the kitchen-garden, in rows a foot and a half or two feet distance, and about fifteen inches distant in the line."

The support of peppers. As the plants begin to grow, some method of supporting them must be adopted. William Hanbury commented on this in *A Complete Body of Planting* (1773): "Capsicums are very easily raised from seeds, but it requires nice attendance and management to bring them to perfection. It is naturally an irregular-growing plant; and if it meets with bad management, or is checked in its progress, it will then be deformed, and excite but little pleasure to behold it."

Rev. Hanbury was growing peppers as ornamentals, but those intended for cookery will also need some type of support to keep them from breaking apart in summer storms. We have found that a teepee of five sticks placed firmly in the ground and tied together at the top over each plant is a quick, easy way to support them.

Peppers in hotbed; pepper supports; pulling pepper plants at end of season

The watering and harvesting of peppers. Once the plants begin to flower and set fruit, careful attention must be paid to watering. Philip Miller instructed in *The Gardeners Dictionary* (1768) that the plants must be "duly watered in dry weather; which will greatly promote their growth, and cause them to be more fruitful, as also enlarge the size of the fruit." If the larger peppers, such as bell peppers and pimientos, form dark sunken spots on their fruit, it will be a sign that the watering has not been sufficiently uniform.

In Williamsburg, the first peppers are ready for harvest by the middle of July, and the plants will continue to produce through September, when they are pulled up to make room for the winter garden. The fruit is attached to the plants by tough stalks, and pepper stems are quite brittle and easily broken. A sharp knife or a small pair of secateurs (pruners) will greatly facilitate the harvest.

PEPPER ESSENTIALS

PLANTING Sow pepper seeds in a hotbed or indoors, when daffodils bloom. Sow seed ¼ inch deep and keep the soil continually moist. Transplant to the garden after nighttime temperatures remain above 60°F.

SPACING There is some size difference among varieties, but placing plants 15 inches apart in rows 2 feet distant will serve for most.

FOR BEST GROWTH Peppers require a rich, moisture-retentive soil to produce quality fruit in the hottest months. Mulch can be particularly beneficial.

HARVESTING Most peppers are harvested in a mature stage with fully formed seeds. Sweet peppers for pickles or hot peppers for green chile peppers are harvested as immature fruit. For the hotter varieties, thin disposable gloves are a good idea.

TO RAISE PURE SEED Separate pepper varieties by 500 feet.

COLLECTING AND STORING SEED Harvest seed when peppers are fully mature. Carefully separate the outer flesh from the internal core to which the seeds are attached. For the larger peppers, the seeds can be scraped from the core with a paring knife. Place the smaller peppers in a blender and process at a slow speed until the seeds are separated. This should be done in a well-ventilated place for the hotter peppers, as the fumes are dangerous. Gloves should also be worn when processing the hotter varieties. The good seeds will sink to the bottom of the solution. Pour the top off and repeat until the seeds are clean. Allow the seeds to dry thoroughly before storing in refrigerated airtight containers. Completely dry seeds will snap in two when folded.

SEED VIABILITY 3 years

Seed Varieties

Varieties listed in 18th-century Virginia

♦ '**Cayenne**', '**Indian**', '**Piperone**'

Heirloom varieties for the modern gardener

♦ '**Cayenne**': A hot pepper that has changed little from the 18th-century type

♦ '**Bull Nose**': A sweet pepper similar to bell pepper

♦ '**Tomato**': Pimiento-type fruit

♦ '**Scotch Bonnet**'

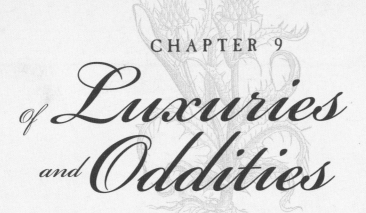

CHAPTER 9
of Luxuries and Oddities

Among the vegetables that distinguished a gentleman's garden in 18th-century Virginia were the artichoke and closely related cardoon; celery and closely related celeriac; and asparagus. Artichoke, celery, and asparagus have long been associated with wealth, partly because they require specialized techniques to cultivate successfully. Cardoon, a popular vegetable in southern Europe, and celeriac, best known in northern Europe, were both oddities in 18th-century Williamsburg gardens and remain so today.

Both the artichoke and cardoon evolved from a Mediterranean plant, *Cynara cardunculus* var. *sylvestris*. This very prickly ancestor is found over a wide area of the Mediterranean basin and has been cultivated or collected in the wild by southern Europeans for thousands of years. The artichoke was probably domesticated in the 1st century CE in Sicily. The cardoon was domesticated somewhat later in the western Mediterranean, likely in Spain. Both celery and celeriac were developed from wild populations of *Apium graveolens*, known to the ancient apothecaries as smallage. Smallage was used almost exclusively as a medicinal plant. Celery was developed in Italy, probably in the 16th century, but it was not until the 18th century that celery was accepted by the English as a culinary crop. Once adopted, it quickly became a common ingredient in English soups and salads. Asparagus has undoubtedly been gathered in the wild for thousands of years, but the earliest descriptions of asparagus seem to refer to the spiny asparagus (*Asparagus acutifolius*). It is not clear when or where the modern asparagus (*A. officinalis*) emerged as a domesticated plant. It may be yet another vegetable introduced into Europe from Moorish Spain.

Both the artichoke and asparagus were introduced into Virginia gardens in the 17th century. As in England, celery did not appear until the 18th century.

ARTICHOKE and CARDOON
Cynara cardunculus

Artichoke and cardoon are both members of the thistle family, which includes some of the most painfully pernicious weeds known to humankind. While thistles have long been used in medicine, the use of the primitive artichoke as a culinary plant, reserved for the wealthy, was a source of amazement to Pliny the Elder. He wrote in his *Natural History* (circa 77 CE): "Alas for the monstrosities of gluttony! It would surprise us if cattle were not allowed to feed on thistles, but thistles are forbidden to the lower orders! . . . we turn even the monstrosities of the earth to purposes of gluttony, and actually grow vegetables which all four-footed beasts without exception shrink from touching."

An Ancient Thistle

At one time, the artichoke and cardoon were considered to be different species: Artichoke was *Cynara scolymus,* and cardoon was *C. cardunculus.* DNA analysis has reunited them as varieties of the same species. Artichoke is now classified, depending on the author, as *C. cardunculus* var. *scolymus*; Cardoon is now classified as *C. cardunculus* var. *altilis.*

Both Greek and Roman writers recorded eating a thistle that often has been identified since as the ancestor of the artichoke and cardoon, but interpretations of the ancient literature are uncertain. Sir Arthur Hort's 1916 translation of Theophrastus's (371–287 BCE) work, *Enquiry into Plants,* reported: "But the plant called *kaktos* grows only in Sicily, and

> "The *cinara* is a kind of cultivated *carduus* of which we eat the topmost fruit."
>
> —Charles Estienne, *De re hortensi libellus* (1536)

not in Hellas [Greece]. It is a plant quite different from any other; for it sends up straight from the root stems . . . its leaf is broad and spinous: these stems are called *kaktoi*; they are edible, if peeled, and are slightly bitter." A characteristic of the cardoon that is either prized or disliked by modern diners is the bitter taste of the stalk, which as Theophrastus pointed out, must be peeled. If this is a reference to a primitive *Cynara,* it suggests that the first use of the plant was for its leaf stems, as cardoon is used today.

The Artichoke Travels North

The artichoke apparently remained a local specialty of Sicily and perhaps southern Italy for hundreds of years. Arabs, who controlled Sicily for just over 200 years beginning in the 9th century, likely introduced the artichoke into the rest of Italy. The modern name *artichoke* derives from the Arabic *al kharshuff.* The first reliable record of the artichoke in Italy came from Filipo Strozzi, who recorded artichokes in Florence in 1460. Pietro Matthioli, a 16th-century doctor and naturalist, recorded that the artichoke was introduced into Florence in 1466 from Naples, again suggesting a southern origin. Hermolai Barbari wrote in *In Dioscoridem corollariorum* (1530) that artichokes were not always found in Italian gardens in Venice but more commonly in the Moorish quarter, suggesting that it was Arabs living in Italy who introduced the custom of eating artichokes to the Italians.

The Artichoke in England and Its Several Forms

From Italy, the artichoke spread to the rest of Europe. The first reference to the artichoke in England is found in Thomas Fromond's "Herbys necessary for a gardyn by letter," written about 1500. By the end of the 16th century, the artichoke was a well-known luxury, according to *The Gardener's Labyrinth* (1577): "The Artochoke which before grew wilde in the fieldes, came by diligence . . . to bee carefully bestowed in the Garden, where through travell, broughte from his wildernesse, to serve unto the use of the mouth and bellie. The Artochoke growing with thicke scalie eares, in forme to the pinaple, and sufficiently knowen to most persons."

By the 16th century, several forms of the artichoke had been developed. Richard Surflet recorded in a 1616 English translation of the 1564 French work *L'Agriculture et Maison Rustique*: "For of Artichokes there be divers kinds; as the round and the long, the red and the greene: the round, which is greene, is a good Artichoke, so is the red, although it be long, yet the soale is but thinne, neither is the leafe verie substantiall, only it is exceeding pleasant in tast: the greene, which is long, is of all sorts the worst." John Gerard listed two types of artichoke, and for the first time, mentioned the cardoon in *The Herball* (1597): "There be three sorts of Artichokes, two tame or of the garden; and one wilde, which the Italian esteemeth greatly of, as the best to be eaten rawe, which he calleth *Cardune*."

A Rare and Expensive Delicacy

In England, as it had been in Italy, the artichoke was a delicacy reserved for the aristocracy. At Wimbledon Manor in the south of London, an entire garden was given over to artichokes. As recorded in the Parliamentary Survey done in 1649: "There is one parcel of land belonging to the said upper garden, containing forty four perches of land, called the Hartichoke Garden . . . the ground whereof is ordered for the growth of hartichokes . . . but the roots and plants of hartichokes therein now growing and planted we value at £1. 10s." John Evelyn wrote in *Acetaria* (1699): "'Tis not very long since this noble *Thistle* came first into *Italy*, Improv'd to this Magnitude by Culture; and so rare in *England*, that they were commonly sold for *Crowns* a piece."

The cardoon was much less familiar to the English than was the artichoke. John Parkinson recorded in *Paradisi in Sole* (1629): "The Chardon as they call it. . . . John Tradescante assured mee, hee saw three

'Green Globe' artichoke; cardoon flowers

acres of Land about Brussels planted with this kinde, which the owner whited like Endive . . . Wee cannot yet finde the true manner of dressing them, that our Countrey may take delight therein." Attitudes toward the cardoon changed little over the centuries. In 1790, John Abercrombie wrote in *The Garden Vade Mecum*: "[Cardoon] is but in small request, only in some particular families." To this day, those families are most commonly of southern European descent.

The Artichoke in America

The artichoke was introduced into the American colonies by the middle of the 17th century. An anonymous work titled *A Perfect Description of Virginia* (1649) listed a number of vegetables found in Virginia gardens: "That they have Roots of severall kindes, *Potatoes, Sparagus, Carrets Turnips Parsnips Onions*, and *Hartichokes*." This work was written in England as an advertisement for prospective immigrants to Virginia, so it cannot be considered a first-person account. A more reliable account was that of Adriaen van der Donck, a former resident of present-day New York, who recorded artichokes in *A Description of the New Netherlands* (1655).

As in Europe, the artichoke was a luxury found only in the gardens of the gentry. William Hugh Grove, a visitor to Tidewater, Virginia, in 1732, recorded: "Curl'd Savoys are Plenty but few Colyflowers or Hartichoak tho' the Gentry sometimes rayse a few." This was probably because artichokes are difficult to raise in Virginia, and it was only the gentry who had leisure to attempt so extravagant a crop. This was also suggested by Hugh Jones in *The Present State of Virginia* (1724): "The worst Thing in their Gardens, that I know, is the Artichoak; but this I attribute to Want of Skill and good Management." Nevertheless, artichokes were clearly an important part of a gentleman's garden and a popular vegetable on his table. William Byrd II, a member of the Governor's Council and one of the wealthiest men in Virginia, recorded in his diary in 1711: "I ate some boiled pork for dinner and was angry with Moll for neglecting to boil some artichokes."

The artichoke never became a common vegetable in the American garden. In 1847, Robert Buist wrote in *The Family Kitchen Gardener*: "THE Artichoke is principally cultivated in the gardens of the French, by whom it is considered more as a luxury than a profitable esculent [vegetable fit to be eaten]." The cardoon is even rarer in the American garden; when it is grown today, it is often grown as an ornamental and not eaten at all.

Seed Varieties

Varieties listed in 18th-century Virginia

♦ Artichokes: **'Artichoke'**, **'Globe Artichoke'**

♦ Cardoons: Individual varieties were not specified.

Heirloom varieties for the modern gardener

♦ Artichokes: **'Green Globe'**: Round artichoke that will usually set fruit in first year

♦ **'Violetta di Chioggia'**: Purple artichoke with pointed head

♦ **'Romanesco'**: Southern Italian artichoke with red-

dish coloration, similar to the 18th-century artichoke; difficult to grow in Virginia

♦ Cardoons: Cardoons are generally divided between spiny and spineless varieties.

♦ **'Giant Roman'**: few spines

The Williamsburg Gardener's Assistant

A perennial for the South, an annual for the North. Ideal artichoke weather is cool and moist: days of about 70°F and nights in the mid 50s. Artichokes will tolerate temperatures in the 80s, but in hotter weather, they often become tough and bitter. Artichokes are perennial plants, and for the production of premier flower buds (which is what artichokes are), the plants must be overwintered. This becomes very difficult north of Virginia, and in colder climes, artichokes must be grown as annuals. Fortunately for the modern gardener, the variety 'Imperial Star' was developed to be grown as an annual and reliably forms flower buds within 90 days of setting out. The most commonly available variety today is 'Green Globe', and it, too, can generally be grown as an annual coming to flower somewhat later than 'Imperial Star'.

The 18th-century gardener almost always propagated artichokes from divisions, or slips, taken from mature plants. On some Virginia plantations, they were grown on a large scale. Landon Carter produced enough slips to provide for his own plantation and to share with his neighbors. As he recorded in a 1772 letter: "I sent Giberne 2 dozen Artichoke slips and Dr. Jones one dozen yesterday; and to Mr. Lee of Stratford this day 19 dozen."

What skills are necessary to divide your artichokes. The method of dividing artichokes for slips was explained by Philip Miller in *The Gardeners Dictionary* (1768): "Remove all the earth from about your stock, down below the part from whence the young shoots are produced, clearing the earth from between the shoots with the hands." Once the roots are revealed, Miller directed: "Then make choice of two of the clearest, straitest, and most promising plants that are produced from the under part of the stalk,

Dividing artichokes

which are much preferable to the strong thick plants which generally grow upon the crown of the roots." We use a spade to split the most promising slips from the plant. Artichokes and cardoons are best divided in spring, while they are less than 1 foot tall.

The proper situation for artichokes. Artichokes are large plants that require lots of sun, moisture, and nutrients. For location, John Abercrombie suggested in 1778: "With respect to situation and soil for these plants . . . they are the most prosperous in a some-

what moist soil; but, if possible, avoid planting them in wet ground, as in such the plants would be in danger of rotting." In heavy clay soils, artichokes are best grown in raised beds or on large hills.

"Having fixed on the ground," Abercrombie continued, "lay thereon a considerable coat of rotten dung [compost], spreading it equally over every part; then trench the ground one good spade deep . . . as you proceed, bury the dung equally in the bottom of the trenches." Soil preparation is particularly important for gardeners who are able to overwinter artichokes, as

(Top) Seedling artichoke with crown above ground; multiple artichokes on stem; (bottom) artichoke cut down and sprouting in fall; twig dome; spring artichokes under bells

the plants will need to remain productive in the same spot for 3 or 4 years before they are lifted and divided.

In 18th-century Williamsburg, John Randolph recommended planting three slips per hill: "If you have plenty of ground put three slips in a hill and let the hills be four feet asunder, and the rows the same, but if you are scanty with regard to your land, you must cut your coat according to your cloth."

Growing artichokes from seed. Today most gardeners start their artichokes from seed, which should be sown for a spring planting 6 to 8 weeks before the last frost. Artichoke plants require 8 to 10 days of about 50°F nighttime temperatures to initiate the formation of flower buds, so the plants should be set in the garden before the weather becomes too warm. Artichoke seed does not produce reliably uniform plants; up to 20 percent of artichokes started from seed will produce plants with inferior traits. Choose only the largest, best-formed plants to transplant to the garden. When planting out, make sure that the crown of the plant is not buried, as this will retard its growth.

A strategy for artichokes in smaller areas. Because of the large area required for growing artichokes, many 18th-century market gardeners would double-crop the artichoke bed. As explained in *The Universal Gardener and Botanist* (1778): "If it is necessary to make the most of every piece of ground, as is consequently the case with the market gardeners, you may sow between the rows a crop of round-leafed spinach, with some short-topped radish, and a sprinkling of coss lettuce, mixing the seeds together, and sow them by broad-cast." These will be ready for harvest in early spring, before the artichokes start to produce their flower buds.

Several methods for the harvesting of artichokes. Once the flower buds start to form, the ground must be kept continually moist to produce the highest quality artichokes. In addition, a layer of mulch will be beneficial. As explained by Stephen Switzer in 1727: "As soon as the fruit . . . begin to appear, they must be watered plentifully, especially if it be a dry soil,

and a dry season, laying grass-muck, or any other long stuff or dung [compost], to the roots, to keep them moist, for herein depends the largeness and goodness that is to be expected in a good artichoke."

The terminal, or top, artichoke will be the largest one on the stem. The artichokes formed below this terminal bud will be progressively smaller. Many 18th-century gardeners raised their plants to produce only the terminal bud. To produce the largest artichoke, the lateral buds that sprouted along the stem were removed. As instructed by Abercrombie in 1778: "Observe, that, besides the principal or top fruit, several collateral small heads often arise from the sides of the main stem, which side-shoots, or suckers, being displaced, the whole nourishment is consequently directed to the principal head; therefore if you prefer one large handsome head to three or four small ones, the above culture should be constantly practiced, from time to time, before the side heads exceed the size of a hen's egg."

Abercrombie also gave the gardener another option: "But some persons, not anxious about having very large heads, suffer the above mentioned side-shoots to remain, rather preferring three or four middling ones, from the same stem." This is how we manage our artichokes in Williamsburg.

The artichokes will be ready to harvest when the bottom scales begin to open. As Abercrombie explained: "The maturity of the Artichoke heads, is, when arrived to their full magnitude, discoverable by the scales diverging from each other considerably, but before the centre or crown opens. . . . When the heads are to be gathered, you should cut them with six or eight inches of the stalk." After the artichokes are harvested, cut the flower stems to the ground. As Abercrombie concluded: "As the heads are gathered, the whole stalk should always be broken down close to the ground, being absolutely necessary to the welfare of the plants, by encouraging their stools to produce some new shoots more freely before winter."

Preserving artichokes for winter. In Williamsburg, we cut the entire plant to the ground after the last artichoke is harvested. The plants typically go dormant in

August and then start growing again as the weather cools in fall. By late November, the plants are grown to their full size and must be made ready for freezing weather. To protect them for winter, remove the larger, outer stems and pull soil up around the plants. At the same time, refresh the mulch. As John Randolph advised in 18th-century Williamsburg: "The best way to preserve them is by laying straw on the surface of the ground over their roots. This preserves the leaves from rotting, which fall down from the frost, and united,

afford such a protection to the plant that not one in fifty will perish." We have not had as good a success rate as Randolph, so we provide additional protection with a dome made from sticks, over which we lay canvas at night when the temperature is forecast to go below 28°F.

Even with this added protection, the plants do not always survive winter. In January, artichokes are started from seed in the hotbed frame and are ready to be set out in early April. The mature plants that passed winter in the open ground will produce the first and largest artichokes of the season in May, followed in June by the plants sown on the January hotbed.

The raising and blanching of cardoon. Cardoon was almost always grown as annuals by 18th-century gardeners. John Rutter gave these instructions in *Modern Eden* (1767): "About the twentieth of March, dig up a bed for the seed one spade depth . . . scatter on the seeds not too thick. When the plants appear, thin them to three or four inches distance. . . . When they are strong enough to transplant, dig up a fresh bed . . . and mark it out by lines a yard and half asunder. Take up the plants, and set them carefully at a yard distance."

By midsummer, the plants will be ready for blanching, which greatly lessens the bitterness so characteristic

(Top) Preparing cardoons for blanching; (bottom) cardoons tied up for blanching and harvested

of cardoon. Rutter explained the process: "As they grow up the mould must be drawn up about them in a kind of hills, to near the tops of the stalks. When they are thus brought to be tall and strong, the tops of all the foot-stalks must be gathered together, and tied round with a parcel of bass [twine], and the mould [soft, loose soil] then is to be drawn up about them in a large hill, nearly to their tops. They will thus blanch very perfectly, and will be a yard high, and as white as cream, perfectly tender, and fine tasted: to keep up a succession of them for a considerable time, there need not be repeated sowings of the seed; only the plants should be earthed up in succession, a certain number every fortnight or three weeks." In Williamsburg, we do not have much call for cardoon at the table, so we grow it as both a summer ornamental and a fall vegetable. The plant is allowed to grow to its full size and come to flower in July. The spectacular show of bright blue thistle flowers on 5-foot stems is a marvel to visitors to the garden. After the blooms have faded, the plant is cut to the ground, and like the artichoke, will go dormant for the hottest weeks of summer. In fall, cardoon will resume growth, and once the leaves are about 3 feet tall, we select two well-spaced shoots springing from the mother plant and remove the rest. These two shoots are tied up and then wrapped with paper to exclude the light. In 5 or 6 weeks, the stems will be sufficiently whitened to be harvested. After they are cut, the stems are peeled with a sharp knife and are then ready for the chef.

Cardoon is more cold-hardy than is the artichoke, and a simple mulch of pine straw is generally sufficient to overwinter it in Williamsburg.

ARTICHOKE AND CARDOON ESSENTIALS

PLANTING Divide artichoke plants in early spring, before the shoots are 1 foot tall. Seed artichokes on a hotbed in January before the crocuses bloom, and in a seedbed in August when the phlox and asters are at their height of flower. Cardoon is started from seed sown in the open ground in late March or early April, when the first tulips bloom.

SPACING Artichokes and cardoons are both large plants and should be spaced a minimum of 4 feet apart. Cardoons that are grown as annuals for their blanched stems can be spaced 3 feet apart.

FOR BEST GROWTH Artichokes and cardoons are heavy feeders with an extensive root system and require a deep, rich soil. Both suffer in a poorly drained clay soil. Artichokes, in particular, must be kept continually moist when the flower buds are forming.

HARVESTING Harvest artichokes when the bottom scales begin to spread but while the central scales are still tight. Cardoon requires 4 to 5 weeks to blanch.

TO SAVE PURE SEED Artichokes do not usually come true from seed, so in order to save a desired cultivar, they are best propagated from divisions. To collect seeds from artichoke or cardoon, the flower heads are best enclosed with plastic bags to prevent cross-pollination. Once a day, remove the bags and brush the flower heads back and forth, to transfer the pollen within the individual heads. We have not had very good luck raising viable seed in Williamsburg for either cardoon or artichoke.

COLLECTING AND STORING SEED After the flowers have been pollinated, allow them to mature and produce their white dandelion-like seed plumes. Once the heads are completely opened, they are cut with about 6 inches of stem. They are hung or stored in a dry room, out of the sun, until they are hard and brittle. Put each head in a burlap bag and bang the base of the head with a hammer. This will dislodge the seed and help to separate the seed plume. Refrigerate seed in airtight containers.

SEED VIABILITY Both artichoke and cardoon seed will remain viable for 7 years.

CELERY and CELERIAC
Apium graveolens

Celery, in its primitive form, was well known to the ancient Greek and Roman writers as a medicinal plant and was recommended for every malady from kidney stones to hangovers. Leonhart Fuchs recorded one of its more popular uses in *De Historia Stirpium* (1542): "It makes women more eager for love-making." By the 17th century, the first modern-looking celery plants found their way to the kitchen. These celery plants still retained some of their medicinal virtues, as explained by Giacomo Castelvetro in 1614: "It is warm, and has great digestive and generative powers, and for this reason young wives often serve celery to their elderly or impotent husbands."

How a Medicine Was Brought to the Table

The wild form of celery, known as smallage, is found over a wide range of Europe and western Asia, from Sweden to Iran and west to Pakistan. Theophrastus (371–287 BCE), the Greek philosopher and father of botany, listed horse celery, mountain celery, and marsh celery in *Enquiry into Plants* and wrote that there were both wild and domesticated forms of the marsh celery. Horse celery was likely an alexander, mountain celery was probably parsley, and marsh celery was probably the ancient celery known by the English as smallage. Smallage is a highly aromatic and bitter herb used almost exclusively as a medicine.

The first writer to suggest a culinary use for smallage was John Gerard in the 1597 *Herball*: "This is not wonted to be eaten, neither is it counted good for sauce, but it is not unprofitable for medicine." Gerard's intimation that it was eaten at all probably came from its use in Italy. It was during the 16th century that the modern celery (*Apium graveolens* var. *dulce*) began to emerge as a culinary plant in Italy, but

it remained a rarity on English tables until the 18th century. John Laurence wrote in *A New System of Agriculture* (1727): "It . . . hath not been long from *Italy* introduced amongst us: But now it most deservedly obtains a Place not only in raw Sallads, but also in Soops and Pottages." By the end of the century, celery had become an indispensable part of English cookery and was planted and harvested nearly year-round. John Abercrombie observed in *Every Man His Own Gardener* (1776): "In some families, these plants are required every day."

A Late Arrival to North America

When celery first came to North America is a mystery. It was not recorded in Virginia until 1759, when "Italian Cellery" was included in a list of vegetable seeds advertised for sale in Williamsburg in the *Virginia Gazette* by Christopher Ayscough. Ayscough was the gardener at the Governor's Palace and presumably was ordering extra seeds to sell along with the seeds ordered for the governor's household. This suggests that celery was still a rarity in Virginia and likely found primarily in gentry gardens. Celery in the 18th century had to be blanched, or it would be strong flavored and stringy. This may explain why it was found only in gardens whose owners had the leisure or the labor for such work. For those who could afford it, however, celery was a prized esculent, or edible vegetable. Thomas Jefferson, while serving as secretary of state during the Washington administration, wrote home to Monticello to remind his son-in-law, Thomas Mann Randolph: "From a feeling of self interest I would propose a great provision of Celery plants to be made."

The original celery had pithy, hollow stems, but by the 18th century, improved varieties with solid stems had been developed. Bernard McMahon recorded several forms in *The American Gardener's Calendar* (1806): "There are several varieties, viz. common upright celery with hallow stalks, solid-stalked celery; red-stalked solid celery, &c [etc.]." McMahon also observed that "The best kinds to sow, are the solid, and red stalked celery." Solid-stalked celery entirely replaced the old hollow-stemmed variety by the middle of the 19th century.

A Curious Root

Celeriac (*A. graveolens* var. *rapaceum*) may have been used as a culinary crop for its root for longer than celery has been used for its stem. In 1536, Ruellius recorded in the French work *De natura stirpium* that the root of smallage is eaten, both raw and cooked. In Germany, Jo. Baptista Porta wrote in *Villae* (1592) what has been translated as: "There is another kind of celery called Capitatum, which is grown in the gardens of St. Agatha, Theano and other places. . . . Its bulb is spherical, nearly of the size of a man's head. It is very sweet, odorous and grateful."

In England, celeriac was a rarity. Stephen Switzer wrote a curious little book in 1729 entitled *A Compendious Method for the Raising of the Italian Brocoli, Spanish Cardoon, Celeriac, Finochi, and Other Foreign Kitchen-Vegetables.* These were the newest and most exotic vegetables of the day. Celeriac was so unusual that Switzer had never actually seen the plant; he gave an account of an entirely different plant in its place. He wrote: "The Celeriac is the next Herb I have endeavoured to promote the Use of; those who have eat it abroad say, that it is much better than common Celery. . . . I must confess I don't know it by that Name, nor do any of the Seedsmen that I have met with at this End of Town." The plant Switzer had acquired from Alexandria in the mistaken belief that it was celeriac was actually Italian celery, used for its stalk. Thomas Knowlton, who Switzer described in 1727 as "a very ingenious Person in the *North*, who has the Care of some considerable Gardens belonging to a Noble Lord [Earl Burlington]," wrote to correct the

Celeriac

mistake: "The Description of that good Plant which you suppose to be the *Italian-Celery*, (tho' very different from it) I presume to send you this Account of it." He then went on to give an accurate description of celeriac.

By the middle of the 18th century, celeriac was listed by most English garden writers as an easy to grow but inferior substitute for celery. John Rutter summed up the general opinion in *Modern Eden* (1767): "Some are fond of the thick-rooted celery, which is called celeriac; but it is less delicate than the former. However as it is raised with little trouble, it is worth while to have a bed of it."

Celeriac was even less common in North America. In Williamsburg, celeriac seed was listed for sale only at the John Carter store. Randolph included celeriac in his *Treatise on Gardening,* but Thomas Jefferson, who experimented with virtually every vegetable variety of the time, did not mention celeriac in his *Garden Book* (1766–1824) or in his correspondence.

The Williamsburg Gardener's Assistant

Celery as a demanding crop and a reluctant seed. Celery is not the easiest vegetable to grow. It requires a long cool season, ample moisture, and abundant fertility. English gardeners had the benefit of a nearly perfect climate and grew celery year-round in the 18th century. Most parts of America present a more challenging climate.

In the northern states, celery is best grown as a spring crop, and the seeds should be sown on a hotbed or in a conservatory 10 to 12 weeks before the date of the last projected frost. Celery seed is very slow to germinate, taking 2 weeks or more for the seedlings to appear. Some gardeners soak the seed overnight, but it is probably more important that the seeds be only lightly covered and kept evenly moist. Germination is stimulated by sunlight, which is why the seeds should not be buried more than $^1/_8$ inch deep. Set the transplants into the garden as soon as nighttime temperatures remain above 50°F.

In Williamsburg, we find that the fall season is the most accommodating for a crop of celery. Germinating seed in late summer for a fall crop, however, is quite a bit more difficult, as celery seed germination is inhibited by soil temperatures above 70°F. If started in an outdoor seedbed, a covering made of a gauzy fabric will help to cool the soil and prevent rain showers from washing the seed from the bed. Seed will often require a month to germinate at this time of year.

For both the spring and fall crop, the seedlings must be managed so that their growth is in no way impeded. For more than any other vegetable in the garden, the quality of the soil will determine the delicacy of the crop. Walter Nicol described the perfect soil in *The Scotch Forcing and Kitchen Gardener* (1798): "The soil best adapted to the production of Cellery, is a rich loam of a middling texture; and the fittest manure is a composition of stable dung, and vegetable earth." Above all, whether or not animal dung is

Celery seedlings under shade

used, the gardener must prepare a deep, organically enriched, moisture-retentive soil.

To prevent the plants from becoming bitter and stringy, they must be shaded in hot weather. In Williamsburg, John Randolph observed: "The sun is a great enemy to Celery, when it is very hot, wherefore I would recommend the covering of you[r] plants with brush, at all seasons of their growth, whilst the weather is hot, from 9 in the morning till 6 o'clock in the evening." We have had good success with fall-grown celery by planting it in a row on the edge of the garden where it receives shade from a nearby hedgerow in the afternoon.

The benefit of blanching celery. The 18th-century varieties of celery had to be blanched to make them palatable. The modern self-blanching celery is not as strongly flavored but is still much improved by blanching. For those who prize the hearts of celery, the entire plant can be made of that quality through blanching.

Gardeners in 18th-century Williamsburg blanched their celery in trenches, in accordance with the instruc-

Celery seedlings; blanching celery in trench; harvested celery

"As the heat of the sun now increases, you must shade the celery seed-bed from ten to three o'clock every day."

—James Garton, *The Practical Gardener, and Gentleman's Directory* (1770)

tions found in *The Gardener's Pocket-Calendar* (1776): "Dig a trench ten inches wide, and about nine inches deep; throw some of the earth out on each side, and loosen the earth at the bottom of the trench. . . . Cut off just the ends of the fibres, and the tops of the long leaves; then plant them at about six inches from each other." After they had taken root, the gardener would begin to fill the trench with dry soil and continue "landing," or mounding the soil, around the plants until they were 20 inches to 2 feet tall.

We use a somewhat different method today. The seedlings are transplanted from the nursery bed to the garden when they are 5 or 6 inches tall. When they have grown to about 1 foot tall, we then dig the trench as instructed above. Once the trench is prepared, we select two or three plants, tie the stems together, and transplant them into the trench. They are then earthed up to where the leaves sprout from the stem. (Be cautious not to let soil fall into the heart of the plant.) In 10 days to a fortnight, the celery will be blanched and ready for the table. Every week or 10 days, transplant two or three more plants into the trench for blanching. This will provide celery until freezing weather arrives in December.

It is of utmost importance that the plants are earthed up in dry weather. William Hanbury warned in 1773 of the danger of keeping celery too moist while it is being blanched: "It is but too often that we see spotted, cankered, and sticky Celery; but that is chiefly owing to the plants being moulded [earthed] up when they are not dry: This should warn all raisers of Celery to perform that business at a suitable time."

To grow celeriac. Celeriac, like celery, is a long-season plant, and the seed is sometimes difficult to germinate. Like that of celery, germination is improved by only lightly covering the seeds so that they are exposed to light. Once the plants are up and ready for transplanting, set them out in 18-inch rows with the plants 6 inches asunder. Celeriac is an easier plant to raise than celery and is not as sensitive to hot weather. It will grow throughout summer and can be preserved long into winter with the aid of a straw mulch. Draw earth up around the plants as they grow to shade their bulbs from the sun, and they will be ready when about the size of turnips.

Seed Varieties

Varieties listed in 18th-century Virginia

♦ **'Italien', 'Solid Celery':** Solid-stem celery was first known as 'Italian' celery.

♦ **'Celleriack', 'Dwarf Celleriack'**

Heirloom varieties for the modern gardener

♦ **'Giant Pascal':** Late 19th-century white-stem variety

♦ **'Golden Self-Blanching':** A 19th-century yellow-stem variety

♦ **'Celeriac Giant Prague':** A late 19th-century variety

CELERY AND CELERIAC ESSENTIALS

PLANTING Sow celery and celeriac seed for the spring crop when the crocuses bloom. The fall crop is sown when the phlox and asters bloom. Presoaking, particularly for the fall crop, may be of some benefit. Cover the seed with ⅛ inch of soil. Light stimulates germination. Seeds germinate poorly in temperatures above 75°F.

SPACING Grow celery in rows 2 feet apart, with the plants 8 inches asunder. Celeriac can be grown in 18-inch rows, 6 inches asunder.

FOR BEST GROWTH Both celery and celeriac require a deep, rich soil that stays continually moist. They are best grown as a spring crop in the North and a fall crop in the South.

HARVESTING You can begin blanching celery when the stems are 1 foot tall. Harvest celeriac when it is the size of a turnip.

TO SAVE PURE SEED Celery and celeriac are cross-pollinated by insects, so varieties must be separated by 3 miles.

COLLECTING AND STORING SEED Celery and celeriac are biennial plants, so must grow over a winter season to produce seed. In the South, they can be overwintered in the ground with some protection if the weather is colder than 28°F. In the North, the plants must be dug and kept in a cellar over winter. Trim the tops off of celery and store it in damp sand with the crowns exposed. Trim back the tops of celeriac to 2 inches and store it in moist sawdust. Maintain temperatures between 32° and 40°F. The plants are placed back in the garden in early spring, and the flower stalks will appear as soon as the weather warms. Once the seedheads (umbels) turn brown, cut and place in a paper bag to fully dry. Shake the seeds into the bag and refrigerate in airtight containers.

SEED VIABILITY 8 years

"Celery is a variety of a common weed called Smallage, and it grows naturally in moist places in many parts of England."

—William Hanbury,
A Complete Body of Planting (1773)

ASPARAGUS
Asparagus officinalis

Pliny recorded in the 1st century CE: "I find it stated that corruda (which I take to be a wild asparagus . . .) will also come up if pounded rams' horns are dug in as manure." The belief that horns spontaneously generated asparagus plants persisted for the next 1,500 years. Thomas Hill wrote in 1577: "Manye Sperages do spring up throughe the hornes of wilde Rammes broken into grosse pouder . . . whiche although it seemed not credible to the worthy Dioscorides . . . if the Gardener or owner shall make a profe or trial, he wyll after confesse (I dare affyrme) thys experimente to bee moste true." While horns do not spontaneously generate asparagus, they are a good fertilizer for asparagus, and this may be the source of the fable.

Out of the Wild

The earliest references by Theophrastus (372–288 BCE) and others were likely for the spiny asparagus, *Asparagus acutifolius*. This is a drought-hardy species found in the Mediterranean basin but not cold-hardy enough for much of Europe. It was almost certainly this asparagus that Pliny wrote of in his *Natural History* (circa 77 CE): "Nature has made asparagus to grow wild, for anybody to gather at random; but lo and behold! now we see a cultivated variety, and Ravenna produces heads weighing three to a pound. Alas for the monstrosities of gluttony!"

Pliny dated the domestication of asparagus to the time of Cato. He wrote: "No subject included by Cato

is treated more carefully, and it is the last topic of his book, showing that it was a novelty just creeping in." Cato's *De Re Rustica* was likely written in the first half of the 2nd century BCE.

A New Asparagus

It was probably the Moors in medieval Spain who first recognized the superiority of *A. officinalis* and embarked upon its domestication. *A. officinalis* is native to Europe, primarily along the coast, but its original range has been obscured by centuries of cultivation and by its adaptability to a wide range of climates that allowed it to greatly expand its natural range. Asparagus now occurs in naturalized populations throughout Europe, western Asia, the Americas, and Australia.

In the British Isles, asparagus has probably been gathered from the wild since prehistoric times. William Turner wrote in *A New Herball* (1551): "Sperage is called in Latin, Asparagus . . . thie is the common sperage which groweth in diverse gardeis in England: and in sume places by the sea side." After this time, asparagus became one of the most popular of all kitchen garden plants, and elaborate means of raising it were developed. Thomas Hill devoted an entire chapter in *The Gardener's Labyrinth* (1577) to: "What singular skill and secretes to be knowen in the sowing, removing, and setting againe of the worthy hearb named Sperage."

Varieties in Name and Culture

By the 18th century, several varieties of asparagus were recognized by English garden writers, though the difference among them was likely due to local soil conditions or the skill of the gardener. It had long been recognized that asparagus could be improved through cultivation. As explained by Giacomo Castelvetro in 1614: "When I see the weedy specimens of this noble plant for sale in London I never cease to wonder why no one has yet taken the trouble to improve its cultivation."

In 1776, Thomas Ellis listed four varieties of asparagus in *The Gardener's Pocket-Calendar*: the 'Battersea', 'Deptford', 'Dutch', and 'Gravesend'. Ellis doubted that they were distinct varieties: "The above Varieties are the same sort of Asparagus, only raised in the different

places, and from the change of soil consequently have some difference in their flavor; each sort has its particular admirers." William Hanbury, who had no patience with the proliferation of varieties, took the same position in *A Complete Body of Planting* (1773): "There is but one real *Asparagus*, and that indeed is the Common Wild *Asparagus* which grows naturally in England, and several parts of Europe."

Asparagus was introduced into North America by the middle of the 17th century and was as popular in America as it was in England. It is the great and ephemeral delicacy of spring, for the season for asparagus is brief and prolific. William Byrd II recorded on April 15, 1709, at Westover, his plantation on the James River in Virginia: "At noon I ate nothing but squirrel and asparagus." Nine days later, while on his way to Williamsburg, he wrote: "We rode home to Colonel Ludwell's again where we dined and I ate fish and asparagus." Four days after this, while staying in Williamsburg, he recorded: "Mr. President and Colonel Duke came to see me at my chambers. . . . we went to dinner and I ate mutton and asparagus."

A Profitable Delicacy

Asparagus was one of the first vegetables to be artificially forced for an out-of-season market. In 1683, Leonard Meager recorded that inventive gardeners were forcing asparagus on piles of rotting dung (manure). He also observed: "But how good I cannot say, but undoubtedly it is welcome to such as love Rarities." By the 18th century, forcing asparagus was a common and profitable business for market gardeners. Richard Bradley wrote in 1718: "THE *Asparagus* is one of the great Dainties of the Spring, and what I account to be part of the most necessary Furniture of a *Garden;* it brings great Profit to the *Gardeners* near *London,* either propagated upon natural *Beds* . . . or when they are forced with Dung in the *Winter.* I have heard that a *Gardener* about *Westminster* has receiv'd above thirty Pounds in one Week for forc'd *Asparagus*." If using fresh manure as a heat source, the asparagus should be grown in soil laid over the manure, so that the plants do not come into contact with the manure.

The Williamsburg Gardener's Assistant

A great apparatus for growing asparagus. Pliny recorded in the 1st century: "Of all cultivated vegetables asparagus needs the most delicate attention." For many centuries, a great deal of effort and elaborate devices were employed in the growing of asparagus. Joseph Prentis, a Williamsburg lawyer, recorded the steps for making an asparagus bed in his "Monthly Kalender" (1775–1779): "Set out asparagus as follows. Dig a trench as wide as you intend your Beds to be, and two feet deep, lay a layer of Oyster Shells, six Inches, then lay on six Inches of Horse Dung [compost], and as much Mould [soil], continue so to do, till the Bed is done."

Archaeologists found the remains of four asparagus beds at the Peyton Randolph House in Williamsburg. Two of the pits were lined with wine-bottle fragments, animal bones, and a few ceramic shards. The two other pits, dug at a later time, were lined mostly with oyster shells and some bone. Excavating and lining beds for asparagus is a very old practice, and until recently, many gardeners recommended that asparagus be planted in trenches up to 2 feet deep that were to be filled in as the asparagus grew. John Randolph, brother to Peyton Randolph, had a very modern approach to growing asparagus. He recorded in *A Treatise on Gardening*: "A great apparatus was formerly made use of but now seems on all hands to be disregarded. Nothing more is necessary than to make your beds perfectly rich and light."

To create a rich and enduring space for asparagus. An asparagus bed will endure in one place for 15 or 20 years, so the ground must be thoroughly prepared. John Abercrombie gave a thorough explanation for planting asparagus in *Every Man His Own Gardener* (1776): "In making plantations of these plants, one great article to be considered is, to make choice of a proper soil; it must not be wet, nor too strong or stubborn, but such as is moderately light and pliable."

After selecting a suitable location, preferably on the north side of the garden where the tall asparagus will not shade other plants, prepare the soil as instructed: "The ground where you intend to make new asparagus beds, should be regularly trenched, and a large quantity of good rotten dung [compost] buried equally in each trench, as least twelve or fifteen inches below the surface of the dug ground." Digging the beds deeply will allow the asparagus to reach its roots down deeply and be less susceptible to drought.

The method of setting asparagus crowns. Abercrombie continued: "The ground being dug, and laid level, divide it into beds four feet wide, with alleys two feet wide between bed and bed." Once the beds are laid out, you will be ready to open the trenches that the asparagus crowns will be set in. "For planting, stretch a line lengthways . . . and with a spade cut out a small trench or drill six inches deep, turning the earth to one side." After the trench is opened, cover the bottom with

Planting asparagus crowns

bonemeal to be ready to plant the asparagus crowns.

One-year-old crowns are preferable, as they generally suffer less transplant shock. Abercrombie explained: "Most good gardeners prefer those that are only one year, which are what I would choose to plant; as, from experience, I have found they generally take root much freer." Space the crowns 1 to 1½ feet apart and fill the trench level to the ground. Once all your rows are planted, water the entire bed thoroughly.

What attention is required for asparagus in the first 3 years. Asparagus is not cut in the first year, giving the plant a year to establish itself, but the plants must be closely managed. As explained by Abercrombie: "Keep them clean from weeds, which must be well attended to, during the summer season." If perennial weeds such as bindweed or nutsedge are allowed to establish in the first year, they will be very difficult to eradicate in future years. After the first year, the asparagus growth will be so dense that it will provide some weed control by shading the ground.

In the second year, the asparagus bed can be harvested for 3 weeks. During the harvest, cut all spears, regardless of size, as recommended by Richard Bradley in 1718: "Not any Bud that appears above Ground must be suffer'd to grow in the Cutting Season."

(Top) Asparagus fruit; preparing asparagus for winter; (bottom) forking the beds and laying on the mulch

When the harvest is over, take care to thoroughly weed the bed before the year's foliage covers the ground. In the third year and every year after, you may cut the asparagus for 6 weeks before allowing the bed to go to leaf.

The old versus the new asparagus. The asparagus known to colonial Virginians was very much like the variety called 'Mary Washington'. A bed of 'Mary Washington' will have both male and female plants and will produce an abundance of red berries. This often leads to the degeneration of the bed, as the berries sap the strength of the female plants, and when they fall to the ground, they germinate to become weeds in the bed. We endeavor to allay this problem by cutting down the berry-producing stems before the fruit ripens. The modern all-male cultivars such as 'Jersey Knight' do not form berries and will outproduce the old-fashioned 'Mary Washington' asparagus three to one.

To dress the asparagus plants for winter. In November, when the asparagus foliage turns a golden yellow, we cut it to the ground. As instructed by John Randolph: "The haulm should be cut down and the beds covered with rotten dung [compost] about six inches, part of which may be taken off in February or March and the remainder forked up in the beds." You must be careful to fork the bed only shallowly, so that the crowns and roots are not damaged. As a further protection from weeds, we top-dress the bed with a fine compost after the beds have been forked over.

ASPARAGUS ESSENTIALS

PLANTING Plant asparagus crowns when the daffodils fade and the soil temperature reaches 50°F. Add phosphorus to planting trench for best growth.

SPACING Asparagus crowns should be planted 6 inches deep and 1 foot apart, in rows 4 feet asunder.

FOR BEST GROWTH Asparagus performs best in a light, deep soil. Top-dress with compost for winter months.

HARVESTING Do not harvest asparagus spears in the first year. Harvest for 3 weeks in the second year and 6 weeks every year after.

TO SAVE PURE SEED Modern all-male hybrids are propagated vegetatively, generally by tissue culture. For seed production, separate varieties by 2 miles.

COLLECTING AND STORING SEED Collect the red berries before they fall from the plant and drop them in a bucket of water. The good seeds will sink. Skim off the sterile seeds. The remaining seeds can be left to ferment, or they can be rubbed over a screen, to separate the pulp from the seed. Rinse the seeds in several changes of water, dry thoroughly, and refrigerate in airtight containers.

SEED VIABILITY 5 years

Seed Varieties

Varieties listed in 18th-century Virginia

◆ 'Asparagus', 'White Asparagus'

Heirloom varieties for the modern gardener

◆ 'Mary Washington', 'Martha Washington': Old-time standbys but inferior to modern all-male varieties

CHAPTER 10
Gardening under Cover

One of mankind's most notable attributes is the ability to alter the environment. About 2,000 years ago, this skill progressed to the sheltering of plants. The first record of an artificial environment created specifically for the benefit of a plant is found in Pliny's *Natural History* (circa 77 CE). He recorded that the gardeners for Roman emperor Tiberius constructed a "specularium" in order to provide the emperor with "cucumis" fruit (melons) throughout the year. From Pliny's description, a specularium sounds like a cold frame on wheels, probably glazed with thin pieces of mica on top.

With the fall of the Roman Empire, such extravagances disappeared, and for most of Europe, the science of horticulture was reduced to providing sustenance. A lone bastion of horticultural experimentation survived in Moorish Spain, and it was there that the next significant advance occurred with the development of the hotbed.

A hotbed is simply a pile of fermenting dung (manure) that generates heat for starting early seedlings or for ripening tender crops. Ibn Bassal, gardener to the sultan of Toledo, explained sometime before 1085: "We use soft, slightly dried-out mule- or horse-dung, free of all foreign bodies." He was using the hotbed for starting gourds (probably melons) and aubergines (eggplants). In chilly weather, he covered the beds with cabbage leaves.

The first reference to hotbed gardening in England is found in Thomas Hill's *The Gardener's Labyrinth*, published in 1577. Unfortunately, he did not give us a description. For that, we have to wait for John Gerard, who recorded in *The Herball; or, Generall Historie of Plantes* (1597): "In the middest of Aprill or somwhat sooner . . . you shal cause to be made a bed or bank of hot & new horse dung taken forth of the stable." Once the heat came up in the pile, Gerard covered the manure with 6 inches of fine soil and started his cucumbers on it. To protect the seedlings from frost, Gerard improved on Ibn Bassal's cabbage leaves with a series of hoops. As Gerard explained, "You shall cover [the bed] with Hoopes and poles, that you may the more conveniently cover the whole bed or bancke with Mats, olde painted cloth, strawe or such like, to keepe it from the injurie of the colde frostie nightes."

The next innovation in hotbed gardening also involved covering, and this time it was in regard to raising melons. In 1629, John Parkinson wrote in *Paradisi in Sole*: "Then having prepared a hot bed of dung in Aprill, set your seedes therein to raise them up, and cover them, and order them with as great care or greater then Cowcumbers." The covering was a new innovation out of France. Parkinson continued: "Some use great hollow glasses like unto bell heads." After this time, the bell glass, or what the French called *cloche,* became one of the most common garden tools in London market gardens.

Bell glasses were used primarily for raising seedlings in spring and protecting smaller plants in winter. Crops such as melons and cucumbers, which were commonly raised to maturity on hotbeds, required a much larger structure. These plants were protected within frames, much like our modern cold frames, and covered with window sashes, or what the 18th-century gardener called lights.

The Types of Hotbeds

There were two types of hotbeds used by 18th-century gardeners: the manure hotbed and what was called the bark bed. In the latter case, manure was replaced with *tanbark,* a waste product from the tanning of leather. Tanbark was used primarily in *stove houses,* or greenhouses, for raising pineapples and other tropical fruit and had the advantage over dung of sustaining its heat for a much longer time.

The manure hotbed was more common in the private kitchen garden. Some of the best instructions for building and maintaining hotbeds came from John Abercrombie's *The Universal Gardener and Botanist,* published in 1778. He began: "As horse-dung Hot-beds are of general utility in gardening, I propose to handle this article at some length, for the benefit of those unacquainted with their nature."

The Quality of Dung

Horse dung was the only type of manure used in these beds, and the straw litter that the horses were bedded in was just as important as the manure itself. Abercrombie wrote: "The sort of horse-dung to be understood for the purpose of Hot-beds, is the dung and wet litter together, daily cleaned out of stables where horses always stand, and are littered down with plenty of straw every night, which being rendered wet by the urine and dung of those animals, composes the principal material for a dung Hot-bed; for the dung alone without litter would do nothing, but the litter being thus moistened, and cleared out along with the dung, are both mixed together."

The difficulty for the modern hotbed gardener, including the gardeners at Colonial Williamsburg, is that today horses are almost always bedded in sawdust rather than straw. Sawdust, in a quantity that can be conveniently collected, will not generate the heat needed for the hotbed and actually retards the heat of the manure. Without the benefit of urine-soaked straw, we use fresh horse manure gathered from our pastures instead. This provides adequate heat for starting seedlings but does not maintain its heat for as long as a manure and straw mix would. Cow manure and most vegetable compost will not generate sufficient heat. Some gardeners have experimented with hay-bale hotbeds with some success. Whenever using fresh manure, normal sanitary precautions should be exercised. Manure may contain E. coli, salmonella, or listeria bacteria. People who handle manure must keep their tetanus shots up to date. And you should, of course, wash your hands after

Steamy dung

working in the garden and before eating. When properly handled, manure poses very little danger to the gardener.

In Williamsburg, we plan to start the first hotbed in January. As the dung must be gathered while it is relatively dry and not frozen, the gardener must not miss the opportunity when the weather is right. Abercrombie advised: "Observe also that the dung must be fresh . . . for the newer the dung the better, its heat proving always the most effectual and durable, provided it is properly prepared . . . therefore always chuse the fresh, or new-made steamy dung."

A minimum amount to make an effective hotbed, 10 feet long, is a full pickup-truck load. For shorter hotbeds, a correspondingly smaller amount is necessary, though it is important to remember that too small a hotbed will not be able to sustain the heat needed to germinate the seeds. Throw the manure into a heap made as tall as possible. According to Abercrombie, "If in six, eight, or ten days, according to the quantity, the whole is turned over, casting it up in a heap again, it will give greater vent to the noxious vapour and burning heat to pass off . . . the whole mass will be every way better prepared for the purpose of a Hot-bed." This will evenly spread the microbial activity and hence the heat throughout the pile.

Constructing the Hotbed

The typical 18th-century hotbed was built all or partly aboveground. The problem, again, is that you can only build an aboveground hotbed with a manure/straw mix. Manure alone will not stack evenly enough to support the frames needed to protect the seedlings. So we have built underground hotbeds similar to the one described in *The Scots Gardener* written by John Reid in 1766: "As for making the hotbed for raising early and tender plants, dig a pit two foot deep . . . and of length and breadth as you have occasion, in a convenient and warm place, lying well to the sun and sheltered from winds. . . . this pit will be so much the more excellent, if lined round at the sides with brick."

Our hotbeds are very similar to the one Reid

Pit hotbed

Loading hotbed

described, being 2 feet deep, 2 feet wide, and 10 feet long and constructed with a double wall of stacked bricks on a sand base. The bed must be in a dry location and oriented so that it receives the southern sun. As Abercrombie explained: "Hot-beds are to be ranged lengthwise east and west . . . that they may exactly front the south for receiving all possible benefit of the sun."

About 4 or 5 days after the manure pile is turned, it will be ready to load into the bed. Philip Miller described the process in *The Gardeners Dictionary* (1754): "Wheel the Dung into the Opening, observing to stir every Part of it with a Fork, and lay it exactly even and smooth thro' every Part of the Bed." We load the bed in layers, packing it with a rake head as we go, in accordance with Miller's instructions: "In the making of these Hot-beds, it must be carefully observed to settle the Dung close . . . otherwise it will

be subject to heat too violently; and consequently the Heat will be much sooner spent." A tighter pack will give a somewhat lower but longer-lasting heat.

Capping the Hotbed and Closing the Frames

After the pit is filled all the way to the top of the bricks, the frames (called sashes) are put on as Miller instructed: "When the Bed is made, the Frames should be placed over it, to keep out Wet; but there should be no Earth laid upon it, till after it has been three or four Days made, and is found of a proper Temperature of Heat." (See instructions below for building the frames.)

Within 4 days, the temperature near the surface of the pile will reach 130°F or higher. It is then ready to be capped with soil. Miller wrote: "Cover the Dung about three or four Inches thick with good Earth, putting on the Frames and Glasses."

Packing dung; closed frames; capping bed

Venting frame; condensation; straw insulation

The soil used for capping the hotbed must be a very light, highly organic mixture. We use the fully composted manure from last year's hotbed. It is of the consistency described by John Abercrombie in 1778: "Hot-bed material; besides, that after having performed its office as a Hot-bed, it becomes rotten and buttery, and the most excellent manure that can be for the garden." This very light, porous soil mix allows the manure pile to breathe and continue to heat.

After the soil mix is laid, it will generally warm up to about 110°F the first day. In the next couple of days, the temperature will settle between 70° and 80°F, and then the seeds are sown. After the seeds are planted, they are gently settled in with water that has been heated to a tepid state in a watering can placed near a fire. The sashes, or lights, are replaced, and the frame is kept tightly closed until the seeds germinate.

Managing the Seedlings

Once the seeds have germinated, it is important that the frames are vented during the day. As described by Abercrombie in *The Universal Gardener and Botanist* (1778): "Fresh air, however, must be admitted daily, at all opportunities in mild weather, by tilting the upper ends of the lights . . . from about half an inch to three or four high, according to the heat and steam in the bed, and temperature of the outward air; shutting all close in due time towards evening . . . cover also the glasses every night with mats." It is particularly important that condensation is not allowed to collect on the underside of the glass panes and drip back down on the plants. Venting the sashes will prevent this. Instead of mats, we cover the sashes at night with straw and cover the whole with a canvas tarp. In addition, we provide the January hotbed with an insulating layer of straw all around the outside of the frame. We hold the straw in place with a woven enclosure of sticks known as a wattle fence.

In the January hotbed, we start our spring crops of lettuce, cabbage, cauliflower, leeks, and artichokes. These will be ready to transplant to the garden in April. The second hotbed is started in the first week of March for the melons, cucumbers, tomatoes, peppers, eggplants, and sweet potatoes.

Building the Frames

There are several things to consider when constructing the frames. If window sashes are used, the frames should be set at a declivity that is sufficient for the

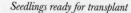

Seedlings ready for transplant

rainwater to run off and not collect in the individual panes. This will greatly prolong the life of the sashes.

The crossbars that support the sashes must be removable, so that you can work in the beds without injuring yourself. Abercrombie described supports very much like the ones we use: "The cross-bars or bearers at top, for the support of the glasses shou'd be about three inches broad and one thick, and neatly dove-tailed in at back and front even with both edges, that the lights may shut down close." Dove-tailing the crossbars into the front and back walls of the frame also helps to keep the two walls in line and square to the window sashes.

Because they are over pits, our frames stay in the garden year-round as a safety precaution. Many 18th-century frames were made to disassemble, so that they might be conveniently stored out of the way and out of the weather when not in use. This is particularly useful for frames, used with or without manure, that are intended to be moved to different areas of the garden.

Finally, the front or south wall of the frame should be made as low as possible while still accommodating the plants you intend to grow. In midwinter, the sun travels low across the sky, and the taller the front wall, the more of the bed will be cast into shade.

Hand-Glasses and Bell Glasses

There were several types of glasses in use to protect young plants in 18th-century England. John Abercrombie described two: "squares, or leaded hand-glasses, and bell glasses." The leaded hand-glasses were made up of small panes set within leaded panels. They were usually made with a square bottom and removable pyramid top. Abercrombie recorded that both hand-glass and bell glass cost 2 to 3 shillings each, which was between $10 and $15 in today's money. He also observed: "London gardeners, some of which work two or three thousand hand-glasses in a season, generally prefer the bells to the other sorts." This was a substantial investment for the market gardener and indicates how lucrative the out-of-season market was around large European towns like London.

Colonial Williamsburg archaeologists found bell-glass fragments at a number of 18th-century properties within the historic area. The largest concentration

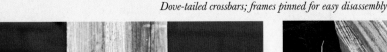

Dove-tailed crossbars; frames pinned for easy disassembly

was in a walled garden within the Governor's Palace property that was likely a nursery. All of the fragments found in town, with one exception, were from green-colored bells. The green color is a result of iron impurities in the sand that was used to make the glass as well as from sulfur from the burning coal that was used to melt the glass. When the glass was intended for window sashes, the iron—and hence the green color—could be leached out of the mixture with a manganese precipitate. This was an unnecessary expense when manufacturing bell glass, however. There were no glassblowers in 18th-century Virginia we know of, so these bells must have come from England, making them even more expensive. In Williamsburg, the gardener to Lord Botetourt ordered 32 bell glasses from England for the royal governor's palace gardens in 1771. They were valued at 5 shillings (today's $25) each.

We use bell glass primarily to shelter plants from frost. They can be used to preserve plants like artichoke and parsley or any seedlings of the cabbage tribe over the winter months, or they can be used to raise transplants in spring. They can also be used to shelter new transplants from the wind. Green bells are preferable to clear bells for this use. Except for recent transplants, the bell glass should be removed during the day. If it is too windy or cold for the seedlings to have the bells taken off, they can be vented by tilting one side up with a shard of pottery or other small prop.

Transplants under bell glass

Vented bell glass

Paper Frames

Paper frames were common in the 18th century, because they were light, portable, and relatively cheap. The paper frames we use in Williamsburg are patterned after an illustration in the 1763 edition of Philip Miller's *The Gardeners Dictionary*. The frame that Miller illustrated was 5 to 6 feet wide and about 10 feet long, while ours are only 2 feet wide and about 10 feet long. Our hoops are made from thinly planed cypress boards that we soak overnight to render them more pliable. They are then mortised to the frame's side rails. A thin center rail across the top holds the hoops together evenly. Before the paper is applied, we tie a string from hoop to hoop about halfway up on both sides of the frame.

Paper in the 18th century was made from cloth of cotton or linen or a cotton and linen blend. We most commonly use a cotton paper, although the modern wood-pulp paper will work nearly as well. It is glued to the frame with hide glue. As described

(Left) String tied hoop to hoop for extra support; gluing paper to frame; oiling paper; (right) frames in winter

by Miller: "In the pasting of the paper on the frames, there should be care taken to stretch it very smooth . . . to prevent the wind from raising the paper, which would soon tear it when it became loose." Miller also gave this advice: "After the paste is well dried, the paper should be oiled over on the outside, which if well done with Lintseed-oil will be sufficient, for the oil will soak quite through the paper, so there will be no necessity for oiling both sides, nor for doing it over more than once. The oil should be dry before the frames are exposed to the wet, otherwise the paper will tear." We have found that frames oiled in November will last until the following August, when mildew finally turns the paper dark and brittle.

The primary use of paper frames in the 18th century was for the growing of melons. The frames were used to shelter the young transplants in spring and again in summer, to keep rain from the plants while the melons were ripening. We also use them to shelter hardy plants, such as endive, over the winter months.

CHAPTER 11
Growing Sticks

There are few items more useful to a gardener than a long, slender, supple stick. Sticks can trellis the cucumbers and the tomatoes. They hold up the peppers, the peas, and the beans. They provide support for innumerable flowers and herbs that would otherwise languish on the ground. At Williamsburg, sticks form the *wattle* (woven branch structure) to hold straw against the frames and to make fences along the garden paths to direct the steps of wayward visitors. Sticks form the lattice to support straw over the broad beans; form hoops to hold tarps over the broccoli; and create domes for canvas over the artichokes. Sticks support the fabric that keeps butterflies from the cabbage and flea beetles away from the eggplant. In short, no garden should be without a ready supply of sticks.

The proper sticks for use in a garden cannot be picked up off the ground; they must be grown from trees selected for this very purpose. Growing sticks is an ancient art that has long provided building material, firewood, tool handles, brooms, and many, many other useful items. It is likely that the first buildings inhabited by humans were made from sticks. *Wattle and daub* construction, in which a lattice of sticks provided the structure for mud-plaster walls, probably dates to the Neolithic period. In medieval Europe, sticks, or *osiers,* were most commonly collected from *coppices.* These were trees such as willows, hazels, alders, and others whose original stems were repeatedly cut to the ground, resulting in a profusion of sucker growth at their stumps that could then be harvested as needed.

A *pollard* is simply a coppice raised aboveground. As explained by Thomas Hale, Esq., in *A Compleat Body of Husbandry* (1756): "FROM the Management of Coppice Wood we are to advance to the Consideration of Timber Trees; but we are naturally stop'd between both, by a particular Kind of Growth, which is properly speaking, neither of the Coppice Wood, nor Timber Tree Kind: this is the Pollard; a Tree of any Sort cut off at ten or twelve Feet Distance from the Ground, and shooting out from that Part a Number of Branches or Poles. These Poles or Branches are called Shrowds, and the lopping them off is called shrowding of the Tree."

The advantage of the pollard to the 18th-century *husbandman* (agriculturist) was that the stems were out of the reach of livestock. Cattle and sheep relish the young and supple shoots of coppiced trees, requiring that the coppiced wood be fenced all around. Hale observed: "Pollards are inferior to Coppice Trees in the Quantity of Wood they yield, and in its Value . . . but on the other hand, Pollards are maintain'd . . . at a smaller Expence . . . for they require no Fences, they take up no Quantity of Ground; and they are in their Shoots above the Reach of Cattle."

The most common use of pollard trees was for producing firewood, and the preferred tree for this was the ash. As explained by William Hanbury in *A Complete Body of Planting and Gardening* (1773): "Pollards are of great service where fuel is scarce: A few of these trees will turn out many loads of lop; and the wood of them makes the sweetest of all fires, and will burn well either green or dry."

To form a pollard, allow the tree to grow to the height you desire, and then head it back (prune off the branch tips) before the limbs become too large. This was described in *Chiltern and Vale farming explained,* published for William Ellis in 1745: "The Pollard Ash is that which is made by cutting off the Standard's Head, and should be lopt for that purpose, before it arrives to a very great Body; else the Wets will be very apt to get in between the Rind and the Body." If you allow the stems to grow too large before you cut them, the large wounds that you will necessarily make will invite decay.

Pollarded sycamore

Traditionally, pollards were formed at about 10 feet tall. Since we are not troubled by cattle in the Williamsburg garden, we make ours at about 5 feet, where they can be conveniently reached. To produce firewood, the pollard would have been allowed to grow for about 10 years before its stems were cut. For tool handles, 3 to 5 years are sufficient. To produce the slender sticks we require in our garden, the plants are cut back every year. As the years pass, and as the plants are repeatedly cut, the number of sticks arising from each cut becomes greater and greater. For generating small slender sticks, and for the health of the tree, the plants must be cut back to the same spot every year.

Every time a limb is cut, it produces callus tissue to close its wound. Over time, this results in the large, gnarled, knucklelike knob on the end of the branch where the cuts are made. Moses Cook gave an interesting explanation for this and the subsequent production of shoots in *The manner of raising, ordering and improving forest-trees* (1724): "The Sap riseth into the Head of the Pollard . . . and so into the Boughs, but finding the Boughs cut off, it filleth the Head so full, that it causeth it to swell in the Spring: and this is the reason

Pollard-heads are bigger than any other part of the Body of the Tree; the Head being so full that it can contain the Sap no longer, it then breaketh out into abundance of young Shoots." Modern plant physiology attributes the swelling of the pollard's head to layers of callus tissue and the abundance of shoots to the loss of *apical* (apex or growing tip) dominance.

Some types of trees make better pollards than others. We prefer sticks that are long and slender, with a minimum of twiggy growth sprouting along their length. Also, some trees recover better from being repeatedly cut than others do. Maples, for example, are notoriously bad at callusing over wounds, and their main limbs quickly become hollow and weak. One of the most popular European pollards today is the littleleaf linden (*Tilia cordata*). This attractive little tree is exceptionally good at healing after repeated cuttings. Most of our sticks come from pollarded chaste trees (*Vitex agnus-castus*) and sycamores (*Platanus occidentalis*). Fruit trees also make good candidates: If you have despaired of growing apples, you can easily grow sticks.

For those adventurous enough to try a pollard or two, we must warn you: The neighbors may talk. Modern gardeners have been schooled to avoid just this sort of pruning technique. John Dicks gave a similar warning in *A new gardener's dictionary* (1769): "This lopping of trees is only to be understood for pollard-trees; because nothing is more injurious to the growth of timber-trees, than that of lopping or cutting off great branches from them."

The wanton butchery that we see so often practiced on our landscape trees, for the sake of an overhead electric power line or from the lack of skill and/or discernment of the property owner, is to be in all ways discouraged. In the first case, this can be achieved by not planting trees under power lines; and in the second case, by educating the property owner in tree selection and pruning.

Pollards are altogether different, and the thrifty gardener will want a few. As Abercrombie observed in *The Universal Gardener and Botanist* (1778): "Oiser twigs being useful in many gardens for various tyings . . . it is eligible to cultivate a few of the best osiers in most gardens, to furnish a supply for the different purposes."

Vitex knuckles (left); Vitex pollards (right)

ABOUT THE AUTHOR and THE COLONIAL WILLIAMSBURG FOUNDATION

Wesley Greene has spent 30 years researching the plants, architecture, and culture methods used in 18th-century Virginia gardens. He studied botany and plant and soil science at the University of Maine. Originally hired by The Colonial Williamsburg Foundation as garden foreman for the Governor's Palace, a 10-acre garden in Williamsburg's Historic Area, Greene founded the Colonial Garden and Plant Nursery on Williamsburg's Duke of Gloucester Street in Colonial Williamsburg in 1996. At this experimental garden, he and another gardener, Don McKelvey, study and interpret 18th-century plants, tools, and cultural techniques.

The Colonial Williamsburg Foundation is a private, not-for-profit educational institution that preserves and interprets the 18th-century capital of Virginia. In addition to the Historic Area, the Foundation operates the DeWitt Wallace Decorative Arts Museum, the Abby Aldrich Rockefeller Folk Art Museum, Bassett Hall, and the John D. Rockefeller Jr. Library.

Colonial Williamsburg actively supports history and citizenship education through a wide variety of educational outreach programs. Programs for students include *The Idea of America*, an interactive, fully digital, Web-based curriculum for high school students, and electronic field trips, which transport students from across the country into American history. Programs for teachers include the Williamsburg Teacher Institute and workshops in school districts nationwide.

The Colonial Williamsburg Foundation relies on and encourages tax-deductible gifts and bequests. For more information, go to www.history.org/foundation/development, e-mail gifts@cwf.org, or call 1-888-CWF-1776.

Work on this book was funded in part by a generous grant from Teresa and Ken Wood, longtime supporters of Colonial Williamsburg's gardens and educational outreach efforts. Members of the National Advisory Council for The Colonial Williamsburg Foundation, the Woods are active in horticultural organizations. Ken is a member of the Pennsylvania Horticultural Society's Board and Executive Committee and Teresa is treasurer of their local community land trust.

A SELECTED BIBLIOGRAPHY

In addition to the historic works cited in this book, the author consulted many modern authors including:

Amherst, Alicia [Evelyn Cecil]. *A History of Gardening in England*, London, 1895.

Andrews, Jean. *Peppers: The Domesticated Capsicums*. Austin: University of Texas Press, 1984.

Ashworth, Suzanne. *Seed to Seed: Seed Saving and Growing Techniques for Vegetable Gardeners*. Edited by Kent Whealy. 2nd ed. Decorah, IA: Seed Savers Exchange, 2002.

Bailey, L[iberty] H[yde], and Ethel Zoe Bailey. *Hortus: A Concise Dictionary of Gardening, General Horticulture and Cultivated Plants in North America*. New York: Macmillan, 1930.

Campbell, Susan, *Charleston Kedding, A History of Kitchen Gardening*, London: Ebury Press, 1996.

Candolle, Alphonse de. *Origin of Cultivated Plants*. New York: D. Appleton, 1885.

Dane, Fenny, and Jiarong Liu. "Diversity and Origin of Cultivated and Citron Type Watermelon (*Citrullus lanatus*)." *Genetic Resources and Crop Evolution* 54, no. 6 (September 2007): 1255–65.

Gray, A. R. "Taxonomy and Evolution of Broccoli (*Brassica oleracea* var. *italica*)." *Economic Botany* 36, no. 4 (October–December 1982): 397–410.

Grieve, M. *A Modern Herbal: The Medicinal, Culinary, Cosmetic and Economic Properties, Cultivation and Folk-Lore of Herbs, Grasses, Fungi Shrubs and Trees with All Their Modern Scientific Uses*. 2 vols. New York: Dover, 1981. Originally published New York, 1931.

Harvey, John. *Mediaeval Gardens*. London: B. T. Batsford, 1981.

Lacaita, C. C. "The 'Jerusalem Artichoke' (*Helianthus tuberosus*)." *Bulletin of Miscellaneous Information* (Royal Gardens, Kew) 1919, no. 9 (1919): 321–39.

McCue, George Allen. "The History of the Use of the Tomato: An Annotated Bibliography." *Annals of the Missouri Botanical Garden* 39, no. 4 (November 1952): 289–348.

Paris, Harry S., Marie-Christine Daunay, Michel Pitrat, and Jules Janick. "First Known Image of *Cucurbita* in Europe, 1503–1508." *Annals of Botany* 98, no. 1 (July 2006): 41–47.

Paris, Harry S. "Paintings (1769–1774) by A. N. Duchesne and the History of *Cucurbita pepo*." *Annals of Botany* 85, no. 6 (June 2000): 815–30.

Paris, H. S., and J. Janick. "Reflections on Linguistics as an Aid to Taxonomical Identification of Ancient Mediterranean Cucurbits: The Piqqus of the Faqqous." *Proceedings of the IX EUCARPIA International Meeting on Cucurbitaceae*, Avignon, France, May 21–24, 2008: 43–51.

Paris, H. S., and J. Janick. "What the Roman Emperor Tiberius Grew in His Greenhouses." *Proceedings of the IX EUCARPIA International Meeting on Cucurbitaceae*, Avignon, France, May 21–24, 2008: 33–41.

Roberts, Jonathan. *The Origins of Fruit and Vegetables*. New York: Universe, 2001.

Root, Waverley. *Food: An Authoritative and Visual History and Dictionary of the Foods of the World*. New York: Simon and Schuster, 1980. Republished by Smithmark, New York, 1996.

Sauer, Jonathan D. *Historical Geography of Crop Plants: A Select Roster*. Boca Raton, FL: CRC, 1993.

Smartt, J., and N. W. Simmonds, eds. *Evolution of Crop Plants*. 2nd ed. Essex, England: Longman Scientific and Technical, 1995.

Smith, Andrew F. *The Tomato in America: Early History, Culture, and Cookery*. Columbia, SC: University of South Carolina Press, 1994.

Sonnante, Gabriella, Domenico Pignone, and Karl Hammer. "The Domestication of Artichoke and Cardoon: From Roman Times to the Genomic Age." *Annals of Botany* 100, no. 5 (October 2007): 1095–100.

Stuart, David C., *The Kitchen Garden*, London: Robert Hale, 1984.

Sturtevant, E[dward] Lewis. *Sturtevant's Edible Plants of the World*. Edited by U. P. Hedrick. New York: Dover, 1972. Originally published as *Sturtevant's Notes on Edible Plants* in Albany, NY, 1919.

Swem, E. G. *Brothers of the Spade: Correspondence of Peter Collinson of London, and of John Custis, of Williamsburg, Virginia, 1734–1746*. Barre, MA: Barre Gazette, 1957.

Wasylikowa, Krystyna, and Marijke van der Veen. "An Archaeobotanical Contribution to the History of Watermelon, *Citrullus lanatus* (Thunb.) Matsum. and Nakai (syn. *C. vulgaris* Schrad.)." *Vegetation History and Archaeobotany* 13, no. 4 (November 2004): 213–17.

Weaver, William Woys. *Heirloom Vegetable Gardening: A Master Gardener's Guide to Planting, Growing, Seed Saving, and Cultural History*. New York: Henry Holt, 1997.

Index

Boldface page references indicate photographs. <u>Underscored</u> references indicate boxed text.

K

Kale
essentials, 26
  for best growth, 26
  harvesting, 26
  planting, 26
  saving pure seed, 26
  seed collection and storage, 26
  seed viability, 26
  spacing, 26
flowers and sprouts, **25**
history, 23
varieties, <u>26</u>
  'Black Tuscan', <u>22</u>, **22**
  Siberian, **25**, <u>26</u>
  Williamsburg Gardener's Assistant,
    24–25, **24–25**
    harvesting, 25
    seasons, 24
Kidney bean, 1, 13–14, **14**
Kohlrabi
essentials, 43
  for best growth, 43
  harvesting, 43
  planting, 43
  saving pure seed, 43
  seed collection and storage, 43
  spacing, 43
history of, 42
seedlings, **43**
varieties, **42**, <u>43</u>
  Williamsburg Gardener's Assistant,
    43

L

Lactuca sativa. See Lettuce
Lagenaria siceraria. See Gourd
Lamb's lettuce. *See* Corn salad
Leek
essentials, 135
  for best growth, 135
  harvesting, 135
  planting, 135
  saving pure seed, 135
  seed collection and storage, 135
  seed viability, 135
  spacing, 135
history of, 131–32
origin of, 132–33
varieties, 132, <u>135</u>
  'London', 132, <u>135</u>
  'Scotch' (flag), 132, **132**
  'Yorktown', 131, **131**

Williamsburg Gardener's Assistant,
  133–34, **133–34**
  blanching, 133
  harvesting, 133–34, **134**
  hotbed, 133, **133**
  planting, 133, **133**
  trimming, 133
Legumes, 1. *See also* Broad beans; New
  World beans; Peas
Lepidium sativum. See Garden cress
Lettuce
essentials, 53
  for best growth, 53
  harvesting, 53
  planting, 53
  saving pure seed, 53
  seed collection and storage, 53
  seed viability, 53
  spacing, 53
history of, 46–47
varieties, 46–47, <u>53</u>
  'Brown Dutch', 47, **47**, <u>53</u>
  'Cabbage' lettuce, 46–47, <u>53</u>
  'Capuchin', 47, <u>53</u>
  cos, 46, **47**, 48–49, **49**, <u>53</u>
  romaine, 48–49
  for summer crop, 51
  'Tennis Ball', 47, **47**, <u>53</u>
  Williamsburg Gardener's Assistant,
    46–52, 48–52
    blanching, 48–49, **49**
    growing in fall, 48, **48**
    slug and snail traps, 49, **50**
    starting spring lettuce in hotbeds,
      49–51, **51**
    summer harvest, 51–52, **52**
    transplants, 48, **48**
    winter crop, 49, **50**
Lima bean, 15, **15**
Lycopersicon lycopersicon. See Tomato

M

Manure, hotbed, 227–29, **228**
Melons
essentials, 168
  harvesting, 168
  planting, 168
  saving pure seed, 168
  seed collection and storage, 168
  seed viability, 168
  spacing, 168
history of, 153, 161–64
origins of, 153, 161

varieties, <u>169</u>
  'Armenian', 161, **163**, 164
  cantaloupe, 161–62, 168
  'Crenshaw', 168
  'D'Algers', **162**, <u>169</u>
  honeydew, 168
  muskmelon, 162
  'Pineapple', **162**, <u>169</u>
  pocket, **163**, 163–64, <u>169</u>
  'Prescott', **167**
  'Turkey Cucumber', 164, <u>169</u>
  'Valencia Winter', **167**
  'Zatta', **162**, <u>169</u>
  Williamsburg Gardener's Assistant,
    165–67, 165–68
    aging melon seed, 165
    cucumbers planted near melons,
      168
    harvesting, 168
    melon baskets, 165, **165**, 166,
      166
    seedling management, 165
    shingles for protection from rot,
      166, 167–68
    sowing seeds, 167
    summer maintenance, 167–68
    transplanting, 166
    watering, 167, **167**
Muskmelon, 162
Mustard, 73–74
essentials, 77
history of, 73
white, 73, **73**, <u>77</u>
Williamsburg Gardener's Assistant,
  74, **74**

N

Nasturtium. *See* Indian cress
Nasturtium officinale. See Watercress
New World beans
essentials, 19
  for best growth, 19
  harvesting, 19
  planting, 19
  saving pure seed, 19
  seed collection and storage, 19
  seed viability, 19
  spacing, 19
kidney bean, 1, 13–14, **14**
lima bean, 15, **15**
runner beans, 15, **15**
varieties, <u>19</u>
  'Caseknife', 14, **14**, <u>19</u>